Hidden Among The Leaves

Part 2

An Adirondack Justice Story

Book 3

By Jamie S. Farrington

Copyright ©2024 by Jamie S. Farrington
Get It Write Publishing Company

Printed in the United States of America
Cover art by Connie Fitsik (Island Holiday Publishing)

ISBN: 9798337786063

This book is dedicated to my beautiful wife, Sherry, without whose love and dedicated support, this book would not be possible. And to my nephews Christian and Nicholas and my niece Avrey. Watching the three of you as you grow and succeed in each new challenge that you face is a constant source of joy and inspiration to me. The world is yours. Reach out and grab it.

While working on this book, yet another tragic loss of true American heroes occurred in Charlotte, North Carolina. On April 29, 2024, members of the United States Marshals Service Carolinas Regional Fugitive Task Force were attempting to arrest a subject on federal weapons charges. When the task force members approached the subject's residence, they were immediately met with high-powered rifle fire from two subjects. Three task force members died in the exchange of gunfire. When officers from the Charlotte-Mecklenburg police department arrived to attempt to assist their fallen brothers, they too were met with gunfire and lost one of their officers as well. This book is dedicated to these brave men in honor of their service and sacrifice. Killed that day were:

Thomas "Tommy" Weeks- Deputy United States Marshal- Survived by his wife and four children

Task Force Officer Sam Poloche-N.C. Dept. of Adult Correction-Survived by his wife and two children

Task Force Officer Alden Elliot- N.C. Dept. of Adult Corrections-Survived by his wife and child

Officer Joshua Eyer-Charlotte-Mecklenburg P.D.- Survived by his wife and child

"It is not how these officers died that made them heroes. It is how they lived." Inscription on the National Law Enforcement Officers Memorial in Washington D.C. and attributed to Vivian Eney-Cross, the wife of fallen Capitol Police Officer, Christopher Eney.

"Evil is powerless if the good are unafraid."

~ Ronald Reagan

Prologue

Rome, Italy

Andino Fabrizio sat alone in his opulent home office, staring out the window that overlooked Saint Peter's Square and the Basilica. It was approaching midnight, and hundreds of lights within the holy city set the alabaster dome of the basilica ablaze with dazzling light. The cross atop the dome shined clearly against the cloudless night sky. The stars in the heavens twinkled and danced, creating a fitting backdrop to the center of the Roman Catholic world.

A glass of Giacomo Contero Monfortino wine sat forgotten and untouched on the beautiful hand-crafted walnut desk at which the troubled man sat. At twelve hundred euros a bottle, the wine was just one of many displays of the former Roman Catholic priest's wealth and affluence. Andino Fabrizio was the youngest son of the Greek multi-billionaire shipping magnate, Macario Fabrizio. He had grown up in a pampered world of wealth and privilege. Even the vows of poverty he had taken years earlier when he graduated from the Pontifical Roman Major Seminary couldn't separate the unstable man from his decadent upbringing.

At this moment, all the wealth that Fabrizio possessed and all the privileges his elevated place in society had provided him with meant nothing. All that mattered was Evora Cota. He must have her. She must be made to pay for her blasphemous portrayal of the church and its priests. More importantly, she must be punished for the sinful lust she stirred within Fabrizio. The woman was an instrument of the devil himself, and she must be made to repent. It was the only way he could cleanse his own soul.

Somehow, the unholy temptress had managed to escape the elaborate kidnapping plan the Italian gangster L'Avvoltoio had devised. Bombs had been set off all around Vatican City, and there had been a major gun battle that left dead bodies lying broken and bloody in the streets of the ancient capital city of Italy. When the smoke cleared, the girl was gone, spirited away by a highly skilled security team hired to protect her from Fabrizio.

The violence and death left in the wake of the failed kidnapping attempt would draw heavy attention from both the Polizia di Stato, the police force responsible for keeping the peace in Rome, as well as the Carabinoieri, the national military police force. Fabrizio wasn't worried about the police, though. There was no way for the authorities to tie Fabrizio to the violence, and his father's wealth and political connections would shield Andino even if the police somehow managed to learn of his involvement.

Making matters far worse, L'Avvoltoio had been killed after the kidnapping attempt failed. Murdered by Padraig Lowery. Now the violent former PIRA brigade commander was demanding that Fabrizio continue to pay him to locate and kidnap Cota. Though Fabrizio was filled with dread at the thought of being involved with the Irish murderer, his desire to possess Cota was simply too powerful. He could not walk away. He would make a deal with the devil himself in order to have Evora Cota at his mercy. So the deal was struck, and now Andino Fabrizio sat alone in the dark, contemplating what he had set in motion.

CHAPTER ONE

Burlington International Airport
Burlington, Vermont

The Airbus ACJ 350 carrying Christian Vikstrom and the team assigned to protect Evora Cota landed at Burlington International Airport at exactly two o'clock in the morning. The four thousand, one hundred and twenty-seven-mile flight from Rome, Italy had taken just under nineteen hours. Despite the long flight, every team member was still amped up as a result of the firefight they had survived the previous evening.

Evora had been both physically and emotionally drained by the time they had departed Rome. Shortly after taking off, Laura escorted the young actress to the small sleeping area in the rear section of the aircraft. The two women spoke briefly before Evy fell into a deep sleep marred by nightmares of the previous evening's attack.

Once Evora was settled in, the remainder of the ArVal team had a short meeting just to go over the plans for when they landed.

Arthur Valentine had assigned seven people to protect Evy. Christian and Laura Knight would team up with Dexter Choi once they reached the safe house in Lake Placid. Christian had arranged for them to use a beautiful lakefront home situated on the shore of Lake Placid. Steven Paine would be in charge of two Quick Reaction Force, or QRF, teams consisting of himself and fellow ArVal members Jerome Abioye, David Altman, and Pierre Durand. All four men were former members of various Tier 1 special operations forces.

"Dexter has arranged for accommodations for both QRF teams." Christian handed Paine a sheet of paper as he continued. "Team one will be staying at the Lake Placid Club Lodge just off Mirror Lake Drive. It's an exclusive condo complex on Mirror Lake. Team two will be staying at Wildwood on the Lake. That's located on Saranac Ave., and it's only about a half mile from the safe house. They have a small, two-bedroom cottage. Dexter has provided addresses as well as the security code to get into both places."

When Christian finished briefing them on lodging, Paine stood up and went over everyone's assignments for when they landed. When he finished speaking, the small group prepared for the long flight ahead.

Christian went to the small galley, where he poured himself a mug of coffee from the pot that Martin Mathers had started as soon as they boarded the plane. The small computer genius had been conspicuously silent for the majority of the night.

"How are you doing, Marty?" Christian asked.

"Fine, Christian. Thanks."

"Come on. You've been too quiet all night."

"No, really, I'm fine," he insisted.

"We're teammates, Marty. If you're having a problem, we need to know about it." Christian could tell by the man's body language and his tone that Mathers was having some sort of issue.

"I'm a computer tech, Christian, not a special forces guy. I was a poker player and a computer security specialist. I'm not sure I'm cut out for shootouts and people dying." The low lighting in the small galley reflected off the top of Mathers' bald head as he looked down at the floor.

"You're not the one who has to deal with the violent end of this job, Marty. That's for guys like Steven and me. Arthur hired you because of your computer skills, not to be a shooter."

"I know, but what if something happens while we're protecting Evy, and I just get in the way?"

"That won't happen. First of all, once we're in the States, you'll be heading back to Washington, D.C. to try to figure out who this stalker is. You won't be on the ground with us after we reach Vermont. Secondly, I think you're selling yourself short. I think that if shit hits the fan, you'll do just fine."

Mathers didn't buy everything Christian had said, but he felt better after they spoke.

Laura turned sideways to let Marty pass as she approached the galley, where Christian stood enjoying his coffee. "What was that all about?" she asked.

"Marty isn't quite sure all of this is his cup of tea."

"Hmm. Is it going to be a problem?"

"Nope. He'll be fine. He just has to remember his role in all of this."

"True. And you? How are you dealing with it?"

"I assume you're referring to the ambush."

"What else?"

"I'm fine. It's strange, I guess. Maybe I should feel guilty about shooting those men, but I don't. They made the choice to try to grab Evora. I made the choice to protect her. In the end, they're responsible for how things turned out."

Laura searched Christian's face for any sign that he was trying to hide anything. What she saw convinced her that the newest ArVal team member was being truthful with her. "I read your file before Arthur reached out to offer you a job. As far as I can see, the only time you ever had to shoot anyone was just recently while looking for that missing girl."

"Cynthia Haynes. Good kid. Chose the wrong asshole to fall in love with."

"And you saved her."

"Yeah. Her grandfather was beside himself. The cops weren't doing enough as far as he was concerned, so he hired me to find her."

"And you did."

"I did. I shot her dirtbag boyfriend, Jeffery Lint, while he was driving her out into the Adirondacks to kill her and bury her on his grandfather's land." Christian gazed beyond Laura, and she could tell he was seeing something other than the inside of the luxury jet. "It's strange."

"What is?"

"Years of hunting the worst, most dangerous criminals in the world, and I never had to shoot anyone. The only shooting I was actively involved in was the Coates arrest, and I didn't fire a shot that night. Now, I've had to shoot four people. It's just strange how it all works out."

"Any regrets?" Laura wanted to be sure Christian wasn't questioning what he'd done. If he had any doubts, it could cause him to hesitate the next time things got hot.

"No. Each time, the person I shot made a choice. They didn't leave me any other options. Lint kidnapped an innocent girl, and when I tracked him down, he shot at me, so I had no choice but to put him down." As he spoke, Christian's fingers subconsciously traced the scar running down his left cheek—a permanent reminder of how close Jeffery Lint had come to ending his life that fateful night. "As for last night. . . Like I said, those men made a choice, and it forced *me* to make a choice. I don't have any regrets."

"Good, because from what I've seen, I think you're a good man. We're lucky Arthur brought you aboard." Laura reached out and ran her fingers along Christian's scar. "For what it's worth, I think the scar's kind of sexy." She chuckled at the surprised look on Christian's face as she grabbed a bottle of water from the refrigerator and headed back to her seat to try to catch a few hours' sleep.

Once they landed, the pilot slowly maneuvered the luxury jet from the runway into a cavernous hanger Dexter had arranged for them. As the jet's tail assembly passed completely into the hanger, the massive sliding doors began to close. When the doors finally came to rest, the noise from the motor driving them ceased to echo throughout the hanger, throwing the huge structure into an eerie silence.

As soon as the plane came to rest, everyone gathered their belongings and filed down the staircase. Evy came down the steps with her carry-on bag in her hand, followed closely by Laura. The two women joined the rest of the team where they had gathered in the small pool of light provided by one of two sets of overhead lights that had been activated upon their arrival. Deep, dark shadows hid the true size of the building.

Evora had slept for almost ten hours when the flight took off, and once she woke up, she spent the remainder of the flight either alone with her thoughts or quietly talking with Laura.

The stress of the previous evening had taken its toll on the young woman. She was frightened and alone with a group of people she had just met. Christian was glad to see that she had begun to bond with Laura. He knew from experience that protecting someone who didn't want to be protected could be a challenge. Christian was hoping Evy would become close enough to Laura to help assure her cooperation.

As the group stood beside the now silent aircraft, the rest of the ArVal team assigned to the detail emerged from the darkness. Christian recognized Jerome Abioye. The stocky former member of the South African Army's sixth special forces had been with Paine when they picked Christian and Dexter up at the airport in Virginia. With him were two additional men Christian had never seen before.

Paine motioned for Christian to follow him over to the waiting men. "Vikstrom, I'm sure you remember Jerome Abioye." He indicated the stocky South African.

"Of course. Good to see you again, Jerome."

"And you, Christian. Will we be stopping for breakfast on our trip this morning?"

The look of annoyance that flashed across Steven Paine's face was more than Christian could handle after the stress of the previous evening, followed by the long, boring flight, and he burst out laughing.

"When you two assholes are done playing grab ass, we can move along." He glared at both men before continuing. Once he was sure the wise remarks were over, he pointed to a tall, thin white male with shoulder-length brown hair and a two-day growth of facial hair. "This is David Altman. Don't let the 'just climbed out of a Salvation Army donation box' look fool you. Altman was a Marine Raider prior to spending a few years with the CIA's Special Activities Division." Altman nodded and offered his hand.

Paine next placed his hand on the thick shoulder of one of the darkest-skinned men Christian had ever seen. "This is Pierre Durand. Durand spent ten years with the French GIGN. He's as tough as they come."

Christian was familiar with the Groupe d'Invention de la Gendarmerie Nationale, or the GIGN, as they were more commonly referred to. The GIGN is responsible for counter-terrorism operations within France and has a fearsome reputation.

Durand was a couple inches shorter than Christian but had at least twenty pounds on him. The muscular Frenchman had a shaved head, and a neatly trimmed goatee framed his wide mouth.

"Gentlemen, this is ArVal's newest member, Christian Vikstrom. Vikstrom was with the United States Marshals Special Operations Group."

"Bonjour," Christian greeted the men as he shook their hands.

"Bonjour. Jerome has been telling us a bit about you,"

Durand said in strangely accented French.

"That he has," agreed Altman. "Will we be stopping for breakfast on the way to Lake Placid?"

Christian could tell Paine was struggling not to explode.

"The next person who mentions fucking breakfast will be eating my fucking boot."

The outburst did nothing to wipe the grins off of the men's faces.

Paine led the small group to three vehicles that had been staged inside the hanger. "Vikstrom, you and Laura will take Cota in the Grand Cherokee. I will be in the expedition with Durand, and Abioye will take Altman with him in the Tahoe. All the vehicles are equipped with run-flat tires. They each have a gun vault in the back. We have portable radios for everyone, and each vehicle has a mobile radio system."

"Radios aren't always reliable in the mountains between here and Placid," Christian said.

"We're prepared for that as well. Each vehicle has a satellite phone."

"Weapons?"

"Abioye will get you sorted out. I need to speak with Arthur before we head out."

"Let's get you set up," Abioye said as he led Christian to the rear of the Jeep he would be driving. Abioye opened the rear hatch, revealing a multi-level weapons vault. "The code for the gun vaults in all three vehicles is set to 1-7-7-6." He entered the code and opened the top tier of the unit. From the vault, he pulled out a set of soft body armor, which was designed to be worn under clothing to allow the wearer to remain low-key. He handed the body armor to Christian and said, "This is Safelife's best concealable armor. If things heat up, there's a set of FRAS flexible rifle armor with FRAS rifle plates in the vault as well." He tossed the soft armor to Christian and shut the top drawer.

While Christian was adjusting the straps for the body armor, Abioye opened the bottom section of the vault. "We have a Daniel Defense MK18 fitted with an EOTech HWS EXPS3 holographic sight. It's also fitted with an G33 magnifier on a switch-to-side mounting system. The sight is compatible with night vision."

Jerome reached back into the vault and lifted out a handgun. "I know you carry the Glock 43 with you. We've provided you with a Gen5 Glock 17 MOS for bigger jobs than that baby gun can handle." Abioye's comment earned him a one-finger salute from Christian.

"Ammo?" he asked as he took the rifle from Jerome's hands.

"You've got a dozen thirty-round Magpul magazines loaded out and an additional thousand rounds of Hornady 5.56. There are ten fully loaded 17-round magazines for the Glock and another five hundred rounds of Speer 147-grain GDHP in the vault."

"Nice," Christian said approvingly.

"We spared no expense, my brother."

Valentine walked over to the group, with Paine trailing right behind. "We all set, gentlemen?"

"Good to go," answered Abioye.

"Okay. Once you're on the road, Paine and Durand will be the lead vehicles. Vikstrom, you and Laura will follow, with Abioye and Altman watching your six."

Christian checked his watch. "It's a little after zero two hundred now. It's around a half hour to the Grand Isle ferry. They run twenty-four/seven, and according to their online schedule, they have a boat departing for Plattsburgh at zero three-o-five. We have plenty of time to get there."

"Alright, people; let's get mounted up." Valentine looked for and found Laura leading Evy across the hanger toward the group. "Are you all set?"

"We're all set, Arthur. Evy wanted to speak with you before we split up."

"Of course." Arthur turned to the young girl and gave her an appraising stare. "How are you holding up, Evy?"

"I'm fine, Mr. Valentine. Just a little stressed out right now."

"That's completely understandable, considering everything that's happened in the past twenty-four hours."

Evy paused before continuing. "I'm still not a fan of this entire plan, but I'm committed now. I just want my parents to know I'm okay."

"I'll have Martin contact your parents through the system we have set up. They'll believe you're in Switzerland, but they'll know you're okay. Once you get settled in Lake Placid, our computer guy there will arrange for you to contact your parents."

"Do you think what happened in Rome will be in the news?" Evora had been worried ever since the attempted kidnapping that her parents would learn about it all from a news broadcast.

"There was major news coverage of the event, but just as Signore Milazzo promised, the entire event is being portrayed as a domestic terrorist incident. There has been no mention of you in the press at all."

Evora's face reflected the immense relief she felt. "Thank you, Mr. Valentine."

"Of course, Evy. Now we have to get you on your way. I want you safely tucked away in Lake Placid within the next couple of hours."

Laura took the young actress by the elbow and led her over to the assembled vehicles. By the time they reached the Jeep, Christian had just finished loading their bags.

"How are you doing, Evy?" he asked.

"I've been better, but I guess it could be worse."

Christian admired the bravery the young woman was displaying. "Just settle in and feel free to take a nap. We'll be at the ferry crossing in around a half hour, and we should have you safely in Lake Placid by around four."

"We're taking a ferry?"

"It's either the ferry or a very, very long drive around Lake Champlain." Christian gave Evy a reassuring smile and helped her climb into the vehicle.

"Alright, everyone. Mount up and let's get this show on the road!" Paine yelled to the group. "I'll keep you updated on our progress, Arthur."

"Take your time and drive safely. There's no indication that our unsub has any idea he's been duped. Martin has been on his computer since we landed, checking as many sources as possible. Our stalker hasn't posted any messages or sent any emails to indicate he knows where she is."

"Good. Hopefully we get lucky, and it stays that way."

"Getting lucky isn't a plan, Steven."

CHAPTER TWO

Lake Champlain Ferries

Grand Isle, Vermont

The drive from Burlington International Airport to the Lake Champlain Ferry in Grand Isle, Vermont took just under thirty minutes. Up ahead, a blue sign that read Lake Champlain Ferries with a picture of a ferry boat below appeared in the darkness. Under the picture of the boat, the sign read FERRY TO NEW YORK in yellow with an arrow pointing toward Lake Champlain.

The lead vehicle slowed, and Durand signaled to turn left, with the remaining two vehicles in their little convoy following close behind. The light of the moon reflected off the lake that was just barely visible in the darkness, and Christian saw a large, two-story white building off to his left. Directly in front of them, the road split into three lanes. Each lane led to a white ticket booth. Streetlights along the roadway and a half dozen more standing at regular intervals in a parking lot off to the right attempted to push back the gloom of a light fog that was rising off the water. Due to the early morning hour, only the furthest right-hand lane was active. A small delivery van had just exited the ticket booth, allowing the Expedition that Paine was driving to pull forward. Once Paine cleared the ticket booth, Christian pulled ahead. The young man manning the booth looked to be in his early twenties. His dirty-blond hair spilled out from under the Lake Champlain Ferries bucket hat he wore. The toll collector informed Christian that they had arrived just in time to purchase tickets for the 3:05 a.m. crossing. Once the small convoy had paid the fee, all three vehicles pulled up to join the small queue of vehicles waiting to be directed aboard the big boat. Christian was surprised by the number of vehicles making the early morning crossing. Several delivery trucks and an electrical contractor's van were mixed in with a half dozen private vehicles.

Once they had the Jeep parked on the ferry, Laura turned to Evy in the back seat and said, "Let's head up to the lounge and find a comfortable spot to enjoy the ride."

"Can't we just stay in the vehicle? It looks cold outside."

"I'm sorry, Evy, but passengers are not allowed to stay on the transport deck. I'm sure the lounge is heated, and they may even have a snack bar where we can grab a hot drink."

"Not to mention, if we're up in the lounge, you may catch a glimpse of Champ," Christian added.

"Who's Champ?"

"Well, I'm sure you've heard of the Loch Ness Monster?" he asked the puzzled girl.

"Of course. Everyone's heard that ridiculous myth."

Apparently, Ms. Cota was not a big believer in folklore. *Surprising,* Christian thought, *as her television series drew heavily from several myths and centuries-old stories of demons and monsters.*

"Well, I don't know how ridiculous it all is, but I do know that we here in the States have our own sea monster right here in Lake Champlain, and his or her name is Champ."

"And I suppose you've seen this 'sea monster'?" Evy used her index and middle fingers on each hand to throw up a set of air quotes as she spoke.

"Technically, it's a 'lake monster'," he answered with air quotes of his own. "And no. Not personally."

"Do you actually believe the story?" Evy's face held a small smile—the first they'd seen since leaving the hotel in Rome the previous evening.

"I don't know. I'd like to think there could be something out there."

"Why?"

Christian thought she sounded genuinely curious. "Because I'd like to believe there are still things in this world that we haven't discovered yet. A little mystery and a bit of adventure make the world a much more exciting place to live."

The actress seemed to shiver a bit before she replied. "I think last night's adventure was just about as much excitement as I care to experience right now, thank you."

"I'd have to agree with Evy on that one. Let's hope for some relatively boring days ahead," Laura added.

Laura put her arm around Evy and guided the young actress up the stairs to the main deck, where she got her settled in on a comfortably padded bench in the far corner of the lounge. Shadows caused by the overhead lighting helped obscure them from any casual observer.

After checking to ensure Cota was all set, Paine ordered Pierre Durand to go below and keep an eye on the vehicles. "If they give you any problems about staying with the vehicles, offer them some cash. If they still don't want to let you stay down there, come and get me, and I'll handle it."

Durand headed for the stairs leading below, while Paine ordered Abioye and Altman to conduct a roving patrol of the boat without drawing too much attention to themselves.

Christian stepped away from the group and called Dexter. After a brief conversation, he hung up and rejoined everyone.

"I just spoke with Dexter. He confirmed the lodging information for both QRF teams. As per our briefing earlier, Paine, you, and Pierre are staying at the Lake Placid Club lodges on the southeast side of Mirror Lake. Jerome and Dave are staying in a cottage at Wildwood on the Lake. I wrote down the addresses and access codes for both properties." He handed the small piece of paper he'd jotted the information down on to Paine.

"How far apart are we?" Jerome asked.

"Lake Placid is small. You and Dave are about four minutes from the safe house. Paine and Pierre are about ten minutes away."

Once Christian handed out the lodging information, Paine took charge. "Okay, people, let's spread out. Abioye and Altman, cover the stern area. Christian, you and Laura stay with Evy. I'll set up near the stairs."

"Ladder," corrected Christian.

"Excuse me?"

"We're on a boat. Stairs are referred to as ladders. The floor is a deck, and the doorways are hatches."

Paine opted not to reply. He just shook his head slightly and walked off to cover his portion of the lounge deck.

"Why do you do that?" Laura asked.

"Do what?" Christian did his best to sound innocent.

"Why do you egg Steven on? He has a job to do, just like the rest of us. You constantly busting his balls isn't going to improve your relationship."

Christian saw that Evy was watching them closely, and he didn't want to do or say anything that would cause the girl to worry about the people protecting her not getting long.

"You're right. I just like busting his chops. Sometimes he gets wound a bit too tight, and I like to rattle his cage."

"How about we save the cage rattling for after the assignment is over?"

Christian smiled and, with an extravagant bow, said, "Your wish is my command, Ms. Knight."

Laura couldn't stifle the laugh Christian's dramatic bow had evoked, and both she and Christian turned in surprise when Evy joined in their laughter.

"Please don't encourage him," Laura said.

Evy's laughter trailed off, and her amused expression was preplaced with a contemplative one. Christian had walked away to check out the rest of the lounge area, when Evy looked at Laura and asked, "Are you two together?" She nodded her head in Christian's direction when she spoke.

"Christian and I?" She wasn't sure she understood what the girl was asking.

"Yes. You two seem to have a special connection. Not like with the others."

Laura chuckled and shook her head. "No. Nothing like that. Christian just joined our team. We've only just begun to get to know each other. Besides, I'm married."

"Really? What's your husband do?"

Deciding it was a good sign that Evy was showing interest in something other than her present situation, Laura decided to confide a little personal information with the girl. The closer the bond she could forge with Evy, the better chance the fiery young actress would cooperate with them during their time together.

"Wife, actually."

"Excuse me?"

"You asked me what my husband does. I'm married to a woman, and she's a pilot."

"What does she think of you doing this kind of work?"

"She does the same kind of work, so she's fine with it."

Before Evora had time to ask Laura any more personal questions, Christian returned.

"We'll be docking in another five minutes. Let's get our things and move closer to the stairs."

"Ladder," Evy said with a straight face.

Christian just shook his head and walked away, Laura Knight's laughter following him across the deck.

CHAPTER THREE

Cumberland Head Ferry Landing, New York

The bright lights of the Cumberland Head Ferry dock slowly came into view through the mist that shrouded the lake. From where they stood on the upper deck, Christian could just make out the pier, and a couple of dock hands that were preparing to help tie off the big boat. There appeared to be three slips for the ferry boats to dock, and they were approaching the middle one. Christian felt the ferry shudder as it made contact with the dock, and a few minutes later, the speaker located above their heads announced it was now safe to go below and get into their vehicles.

The small group walked down the steel staircase, being careful not to slip on the dampened treads. Abioye had gone down as soon as the boat made contact with the dock to coordinate with Durand, who had been allowed by the ferry crew to remain below with their vehicles for the entire crossing. Once they were cleared to proceed to their vehicles, Paine led the way to the lower deck, with Christian and Laura keeping Evy safely between them as they followed. David Altman remained behind the group on the lounge deck to make sure no one was paying the rest of the group any undue attention. Once he was sure they were clear, he joined the rest of the team below.

The vehicle deck was a beehive of activity as all of the ferry boat's passengers maneuvered between the parked vehicles to get to their own rides. Laura made sure Evy was comfortably situated in the back seat of the Jeep before climbing into the front passenger's seat. Christian stepped up on the running board of the vehicle and looked around to make sure the rest of the team were loaded up before he climbed in behind the steering wheel. The sound of rattling chains and a humming electric motor filled the air as the ramp was being lowered, and vehicles began to slowly work their way forward. Having arrived at the very last minute for loading, the team's vehicles were the last in line to disembark. Paine and Durand drove the big Ford Expedition across the ramp, with Christian following close behind. The Chevy Tahoe, with Altman driving and Abioye riding shotgun, was the final vehicle to reach the shore.

"Is everyone all set?" Paine asked over the vehicle radio.

"Good to go," answered Knight.

"We're set," Abioye acknowledged.

The three-vehicle convoy proceeded toward the exit, passing a small white building on the right that advertised an ATM, restrooms, and travel information within. Due to the early hour, the building appeared to be closed. On their left was a small line of vehicles waiting to load onto the ferry for the trip back to Vermont. Of the seven lanes available for loading, only the first lane was in use, with three vehicles waiting to be cleared to board.

The single exit lane took them past three small white ticket booths on the left and a small, paved parking lot on the right, where a single working streetlight fought a losing battle with the misty early morning gloom in its attempt to illuminate the parking area. They sped north as the exit road became the Commodore Thomas MacDonough Highway, where they crossed Cumberland Head Road. The ferry dock was located on a peninsula, and their small convoy had to head northwest to reach Plattsburgh and the Northway before turning south and heading toward Lake Placid.

"You may as well try to get comfortable," Christian said to Evy. "It's going to be a little over an hour's drive from here. This is a beautiful drive during the day, especially this time of year. We're almost at peak fall foliage, and the spectrum of red, gold, and orange leaves is absolutely amazing. Unfortunately, our leaf peeping will have to wait until the sun is out. There is not much to see driving through the mountains in the dark."

Even though Laura had turned the heat on high as soon as they entered the vehicle, it was still chilly as the heater attempted to overcome the damp and cold that permeated the vehicle from the trip across the lake. Evy pulled her jacket tight as she sank deeper into the comfortable leather of the back seat.

"That's why I picked this place," Evy said softly.

"I'm sorry, Evy. I could barely hear you," Laura said.

"I said, that's why I picked this place."

"The fall leaves?"

"Yes."

"I thought you'd never been to the States before." Christian's confusion was obvious.

"I haven't, but a few years ago I was cast in a play in Madrid. I wasn't the lead, but I was one of the major supporting actresses. There was an actress who had been cast as an extra to help fill in as a background character when needed. She and I were about the same age, and we hung out together during breaks. She was from someplace in the northeast of the U.S. I can't really remember where. What I do remember is that all she ever talked about was how much she missed her home and how great the change of seasons was there. She went on and on about the beautiful fall colors. The silly girl seemed to think only America has changes in seasons."

"I'm sure she was just proud of her home and wanted to share some of that with you," Laura said.

"Probably. It just got so annoying. You Americans are

always so proud of your country. It's like no one in America is even aware the rest of the world has just as much, if not more, to offer."

Christian held back the first response that came to mind. They'd been warned that Cota disliked Americans and thought they were all arrogant and entitled. She was a young woman thrust into a terrifying situation where she had little control over what was happening. Debating with her on the merits of the nation he loved wouldn't help the situation.

"Considering your opinion of us Americans, what made you choose Lake Placid as the place to hide out?" he asked.

"When Alonzo first told me about Mr. Fraser's idea of taking me somewhere that I have no connection to while they search for the maniac who's harassing me, I told him there was no way I'd go along with the idea. Of course, Alonzo, being Alonzo, kept talking and finally got me to discuss where I'd go if I did agree to this nonsense. I was always very athletic growing up, and even though my goal since I was a child was to be a famous actress, I played football—or soccer to you Americans." The darkness inside the Jeep hid the quizzical look that crossed Evora's beautiful face. "I'll never understand why you Americans call it soccer when the rest of the world calls it football."

"We already have football here, and soccer is just starting to really draw a following," Christian provided.

"Typical." She didn't need to finish the sentence to show

her distaste for Christian's reasoning. "Anyway. When I was younger, I enjoyed skiing and cross-country running. I watched a documentary on female athletes training for the Olympics. A couple of the more famous female skiers have trained in Lake Placid, and the documentary showed them training at the Olympic facility year-round. Part of the documentary was shot in the fall, and the mountains around the lake looked so beautiful that it reminded me of that actress and her love for the fall colors back home. I thought that if I ever did take a trip to the U.S., I'd like to visit Lake Placid. So when Alonzo kept pushing me to think of a place I'd never been to before, I said Lake Placid. At the time, I had no intention of leaving Europe because of this guy."

"I guess you're going to have the opportunity to form your own opinion about how beautiful fall is in the northeast."

"I guess." There was little enthusiasm in her voice.

Evy fell silent for the next half hour, and Christian figured the young woman had fallen asleep. While he and Laura chatted quietly, Christian kept an eye on the taillights of the lead vehicle being driven by Pierre Durand while also staying alert for the abundance of Adirondack wildlife that oftentimes wandered onto the highway, causing fatal car accidents.

"How long do you think I'll have to hide here?" Evy asked.

"Hey, I thought you were sleeping," Laura said.

"Not really. Just kind of zoning out and thinking. How long do you think I'll be here?" she asked again.

"We can't be sure, Evy. The authorities in all three countries where you had apartments are working very hard to identify the person harassing you."

"How long does something like that normally take?"

"There isn't any way for us to know that, Evy," Christian said. "This guy appears to be very smart and hides his identity and location very well, but we have a secret weapon."

Laura gave Christian a strange look as Evy said, "What secret weapon?"

"I work with a person who was once a cybercrime investigator with the FBI. He's by far the smartest person I've ever worked with when it comes to anything having to do with computers and tracking people online."

"If he's so smart, how come he isn't still working for the FBI?"

"Because, like me, Dexter has a bit of an issue with authority." Christian was speaking to Evy, but he was looking directly at Laura, who had to stifle a laugh at his words.

"So he got fired?"

"Unfortunately, he did. But the FBI's loss is our gain. Dexter has been receiving daily updates from the authorities in Europe on what they've been able to find. When I called Dexter just before we left Rome, he said he had some ideas about how to figure out not only where the stalker is but who he may be."

"So once you find the guy, I can go home?"

"Once we find *and* neutralize the threat to you, then you

can go home," Christian corrected her.

Evy let out a soft sigh.

"What is it, Evy?" Laura asked.

"I always talk with my mom every night before I go to bed. We were using Facetime and Skype, but in the past month, we've been using an app called JusTalk. Will I be able to do that from here?"

"I asked Dexter to set up a way for you to be able to communicate with your parents while you're here. Unfortunately, you won't be able to tell them where you really are or who you're with. It's imperative that they think you're really in Switzerland. To make sure of that, one of us will have to monitor any contact you have with anyone on the outside."

"I don't think I care for that very much." Evy's tone reminded both Christian and Laura of the young actress's attitude at their original meeting.

Speaking in a calm, reasonable voice, Laura said, "Evy, you have to understand. What we're doing is for your safety. We understand that you need your privacy, but this person has already demonstrated that he has the ability to monitor your communications. We have to make sure you don't inadvertently say something that could give away where we are."

"I understand," she said quietly as she turned back toward the window and fell silent once again. Evy knew arguing with these people would do her no good. She'd have to take it day by day and decide just how much she would cooperate.

The meek way Evy seemed to accept what Laura had said made Christian very uncomfortable for some reason. He couldn't put a finger on it, but he knew the girl's words hadn't rung true.

There was no way Christian could have known just how justified his unease was.

CHAPTER FOUR

Lake Placid, New York

They came into Lake Placid from the north along Route 86, then turned west onto Northwood Road and followed the worn blacktop of the two-lane road to the end. When they reached Mirror Lake Drive, Christian radioed Paine.

"Paine, you and Durand take a left here. The Lake Placid Club lodges will be a few miles down the road on the left. There's no need to have all three vehicles travel to the safe site. It'll just draw unnecessary attention, even at this early hour."

"Copy that. Check in once you're secure."

"Copy."

While Pain and Durand turned left, the other two vehicles turned right onto Mirror Lake Drive and circled around the west side of Mirror Lake, passing the Lake Placid marina. As they drove by the Mirror Lake Inn, Christian wondered if young Sean Thornton or his grandfather, Abner, were up at this early hour making sure their beautiful inn was ready for their guests.

When they turned right onto Sara-Placid Road, Christian radioed Abioye.

"Jerome, Wildwood on the Lake is just up ahead on the right. We'll be turning off at the next roadway after that. There's only one road into the safe site, so I don't want you following me down there."

"Copy that. We'll be close if you need us."

As they passed Wildwood on the Lake, Christian watched in his rearview mirror as Jerome pulled off the main road into the parking lot.

"Jerome's a good man. I'm glad he's here."

"We're very lucky to have him," Laura agreed.

Christian took his cell phone from his pocket and said, "Siri, call Dex mobile."

"Calling Dex mobile," the digital personal assistant said in a sultry voice.

"Umm, my Siri doesn't sound like that," Laura observed.

"I forgot about that. I had Dexter upgrade the encryption and security on my iPhone. He took the liberty of changing Siri's voice as well."

Christian heard a quiet giggle from the back seat, indicating Evy was no longer asleep. "I think I'm going to like this Dexter person."

"Indeed," Laura said. "Dexter sounds like quite the character."

"Oh, he is," Christian said. *I'm going to kick your ass, Dex,* he thought to himself.

"It's about time, brother," Dexter said by way of a greeting.

"We're five minutes out."

"I know. I've been tracking your phone. See ya in a few."

Christian turned right onto Peninsula Way Road and wound his way through the quietly sleeping community. It was too dark for his passengers to see the beautifully wooded properties they were passing or the multi-million-dollar homes they held. They turned right onto Sand Point Way, following the gentle curve of the road until they reached Roland Way. Roland Way curved gently to the left, and as they came out of the curve, their destination came into view.

Laura and Evy both stared in amazement at the beautiful home they were approaching. Exterior lighting cleverly hidden among the landscaping cast the huge house in alternating areas of brightly lit stone and wood, with deep shadows obscuring other portions of the amazing structure.

The large double garage door began to rise as Christian pulled into the driveway, and he could see Dexter standing just inside the garage bay, awaiting their arrival.

When the vehicle came to rest, the large overhead door began its descent. When Laura opened her door to step out, she found Dexter waiting to greet her.

"Dexter Choi at your service," he said, taking Laura's hand and bowing his head slightly as he spoke. Then he moved to the rear door and opened it so Evy could get out. When the tired young woman slid her legs out, Dexter took her hand and helped her the rest of the way.

"Good evening—or, I guess more accurately, good morning, Ms. Cota. Welcome to Lake Placid. I'm Dexter Choi."

Dexter's formality seemed oddly out of place considering the situation, but his infectious smile and easygoing mannerisms made Evy smile.

"It's nice to meet you. Please call me Evy."

"And you both can call me Dex. Go ahead with Christian inside. I'll grab your bags."

Christian led the two women through a door in the back of the garage that led through a laundry room and into the most beautiful kitchen Laura had ever seen. The kitchen was open with what appeared to be all new black stainless appliances and a huge center island that featured a four-burner gas stove and oven unit and a deep farm-style sink. On the far side of the island sat a dining room table big enough to comfortably seat a dozen guests. Beyond the kitchen/dining area, they saw a huge great room with a vaulted ceiling. A large, dark brown leather sofa and two matching oversized recliners sat facing an enormous stone fireplace with a twelve-foot-long mantle. A fire crackled merrily in the cavernous firebox, helping to keep the large space warm.

Even as exhausted and stressed out as Evy was, she was amazed by how beautiful the home was. "This place is amazing, Mr. Choi."

"It certainly is," agreed Laura.

"Evy, please just call me Dex."

"Dex." As she spoke, a yawn overtook her. "Oh, my. I'm sorry. That was so rude."

"Not at all. After the past two days you've had, I'm totally impressed with how well you're doing." Then, taking Evy's hand, he continued. "Let me show you to your room so you can get settled in. We can continue the grand tour later today."

Evy allowed Dexter to escort her up the large wooden staircase to the second floor, with Laura Knight following closely behind with their luggage. Even in her exhaustion, Evy was amazed by the floating staircase bracketed by a mahogany railing that reflected the flickering firelight.

Dexter led Evy to her room and pushed the door open for her. "If you need anything at all, just let me know." He stepped aside to allow Evy and Laura to enter the room.

"I'll be down in a few minutes. I just want to get her settled in first," Laura said as she passed.

"We'll be in the kitchen." He turned to head downstairs.

CHAPTER FIVE

Safehouse, Lake Placid, New York

Christian and Dexter were seated on comfortable-looking leather stools at the kitchen island when Laura came back downstairs.

"How is she?" Christian asked.

"I'd say as well as could be expected. She fell asleep as soon as she laid down on the bed. I wouldn't expect to hear anything from her until sometime around lunch today."

Christian thanked Laura for taking care of getting Evy settled in and offered her a seat. "Okay. Proper introductions are in order, I guess." He put his hand on Dexter's muscular shoulder and continued. "Laura Knight, please meet my closest friend and one of the best computer security specialists and world-class hackers on the planet, Dexter Choi."

"Dexter, this is Laura Knight. She's Arthur Valentine's right-hand person and one hell of an operator."

After they exchanged a handshake, Laura said, "I know quite a bit about Mr. Choi here. We did a deep dive into his background after you insisted Arthur hire him for this job." Turning to Dexter, she continued. "You have some very impressive credentials, Dex."

Dexter's easygoing smile never left his handsome face. "Thank you, Laura. I took the opportunity while I was setting things up here to do some digging of my own, so I know a bit about you as well. Your time with Marine Corp. Intel was very impressive. I was surprised you gave up such a promising career in the military to join Valentine's organization."

"Probably as surprised as I was to learn you were fired by the FBI for insubordination."

"Touché." Dexter laughed.

"When you two are done, can we go over where we stand here so Laura and I can get some sleep? It's been a long day." Christian barely stifled a yawn.

"Certainly. First off, security. When Tyler Matas had this place built, he included a decent security system. He's loaded, and so is his wife. While he'd never received any threats, kidnapping was a legitimate concern. I took what was already here and made some significant improvements." As he spoke, he gave Christian a speculative look. "Actually, I think you should renegotiate what he's charging to lease this place out to us. The lighting and security upgrades I've added are worth far more than he's asking for rent."

"I'll keep that in mind. Now can we get on with the briefing?"

"Just a thought. No need to get testy." The smile on Dexter's face made it clear Christian's outburst hadn't phased him in the least. "Where was I?"

"The security upgrades," Laura supplied.

"Ah, yes. So I've installed upgraded intrusion sensors on all the windows and doors. The windows are high-quality but not bullet resistant. I didn't have time for that, and the cost may have proven prohibitive. I was able to have blast-resistant film applied to all the ground-floor windows. It turns out an old acquaintance from my FBI days owns a private security company now that caters to the ultra-rich and shameless. He sent a crew out and had the film done in a day."

"The film was a good call, Dex. I don't think we need to worry about actual bullet-resistant glass. If this plan works, the unsub will be in custody without ever learning that Cota is here and not in Switzerland."

"That was my reasoning as well. The house already had a high-end fire suppression system installed during the original build. I added additional smoke and heat detection sensors throughout the house. There are motion detectors and pressure sensors located around the property now. I had the cameras that were here replaced with units that provide infrared capabilities in addition to night vision. I'll install the app on both of your phones and pads, so all alerts go to all three of us."

"What about the QRF teams? I think it'd be a good idea if they were tied into the security system," Laura said.

Dexter looked at Christian. "Up to you. It's no problem getting it done."

"It's a good idea. Take care of that as soon as possible. Next?"

"I put motion detectors on the dock as well as the interior and exterior of the boathouse, and I added additional cameras out there as well. We have complete video and audio coverage of the property."

"We had talked about a safe room when we looked at this place. Did you have time to work on that?"

"Unfortunately, Matas didn't think to add a saferoom. The best I could do was to have wood veneer and steel doors installed in each bedroom. I also had floor-mounted drop locks installed. It was the best I could do with the time constraints. It isn't perfect, but it'll slow down anyone trying to get in long enough to give the QRF teams or police time to get here."

"Nice. Look, it's almost zero-five hundred already. Laura and I need to get some sleep. Let's get together again after lunch and go over the rest of your preparations."

"Works for me. I put Evy in the master suite. It's actually more like a small apartment. She has her own bath along with a small sitting area with a fireplace. Laura, I put you in the guest suite on the first floor. It has its own facilities, so you won't have to share a bathroom with us savages."

"Thank you, Dex."

"Christian and I are in the two second-floor bedrooms down the hall from Evy's suite. Unfortunately, we'll have to share a bathroom. The sacrifices I make for the team." Dexter shook his head in mock humility.

Christian chuckled at his friend's comment. "Great work, Dex. I'll give Paine an update, and then I'm getting some sleep."

"Thank you, Dexter. I'll talk to you two in a few hours," Laura said as she headed toward the suite Dex had set aside for her.

Dexter watched the beautiful woman walk across the room and disappear down the darkened hallway.

"Don't get any ideas, Romeo."

"What?" Dexter asked.

"Don't "what" me. She's a teammate. On top of that, she's married to another member of Valentine's people."

"The good ones are always married."

CHAPTER SIX

Rome, Italy

Andino Fabrizio sat quietly in his study, watching the sun rise over the ancient capital of the Roman Empire. The first rays of the morning sun reflected brightly off the dome of Saint Peter's Basilica in the distance, momentarily blinding the troubled man. He had spent all night reviewing the information sent to him by his small team of computer hackers. He'd tasked them with keeping tabs on the Cota girl's online activity now that she was in Switzerland. They were actively tracking every known cell phone, email, and social media account the girl had. Among the treasure trove of data they had obtained thus far were cell phone call records and tower data, as well as transcripts from text messages that had been sent to Cota's family and closest friends. Email accounts had been hacked, and Fabrizio had copies of all of the conversations. In addition to the actual content of texts and emails, he also had the exact coordinates and IP addresses from which the messages had been sent.

Fabrizio was desperate to find a weakness in the girl's protection that Lowery could exploit. He had spent over two hours entering the longitude and latitude connected with every captured contact into a program designed to provide a detailed map of every electronic communication the girl made. He was comparing the information his expensive group of computer experts had provided him with the information Padraig Lowery was providing, and something was troubling him.

Today marked two weeks to the day since the failed kidnapping attempt in Rome. It had taken Lowery two days to get himself and Nessa Keever out of Italy and back to Northern Ireland. The combination of Italian authorities and the surviving hierarchy of Le Ombre searching for them made every step of their journey fraught with the danger of capture or death.

Once back on his home turf, it had taken the cagey Irishman another five days to get himself and a half dozen of his best people into Switzerland. Part of the problem was that Switzerland was not a member of the European Union and thus didn't enjoy the EU's open border policies. Getting the required number of men and material into the security-conscious country undetected required a lot of planning as well as a significant amount of currency.

Another major problem he faced was that almost every member of his organization had been identified by MI6, and their photos had been distributed through INTERPOL to all member nations, including Switzerland. Being labeled as a member of a terrorist organization made international travel difficult.

Once in Lucerne, it hadn't taken Lowery's people long to locate the safe house where Roddy Fraser and his mercenaries were keeping the girl. The majestic villa sat on a heavily wooded, secluded lot in the foothills of the Alps, overlooking the beautiful city and the crystal-clear waters of Lake Lucerne. There was only one small, two-lane road running past the gated driveway, and the nearest home was over a mile away. The isolated area made direct surveillance of the house nearly impossible.

Nessa Keever had drawn on her experience with the Special Reconnaissance Regiment to come up with a workable solution. The fact that all of Fraser's men were either former SAS or other British special operations veterans added to Keever's challenge. Keever had pointed out that the one-lane road running past the property was a double-edged sword for the men protecting Cota. While anyone using the road would come under immediate scrutiny from the men at the villa, it also meant they had only one route of travel available to them when they wanted to leave the villa and go into the city or surrounding area. Keever had been able to find a vacant rental property five miles away from the safe house. The house was situated in such a way that they would see anyone leaving the villa by motor vehicle. Keever had utilized a small drone to do several flyovers of the house. She was able to identify the four vehicles being used by the team. She had also been able to obtain dozens of photos of the property for planning purposes. The photos also revealed several men that Keever identified as being on the protection team in both London and Rome.

After over a week of surveillance, Lowery's team had not only positively identified several of Fraser's men, but they had also been able to identify and photograph Alonzo Perez, Sofia Avelar, and Cota's ever-present bodyguard, Antonio Lacapra. The surveillance team had also provided numerous photos of the subject they claimed was Evora Cota. While the photographs of Fraser's people and Cota's entourage included numerous clear facial shots, in each photo of the girl, her face was obscured by large sunglasses or with her long hair covering portions of her face. Lowery was positive—the girl was Cota. He argued that she never went anywhere without Perez or Lacapra, so it had to be her.

Lowery gave Fabrizio frequent updates on the surveillance operation. The initial reports were promising, and Lowery was confident that it was just a matter of time until the girl's protectors slipped up and Lowery would be able to grab her. At first, Fabrizio had agreed, but doubt had slowly begun to creep in.

Lowery's reports showed that while Cota's people made numerous trips into the city over the past week, Cota herself had only been observed leaving the villa on two occasions.

In contrast, the data from Fabrizio's team of hackers monitoring the girl's online and cellular activity showed her frequently sending text messages and emails from various spots located all around Lucerne and the surrounding area. The data showed numerous days where Cota had contact with her mother via email and texted from a half dozen different spots within the city. The electronic surveillance seemed to indicate Cota was leaving the villa almost daily. When Fabrizio compared these records to the physical surveillance reports from Lowery, a different picture emerged. A detailed comparison of the electronic surveillance being conducted by his team of hackers to the physical surveillance being conducted by Lowery's people revealed that, on many of the days, Cota was reportedly contacting her family and friends from various locations in and around Lucerne, and the physical surveillance teams reported she had never left the villa. It slowly became painfully apparent to Fabrizio that he had been duped. The girl Lowery and his people were watching wasn't Cota at all. Somehow, Fraser had fooled everyone into thinking Cota had traveled to Switzerland with her people and Fraser's team of protectors.

Fabrizio was furious for allowing himself to be fooled by

such a transparent subterfuge. He had relied too heavily on the reports from L'Avvoltoio's people at the airport. Once again, it was clear that the people the Italian gangster had used were incompetent.

Pushing his anger aside, he called Lowery on the secure satellite phone the man had sent him via a private courier company. Fabrizio didn't waste any time on pleasantries. As soon as Lowery answered the phone, he said, "We've been tricked."

"What the hell are you talking about?" Over the past two weeks, Lowery had slowly come to realize the man he was working for was somehow not right in the head. His intelligence was undeniable, but so was his irrational obsession with the Cota girl. Lowery couldn't wait to grab the girl and be done with this maniac.

"Evora Cota is not in Switzerland with Fraser."

"Of course she is. I've sent you photos of her and all of her people."

"That's just it. None of the photos of the girl show her face clearly. They're all obscured by sunglasses and hats, and her hair is always draped around her face. It's not her. It's an imposter."

"What about her people? It's clearly her manager, bodyguard, and personal assistant." Lowery felt the situation slowly slip from his grasp.

"It is her people. That's why they've gotten away with it

for so long. They sent her people with Fraser to Lucerne, but she isn't with them."

"How can you be so sure?"

"I've been getting continuous reports from my technical people showing Cota texting and emailing her family and friends from all over Lucerne."

"That's because she's here," Lowery argued.

"No, she's not. Please just listen." Fabrizio had learned to be respectful when he spoke with Lowery. The man was not L'Avvoltoio. He was an intelligent, battle-hardened, and experienced tactician. He evaluated everything presented to him from every possible angle. He also had a fiery temper that Fabrizio had no desire to ignite.

"When I compare your surveillance reports to the electronic surveillance reports, a very clear picture emerges."

"Explain."

"On many of the days, your people report that Cota's people travel around the Luzerne area while she isn't with them, and electronic surveillance reports indicate Cota sent numerous texts and emails from various locations in the city. Her texts include the restaurants she eats at and the sites she is seeing. There are even photographs of different tourist locations in the region. My people have the geo-coordinates of where the photos are taken and the ISP addresses and cell towers used when the messages are sent."

"So who's sending the messages if Cota isn't there?"

Lowery realized the Italian may be on to something.

"Exactly. Who indeed? My theory is that they used an imposter when Fraser flew Cota's people out of Rome. They set up a way for someone on Cota's staff to send messages to her family and friends, knowing I'm monitoring her social media and cell phone usage. They banked on me using her need to stay in touch with her family to keep track of her. It was a very good plan, but not good enough. The girl isn't in Switzerland."

"Then where is she?" Lowery's anger was clear.

"I haven't figured that out yet, but rest assured, I will. For now, just keep doing what you're doing."

"Why? It's a waste of time if the girl isn't here."

"Because I'm sure Fraser has already identified some of the people you have surveilling him. I'm also sure they have computer experts of their own who have identified at least a few of the traps I've placed on Cota's phone and computer usage. If all of our efforts to track her just suddenly disappear, they'll know we've discovered she isn't in Switzerland."

"How long do we keep this up?"

"I'm not sure. They will eventually slip up and give me a clue as to where they have taken her. I'll just need you to be ready when she does."

Little did Fabrizio know, that in less than twenty-four hours, Evora Cota herself would reveal her location to him.

CHAPTER SEVEN

Lake Placid, New York

A steady rain had begun to fall just after midnight. Now, at six thirty in the morning, the rain had intensified into a steady downpour. For Evora Cota, the weather mirrored her mood. She stood under the covered portion of the expansive back deck of the beautiful lakeside retreat that served as her safe haven. The heavy rain obscured her normally clear view of the majestic camps that sat along the shore of Buck Island, just across the narrow strip of water that separated the mainland from Lake Placid's second-largest island.

She had been hidden away at the beautiful house in Lake Placid for two weeks now. Her protectors, whom she sometimes unkindly thought of as her jailors, had done their best to fill her days with activities designed to try to take her mind off her current situation. Christian had even taught her how to kayak on the tranquil waters of the beautiful Adirondack Lake. Evy had never been in a kayak before, and she enjoyed learning the nuances of maneuvering the small fiberglass craft through the crystal-clear water. She marveled at the array of camps along the shores of the three islands on Lake Placid. The structures ranged from small, modest structures to palatial, multi-building compounds. Evy's favorite camp was situated on Hawk Island, the smallest of the three. The camp was two stories high and sat partially on the shore, with the majority of the structure jutting out from the shore and resting on moorings sunk deep into the lake bed. The camp featured a large sundeck set atop a three-stall boathouse.

During one evening trip around the lake, with Christian and Laura paddling alongside her, they observed the owner of one of the lakeshore camps working on the most beautiful boat Evy had ever seen. After some cajoling, and with a little help from Laura, Evy was able to convince Christian to let them paddle over to the dock and take a closer look. The man was delighted to talk about his latest treasure. The eighteen-foot Chris Craft Riviera was all gleaming mahogany and red leather. After talking non-stop about his newest addition to his small fleet of boats for over thirty minutes, he offered to take them all for a ride, but Christian made up a story about needing to get back to camp, and after the promise of a raincheck, they pointed their kayaks south and headed back to the safe house.

Evy was thankful that she had always been athletic and stuck to a rigid workout regimen because her guardians often took her on day-long hikes. Lake Placid is surrounded by beautiful mountains with hiking trails that range from fairly easy to extremely difficult. Evy enjoyed the chance to get out of the house and experience nature. She found the hikes to be as challenging as they were enjoyable. Evy's favorite place to hike was Whiteface Mountain. When she stood on the stone walkway atop the mountain and looked out over the high peaks of the Adirondacks, it took her breath away. On a clear day from the summit, Evy could see Lake Placid to the southwest and Lake Champlain off in the distant east. Christian could name each of the Adirondack high peaks and claimed he had climbed all twenty-five Adirondack fire tower trails and five more fire tower trails in the Catskill Mountains located in the southeastern part of New York.

During one trip to Whiteface, Laura insisted they take the Cloud Splitter gondola ride. It was midafternoon on a cloudless, sunny day, and the explosion of fall colors that surrounded them as the gondola climbed up the heavily wooded mountainside was indescribable. Evy could see why that young actress all those years ago had gone on and on about the fall foliage back home. It truly was spectacular.

One of Evy's favorite days had been when they hiked the trails and bridges along the Ausable Chasm near Plattsburgh. The drive from Lake Placid took them through the heart of the northern Adirondacks during the peak season for the fall foliage. Once there, they took their time taking the well-worn paths along the Ausable river. Each twist and turn of the trail brought new and wonderful sights. Christian told Evy that during the spring, the runoff from the snow-covered surrounding mountains turned the narrow gorge into a true whitewater rafting adventure. Now, in the fall, the beautiful river flowed slowly between the high stone walls of the gorge, and Evy could look down from any of the bridges over the water and watch as people resting on inner tubes slowly drifted along the scenic river.

Christian even convinced Evy to give rock climbing a try. Evy's natural athletic ability showed itself as she quickly picked up on the technique for working her way up the vertical cliff face she was on.

During these outings, Evy could almost forget why she was hiding in the Adirondack Mountains with three complete strangers as her only companions. Almost.

"It's not looking too good for checking out the ski jumps today."

Evy had been so lost in thought that she hadn't heard the door slide open. She turned and watched as Laura stepped out onto the deck, carrying two steaming mugs. Even from across the huge deck, Evy could smell the hot cocoa.

"I guess not," she replied. The weather had dampened her mood and heightened her sense of loneliness and fear.

"Not to worry. I'm sure our Adirondack tour guide will think of something." Laura nodded her head toward the house where the two women could see Christian standing at the kitchen sink, gulping down a glass of water. He wore a sleeveless, sweat-soaked hoody with '1776' superimposed over a coiled snake emblazoned across the chest and loose-fitting running shorts. His face was red from exertion and sweat covered his exposed muscular arms.

"He definitely knows this area well."

"He should. He grew up in the Adirondacks. He was a Boy Scout and everything." She chuckled as she turned to Evy and asked, "Do they have Boy Scouts in Spain?"

"I'm not sure it's exactly the same, but my younger cousin is in some type of scouting group."

Both women turned when they heard the sliding glass door open. Christian stepped out onto the open portion of the deck and lifted his face to the storm. As rain cascaded over his body, he spread his arms wide, tilted his head back, and began to catch raindrops on his tongue.

"Okay, Thor, step aside," said Dexter as he tried to get around Christian, where he had stopped and blocked the doorway.

"Thor?" Evy giggled.

"Yeah. Thor, as in Norse mythology, the thunder god, son of Odin," Dexter explained. "Of course, if he isn't careful standing there like an idiot catching rain on his face, we may all find out if lightening bothers him."

"I always thought he reminded me more of Ragnar than Thor," Laura said with a smile.

Christian remained as still as stone as he slowly raised the middle finger of each hand without ever opening his eyes. The simple gesture sent Evy into a fit of laughter.

"Please don't encourage his bad behavior," Laura pleaded.

Christian finally lowered his arms and approached the group under the covered portion of the deck. His blond hair was plastered to his head, and rain dripped from the end of his nose. He looked out over the lake as he reached both arms behind his back and grasped his hands. He bent forward and stretched his arms toward the ceiling as he began a series of stretches to cool down from his recent workout. Evy marveled at how the tattoos on his muscular arms and back seemed to come alive as he moved from one stretching exercise to the next.

When he was done stretching, Christian looked to Evy and said, "It's up to you. We can still go see the Olympic ski jumps, but the weather forecast is for heavy rain all day. We can go up to the top, but the rain and clouds are going to limit the view."

"What else can we do?" she asked.

"How about a trip down to Blue Mountain Lake? We can spend the afternoon checking out the Adirondack Experience."

"What's that?"

"It's a really cool museum with exhibits on Adirondack wildlife and the history of the region. They may even have some local artists displaying their work."

"That sounds sort of boring," she pouted.

Laura could tell by Evy's tone and body language that the young woman was starting to feel the strain of her situation. "We don't have to do anything today, Evy. If you'd rather, we can just hang out here and relax. We don't have to constantly be on the go." She gave Christian a hard stare as she spoke.

"I agree with Laura," Dexter added. "I'll get the fireplace in the living room going, and we can sit around and enjoy the rainy day, staying warm and dry."

Evy liked Dexter. He had a carefree attitude, while Christian was always serious. Evy found both men to be handsome, but where Christian really did look like a Viking with his blond hair and penetrating blue eyes, Dexter's Asian features were smoother, and his dark eyes seemed to always be hiding some secret. Both men were muscular, but Christian was taller and more heavily built, whereas Dexter had the build of an endurance athlete. She really enjoyed when Dexter would start to needle Christian.

"I'm not sure just sitting around sounds much better than a boring museum," she said.

"Okay, Evy. What would you like to do?" Laura didn't want the young woman to fall into a downward spiral of boredom and despair. They were all hopeful that her stalker would be identified and located soon so they could put an end to the situation and get Evy back home to her family and life.

Dexter had uncovered some valuable information on how the subject was keeping track of Evy online. He and Christian had provided the information to the authorities in Europe, who were hard at work trying to identify the person.

"I'm not sure. I just don't want to sit around here or go walk around a boring museum."

A smile slowly spread across Dexter's face. "How about a spa day for you two lovely ladies?" he asked.

Evy's face lit up. "That sounds wonderful!" She turned to Laura and asked, "Can we?"

"I don't see why not. Christian?"

"Sounds like a great idea. Let me make a call. The Whiteface Lodge is just down the road, and they have a magnificent spa. It's also secluded and exclusive. It'll be an easy spot to keep Evy secure."

"Come on, Evy. We'll check the place out online and see what we think."

Laura and Evy linked arms and walked to the small office Dexter had set up just off the living room. The computer genius had set up a computer station to allow Evy to have periodic contact with her parents while he maintained the ability to closely monitor anything she did online to ensure she didn't inadvertently give away their location.

"Dex, give Paine a heads up that we'll probably be heading to the Whiteface Lodge at some point this afternoon."

"Don't you want to wait and see if Evy likes what they have

to offer?"

"The place has one of the top-rated spas in the country. She'll love it."

"So if it's so posh and exclusive, what makes you think you'll be able to get them in on such short notice?"

"A couple years before I left the Marshal Service, the local federal judicial circuit held a fall retreat at the lodge. Two of the U.S. Supreme Court justices were invited to attend. The local judicial security inspector contacted headquarters and requested an SOG team be assigned for additional security and overwatch. It ended up being my team that they sent. The head of security at the lodge was a retired major from New York State Police. He'd been the commander of their Special Operation Response Team. We hit it off great with the guy. He told us if we ever needed anything, just give him a call."

"Dude, people say that all the time. They don't normally expect anyone to call them on it."

"Oh, ye of little faith," Christian said as he pulled up the Whiteface Lodge website on his cell phone.

Dexter just shook his head at his cocky friend.

After three rings, an automated answering system picked up. *What the hell?* Christian thought. *One of the high-end spas in the northeast, and they can't have a human answer the damn phone?*

After spending a couple minutes working his way through the automated greeting, a pleasant-sounding woman finally answered the phone. "Good morning. Thank you for calling the Whiteface Lodge. How may I direct your call?"

"Could you connect me with Mr. Alfred, please?"

"May I ask what this is in regard to?"

"Please tell Mr. Alfred that my name is Christian Vikstrom. He'll know who I am."

"Mr. Alfred is a very busy person. Perhaps if I knew what this call was about, I could assist you."

Trying not to let his growing annoyance with the woman show, he said, "Please just tell Mr. Alfred that this is a security matter. As I already said, he will know who I am."

"Of course. Please hold." Without waiting for Christian to respond, the woman placed him on hold.

After patiently listening to elevator music for around three minutes, Christian heard the line connect.

"Anthony Alfred. How can I help you?"

Christian couldn't help but smile at the heavy Bronx accent Alfred still had, even after working the majority of his career in Upstate and Central New York.

"Tony, It's Christian Vikstrom."

Christian waited as Alfred silently tried to place the name. "Ah, yes. U.S. Marshals SOG team, right?"

"Correct." Christian was glad the man remembered him. It would make today's request a bit easier.

"What can I do for you, Christian? Are you guys bringing some more judges up to enjoy the good life in the

Adirondacks?"

"No. Nothing so intrusive, Tony. I'm actually not with the Marshals anymore."

The statement took Alfred by surprise. He remembered Vikstrom as being a hard-charging team member and figured he'd be running the program before his career was over. "Really. So who are you with now?"

"I'm working in the private sector now doing executive protection."

"I see," he said, wondering what would've caused the young agent to leave Federal service. He'd have to make a call and find out more. "So what can I do for you today, Christian?"

"I need a favor, Tony. I have a client here in Lake Placid, and I'd like to get her and one of my people in for a full spa day today if possible."

"Are you staying on the property?"

"No. We have the client secured somewhere else. We had something planned for her today, but the crappy weather ruined that for us."

"Geez, Christian, the spa is normally fully booked, and it takes at least a week to get an appointment if you're not staying on site with us."

"I figured that was the case. That's why I wanted to speak with you rather than someone with reservations. I was hoping you could pull a few strings and help me out."

"What's the threat level on this?" The last thing Alfred

wanted was to bring a problem to the resort. He was making more money as the head of security than he ever did working for the State Police, and he didn't want to do anything to screw that up.

"Low. No one knows we're even in New York right now. I'd just like to get her in for a day at the spa, and if she likes the restaurant, we may even want to dine there."

"How big a team?"

"There'll be a female member of my team with her during the spa treatment, and I'll be staying close. I'll have a computer guy in a van in the parking lot monitoring for any threats and another team close by just in case there's a problem."

"Give me a callback number and let me see what I can do."

Christian rattled off his phone number and thanked the man before hanging up.

"So?" asked Dexter.

"He's going to check. If I were a betting man, I'd wager he makes a call to someone from the Marshals to find out why I'm in the in the private sector now before he tries to get Evy and Laura in."

"You really think so?"

"I do. The resort is really exclusive, with some very wealthy and politically connected guests and condo owners. He isn't going to take any chances on messing up that gravy train."

While they were waiting for Alfred to call back, Evy and Laura came back into the room.

"We just checked the lodge out online. The place looks amazing," Evy said. "It's a perfect way to spend a rainy day."

"Good," Christian said. "I'm just waiting for a call back, making sure they can fit you in today."

"They'd better be able to, or you're going to have a very bad day!"

Laura stepped close and said, "Maybe you should've made sure about that *before* you mentioned it."

"I didn't mention it. Dexter did," he reminded her.

"Dexter mentioned a spa day. You brought up the spa at the Whiteface Lodge. If you can't get us in, who do you think Evy's going to blame?"

One look at Evy's face told him things would be difficult the rest of the day if Alfred didn't come through, and he was sure the young woman's anger wouldn't fall on Dexter.

Twenty long minutes passed before Christian's cell phone buzzed. "Vikstrom."

"Christian, it's Tony. You're all set for this today at ten. Two Whiteface Signature full-day packages. The ladies can check in at ten, and once their treatments are done, they'll have full use of the spa facilities for the remainder of the day."

"Tony, you're a lifesaver. Thank you very much."

"Not a problem. I'll have a couple of my team members assigned to the spa as well. I'm looking forward to having a chat."

"Well?" Evy asked once Christian was off the phone.

"You ladies are all set for a full day at the spa." Christian checked his watch and added, "You'd better get moving. Check-in is at ten."

Laura just smiled at Christian and shook her head. "You pulled that one out of your ass," she whispered as she walked past him on the way to her room to pack a day bag.

CHAPTER EIGHT

"Paine, all you need to do is take a ride over to the resort and have a look. I'm not bringing the entire team into the facility. There's no need."

Dexter could hear the exasperation in Christian's voice. He'd been on the phone with Paine for almost half an hour, answering one question after another.

"You can't just pull this shit," Paine snapped. "We need time to advance the site and find a spot to set up. This should've been done days ago."

"We didn't even know about it days ago, Paine. The weather put a kibosh on the trip to the Olympic ski jump towers. We need to keep Evy active so she isn't worrying about the stalker or being hidden away from her family."

"I'm aware of that, Vikstrom. The issue here is that you didn't run this past me first so we could plan properly."

"Apparently, you've forgotten the set-up, Paine. I don't run anything past you. Once we hit the U.S., I've been in charge. Now you can either take a quick look at the resort and get off site when we arrive, or you can just sit in your room and wait for me to call if and when I need you."

"Give me the phone, please," Laura said to Christian. When he hesitated, she used her hand to gesture for him to give up the phone.

Once Laura had the phone, she told Christian to go and cool down. "Steven," she said as she made sure Christian was out of earshot. "Stop your bullshit. Arthur was very clear. Christian is in charge of this operation, not you."

"I'm aware of that, Laura, but this is ridiculous. He isn't giving me time to properly advance the site and get set up to cover you if needed."

"I'm not disagreeing with you, Steven. I'm just telling you to back off and do what Christian asked you to do. This entire thing was last minute to try to appease Evy."

"We're not supposed to be appeasing the damn girl, Laura. We're supposed to be protecting her!"

"I'm aware of that, Steven, and so is Christian. He has far more experience in protective operations of this type than either of us."

"This is bullshit," the angry snapped. "I'm letting Arthur know what's going on."

"No, you're not, Steven," she said sternly. "What you're

going to do is follow orders. Christian is keeping Arthur informed of things here daily. That's his place as team leader."

"Fine, Laura, but I'm keeping track of everything that goes on, and I'm doing this under protest."

"That's fine, Steven. Just as long as you do what you're asked."

"Fine. Put the *supreme leader* back on the damn phone."

"Thank you, Steven."

Once Christian was back on the phone, Paine said, "We'll do it your way, Vikstrom, but understand I don't agree with this at all."

"Paine, I get it. It's not ideal, but it will keep Cota compliant, and in the end, that's all that matters."

After hanging up with Paine, Christian turned his attention to Dexter. "Dex, I was going to have you set up your equipment in the van, but Tony says he can give you access to their IT area and their secure server. It's up to you."

"I'll take him up on that. As for their 'secure server,' I've already hacked it. It's impressive for a vacation resort, but it isn't nearly as secure as he thinks. I'll use their system to piggyback what I'm running."

Christian had to laugh. He'd expected nothing less from Dexter. He was always a couple moves ahead of just about everyone around him.

At exactly nine forty, both Laura and Evy were standing in the main foyer with one small bag each sitting at their feet.

Laura was wearing a pair of loose-fitting red Adidas wind pants and a matching oversized hoody, while Evy had chosen form-fitting black yoga pants and a dark gray sweatshirt with Mardi Gra theater faces emblazoned on the front. Both women had their hair pulled back into tight ponytails, and neither wore any make-up.

"Well, you both look ready for a day of being pampered," Dexter said.

"More than ready," Evy replied. A brilliant smile lit up her beautiful face.

Christian joined the small group wearing a pair of Ranger green hiking pants and a heavy 5.11 rain jacket covering the Glock secured to his hip. "Are we all set, ladies?"

"Good to go," answered Laura.

Though Evy didn't reply, it was obvious from the look on her face that she was impatient to get going.

Christian led them through the laundry room into the attached garage, where they all climbed into the Jeep Grand Cherokee. Once he made sure everyone was belted in, Christian hit the remote garage door opener. As they exited the garage, Dexter told both QRF teams that they were on the move.

"QRF One copies." Paine's voice came through the radio loud and clear. "All quiet at the destination."

"QRF Two copies. Stand by," Abioye said. He and David Altman were sitting in the Tahoe, parked in the lot of the Dack Shack at the intersection of Saranac Ave. and Peninsula Way

Road.

The heavy rain seemed to intensify as they drove along Peninsula Way. The colorful fall foliage was muted and appeared to sag and curl up in an attempt to protect itself from the deluge. The narrow lane was riddled with deep puddles of water where the blacktop had sagged and rutted since it was laid down. Dexter drove the Jeep while Christian road shotgun with his Daniel Defense MK18 tucked down along his left leg. He didn't expect any issues, but after what happened in Rome, Christian intended to be ready for anything.

"One minute to your location, QRF Two."

"Copy."

When they reached the intersection with Saranac Ave., Christian saw the Tahoe carrying Abioye and Altman parked in the lot of the Dack Shack on their right. Their vehicle was partially obscured between a large green dumpster and a small white Ford Transit van. With the heavy rain and tinted windows, it was impossible to see the two men seated in the vehicle. Dexter turned right onto Saranac Ave., and Jerome waited a full minute to make sure no one was following the Jeep before he pulled out of the parking lot and followed behind.

"Your six is clear," Jerome reported.

"Copy that. There's a parking lot right where we turn into Whiteface Inn Lane. Pull in there and check to see if anyone follows us."

"Copy that. Do you want us to trail you into the resort once we've cleared your tail?"

"Negative. QRF One can cover our arrival. We're going to be here all day, so stay mobile but close by in the event we need you."

"Copy that," replied Abioye.

Dexter slowed on the rain-slicked road and turned onto Whiteface Inn Lane. Fifty yards down the road, he turned left into the resort. They drove past an unoccupied stone and wood guard shack just inside the main entrance and proceeded along the beautifully manicured property. Colorful trees and massive Adirondack boulders lined the road, with well-placed accent lighting spread along the route.

"Stay on the perimeter road," Christian ordered. "Tony said to meet him at the backside of the property, and he'll bring us in through the VIP entrance." Once he'd given Dexter his instructions on where to go, he radioed Paine. "QRF One, we are two minutes from your location."

Paine responded immediately. "QRF One copies. There appears to be a small welcome committee waiting for you."

"Yeah. That's the director of security with a small team of his people."

"That's what I figured. Other than that, the area is quiet."

"Good. Once we're inside, break off and remain mobile in the area until we're ready to leave the resort. I'll keep you posted on what's going on."

"Good copy." Even over the radio, Paine's voice made it clear he didn't like being sent off-site.

The road they were following ended at a small roundabout where Tony Alfred and two of his security team members waited to greet them outside a beautiful log building. Once they'd pulled up to the group, Dexter placed the vehicle in park, and Christian got out.

"Welcome back to the Whiteface Lodge, Christian," Alfred said, offering his hand.

Tony Alfred was a big man with salt-and-pepper hair. Even in his late fifties, the man still appeared to be in excellent shape. He was wearing a pair of khaki slacks with a blue Whiteface Lodge raincoat covering his sport coat.

"It's great to be back. Thanks for this, Tony."

"No worries, buddy. Let's get your people inside." He nodded to the man on his right. "This is Doug Foreman. He's my number two."

Christian shook the man's offered hand. Foreman was shorter than Alfred by about two inches but appeared to be in just as good shape. He too wore a Whiteface Lodge rain jacket over khakis and a blazer. Foreman had a strong handshake, which he held a few seconds longer than necessary. Christian just smiled. Some people just had to try to demonstrate their dominance.

Christian opened the back door of the Jeep, and Evy climbed out with her bag. Laura came around from the far side of the vehicle and joined them.

"I'll show you where to leave the vehicle," Foreman said to Dexter as he climbed into the passenger's seat.

"Doug will show your man where to go once they get the vehicle parked. I'm having him put it inside where we keep our security vehicles. That way, my people can monitor it on camera while you're here."

"Perfect. Thanks. Let's get inside, and I'll make the introductions."

"Of course. Follow me." He led the group through the doors into a small, well-appointed lobby area.

"Tony, this is Laura Knight, a member of my team," Christian said as Laura stepped forward and shook Tony's hand. "And this young lady is our client, Monica Dawson."

"It's a pleasure to meet you, Miss Dawson." Tony caught the momentary look of confusion on Evy's face when she was introduced. It was obvious to the retired cop that Dawson was an alias the young woman wasn't used to.

"It's a pleasure meeting you as well," Evy said, trying to hide her slight lapse. "Thank you for getting us in on such short notice. This place is amazing."

"It was no problem at all. We're quite proud of our resort. The spa is listed in the Top 100 Spas in North America, and you're scheduled for the full day."

"That sounds just like what the doctor ordered," said Laura.

"Well then, let's get going. Ladies, please allow me to show you to the spa."

Tony led the way, with Evy and Laura on either side of him. Christian followed closely behind. The hallways they passed through were a combination of highly polished, v-notched, knotty pine walls and local river stone. Beautiful paintings and sculptures produced by local artisans decorated the walls and tabletops along the way. As they approached the frosted glass doorway that marked the entrance to the spa, they spotted a beautiful Native American woman waiting to greet them.

Alfred stepped up to the woman and said, "Please allow me to introduce you all to Linette King. Linette is our spa manager."

"Good morning," Linette said as she stepped forward to greet them. "I'm glad you decided to join us on this rainy day. We have you all set up for the full spa treatment."

King's Native American ancestry was reflected in her high cheekbones and coppery skin tone. Evy marveled at the girl's beautiful almond-shaped mahogany eyes and her wide, friendly smile. She was tall with an athletic build, and she wore her long, dark hair pulled back into a ponytail that reached her shoulder blades. Her dark green spa polo shirt and tan skirt accented her athletic figure.

"Good morning," said Laura. "We're really looking forward to this."

"Well then, let's get started."

Linette opened the frosted glass door and led the group into the spa. The reception area featured a glass-topped log counter with a large painting of a mountain lake scene on the wall behind it. A small shop area off to the left featured skin and hair care products for sale, while a small gift shop on the right featured casual wear and robes with the spa logo embroidered on them.

Behind the counter was a thin, young black man wearing a light blue polo shirt with the spa logo emblazoned over the left breast. "Good morning. Welcome to the Spa at the Whiteface Lodge," he greeted the group.

"Good morning, Adam," Linette said. "Our guests are Laura and Monica. We have them scheduled for a full spa day today. Can you get them checked in, please?"

"Of course. Ladies, please step up, and we'll get you signed in and off to enjoy a day of pampering unlike anything you've ever experienced," Adam said with an infectious smile.

Once the ladies were signed in, Linette led them back to the changing rooms, while Tony and Christian headed for the security chief's office.

"We can relax in my suite while the ladies are in the spa. I have full camera coverage of the entire facility," he said.

"The entire facility?" Christian asked.

"Except for the treatment rooms, restrooms, locker rooms, and the more private areas of the spa, of course."

"Of course," Christian agreed with a grin. "I remember my last time here. Your video surveillance system is almost as good as the one the Secret Service has at the White House."

While Christian and Tony headed for the security office to meet up with Dexter, Laura and Evy were stripping out of their street clothes and wrapping themselves in the heavy, white cotton robes they'd found inside the spacious lockers Linette had assigned each of them. Once they had changed, they rejoined Linette, where she stood with two young women outside the locker room.

"Okay ladies, are you ready to get started?"

"Yes," they said in unison.

"Great. Here's the itinerary for the day. Your experience is going to begin with a ninety-minute full-body massage. These young ladies are Lilli and Rose. They'll be taking care of you. Once your massage is done, we'll have a light lunch and then move on to the body treatment of your choice. We have several for you to choose from. We'll end the session with facials and mani-pedis. Once the treatments are all over, you'll have full use of the spa's steam room, sauna, and whirlpool therapeutic tubs. Rose will be with you the entire day to make sure you have everything you need."

"This sounds wonderful," Evy said.

"Enjoy your experience, and if you need anything at all, just have one of the girls get in touch with me."

When Laura realized the massage therapists intended to separate them into private rooms, she asked, "Is there any way we can do our massages together?" She wasn't comfortable having Evy out of her sight.

"I'm sorry," one of the women said. Laura couldn't remember if the girl who spoke was Lilli or Rose. "We only have two couples massage suites, and they're both in use."

"Don't be silly, Laura. This is fine," Evy insisted.

"I really am sorry miss. Once the massages are over, you'll be together for the body treatments, mani-pedis, and facials."

"Relax, Laura. I'll see you after the massage."

"Fine," Laura reluctantly relented. Even the knowledge that Christian and Tony Alfred would be monitoring things while she was in the spa with Evy didn't ease her concern.

As they had walked through the beautiful facility, Evy had noticed a cozy little room with a small fire crackling away happily in a stone fireplace. More important to Evy was the fact that the room also contained a half dozen computer terminals.

"You're Rose, correct?" she asked the massage therapist.

"That's right."

"Rose, in that room we just passed with the computer terminals. Is that for guest use?"

"Yes, it is. We have four different locations on the property where guests can access the internet. We also have complimentary Wi-Fi throughout the facility."

"How convenient," said the young actress. As she lay down on the table for her massage, a dangerous plan began to form in Evy's mind—a plan that would inadvertently result in more violence and death before her adventure was over.

CHAPTER NINE

Whiteface Lodge
Lake Placid, New York

Evy sat alone and naked on the massage table, drinking the bottle of ice-cold water that had been left for her. She hadn't had a therapeutic massage in weeks, and her massage therapist had worked wonders during their hour-long session.

Evy slid off the table and stretched her arms over her head as she relished the delicious soreness the deep tissue massage had produced. On the far wall was a full-length mirror. Evy knew she didn't have time to waste staring at her own reflection. If her hastily formed plan was going to work, she had to get moving right now.

Evy's plan was simple. She needed enough time alone to access the web from the spa's internet café, send a message to her mother, and then get back to the lounge area without Laura or Christian knowing what she'd done. Once Evy was alone with Rose, her massage therapist, she asked the girl if she could change her session to sixty minutes rather than the planned ninety. She claimed the longer massage was always too much for her. Rose was used to wealthy, pampered guests and their strange requests. Cutting the massage short was not an issue for her. After all, it'd allow her a much-needed break between clients.

Evy now had thirty minutes before Laura or anyone else would come looking for her. She figured that would be plenty of time for what she had planned. Evy wrapped the plush robe around her small frame and quietly stepped to the door. She slowly turned the knob and peeked into an empty hallway. She needed to act fast as she stepped into the hallway and slowly made her way to the small seating area, where several women sat chatting as they waited for their appointments with the massage therapists. Linette King, the spa manager, was nowhere in sight. So far, Evy's luck was holding.

"Can I help you?"

The voice startled Evy, and she turned, finding herself face-to-face with a young girl wearing a white Whiteface Lodge polo shirt and a small name tag that identified her as Lisa. Evy hadn't heard the girl approach. She was very pretty, with skin the color of cocoa and eyes such a light brown they appeared almost golden. She wore her dark hair in rows of tight braids with colored beads woven in.

"Yes, Lisa. My friend has another half hour before her session is through. If it's possible, I'd like to use one of your internet terminals while I'm waiting." Evy's heart was pounding in her chest so hard that she was positive Lisa could hear it.

"Of course. We have a small internet suite right around the corner." As she spoke, she turned and led Evy down the hallway.

Once they reached the computer room, Lisa said, "Here you go. The password for each terminal is written on a small card taped to the monitor. Will there be anything else?"

"No, thank you. I'll be fine."

Evy waited for the girl to walk away before she chose the terminal the furthest from the door and sat down. As promised, there was a small white laminated card taped to the terminal with the password for the internet connection. Evy tapped the return key, and the monitor came to life. She entered the password and was rewarded with a panoramic picture of the resort that was set as the screen saver. Evy quickly opened a web browser and typed in the address for an online game she and her mother often played when they were apart. The game "Guess Where I Am?" was designed for each person to provide clues to where they were. The other player had up to ten guesses to try to figure out the location. While the game was fun to play, it contained one particular feature that Evy was planning to use today. There was a chatroom integrated into the game that allowed Evy and her mother to message each other as they played. As both women traveled extensively, the game had become one of their favorite methods of keeping in touch. Evy hadn't had the time to play the game with her mother over the past couple of months. The demands of filming the show and the constant strain of her unknown stalker had limited Evy's online activity, and she could only hope her mother would log on sometime soon and check the game for messages.

Dexter had provided Evy with a couple of ways to send her mother messages, and she could even chat over a video messaging system he had set up. Evy's mother was her best friend and biggest supporter, and she normally spoke with or messaged her several times every day. The problem was that Evy had to lie to her mother about where she was, and she hated that. She wasn't allowed to contact her mother without one of the team members present to monitor what she said or typed. Dexter told her he had built a slight delay in the system so they could delete or block any information Evy might pass on to her mother that could accidentally give up their location. Evy wanted her mother to know the truth. She wanted her to know about the attack in Rome and that she was now hiding in America. As the days went by, she became more and more determined to let her mother know the truth. She was her mother, after all. If they couldn't trust her, who could they trust?

Evy checked the clock located at the bottom of the screen and saw that her massage had ended twenty minutes ago. In ten minutes, Laura would be done with her treatment, and she'd come looking for her. She had to send her message and get back to the small sitting room before Laura found her missing and came searching for her.

She quickly typed out her message and then exited the program. She opened the settings feature and erased her browser history, just in case someone had observed her on the computer. Once she was satisfied that she had cleared her internet trail, Evy walked back to the waiting area.

As she entered the small sitting room, she found Linette King waiting for her.

"Was everything okay? Rose tells me you cut your massage short."

Damn it! she thought. She had hoped the girl would keep her mouth shut. After all, she did get a half-hour break because Evy had shortened the session.

"The massage was wonderful. I just never cared for more than an hour at a time."

The lodge welcomed rich and powerful people daily. It wasn't among Linette's duties to ask her guests why they did what they did, so she accepted Evy's lie at face value and moved on.

"I'm glad you enjoyed the massage. Can I interest you in a drink or a light snack while we wait for Ms. Knight?"

"If you have any orange juice, that would be great."

"Of course. Coming right up."

Evy breathed a small sigh of relief once Linette had gone to get her juice. She hadn't been prepared to explain where she had spent her last half hour, and she wasn't accustomed to coming up with excuses for her actions. She sat down in an overstuffed lounge chair right next to the crackling fire and tried to relax while she waited for Laura to appear.

CHAPTER TEN

Rome, Italy

Forty-two hundred miles away, Andino Fabrizio was also sitting by a warm fireplace. He was pouring over the reams of intelligence that his computer experts and Padraig Lowery had provided him with. The more he reviewed the information, the more he was convinced Cota and her protectors had deceived him. Now the task was to determine where the harlot had actually gone. It may take some time and effort, but Andino would possess the girl! She must pay for her sins. She must pay for the desires she aroused in him. Only her atonement could cleanse his soul.

Andino had just finished compiling a list of possible locations where Cota may be hiding, when a secure messaging app on his computer chimed to notify him that he had a new message. He scrolled the mouse over the application icon and opened it. He could barely believe what he was reading. They found her. The stupid girl had sent her mother a message through a gaming chatroom. She had handed herself to him. God truly did work in mysterious ways.

"I've got you now!" he shouted to the empty room in which he sat.

He read and reread everything his spy had sent him. The computer hacker provided him with a printout of the entire message Evy had sent her mother. It was short, but it provided everything he needed to bring this game of cat and mouse to an end.

Mama, please don't tell anyone about this message. It's taken me two weeks to find a way to contact you without anyone knowing about it.

I'm not in Switzerland. I've been sending you messages pretending to be there, but I'm not. Did you hear about the shootout in Rome? The one where a bunch of men got killed? That was me. The animal tormenting me hired men to try to kidnap me, but the people protecting me stopped them. After the attack, Alonzo, Antonio, and my dear, sweet Sofia were flown to Switzerland with a woman pretending to be me. Roddy Fraser and his people are there as well. All of the social media posts you are seeing from me are actually being done by their computer experts to make it appear as if I'm hiding in Lucerne, but I'm not. The messages I have sent you are closely monitored to make sure I'm not telling you where I really am.

You are not going to believe where I am. I'm in America. Unbelievable, right? You know how I feel about Americans. Fraser hired an American to bring me to the U.S. secretly and hide me here. I'm currently staying in the most beautiful house in Lake Placid, New York.

I have three people with me constantly, and there are a few more men close by just in case there is a problem. You should see these people, Mama. There is a woman who used to be in the American Marines. She is gorgeous and badass all at the same time. There are also two men. One is Asian and he's some sort of computer genius who used to work for the FBI. The guy in charge right now looks like he walked off the set of The Vikings television show. He's huge and even has a scar running down his face. He has that typical American arrogance, but he appears to know what he's doing. Roddy Fraser told me he used to protect federal judges here.

They treat me well and try to keep me occupied. We go hiking and kayaking. Today we're at a beautiful resort on the lake for a spa day. None of it matters, though. I just want them to catch the madman whose stalking me so I can come home.

I have to get going before they realize I'm not where they think I am. I'll try to leave you more messages once in a while just so you know what is really going on. PLEASE DO NOT TELL ANYONE! The guy tormenting me is as dangerous as

they have been trying to tell me. Hopefully, they catch him soon
so I can come home.

I love you so much.

Evy

Andino's hands were shaking with excitement as he picked up the secure satellite phone the Irishman had provided him with. He pulled up the only contact number programed into the phone and hit the green phone symbol to call Lowery.

"Priest," the man answered. "Tell me you have news. I'm getting tired of the charade we're playing in Lucerne."

"I have excellent news, my friend." Andino paused to see how Lowery would react.

"Well, spit it out then. Don't make me drag it out of you." Lowery was angry. His grandson was dead, and he and his current employer had been tricked into wasting time and resources to move men into Switzerland when their target wasn't there. He was in no mood for the priest's theatrics.

"She is in America."

The news shocked Lowery. "Are you positive this time?"

"Yes, of course."

"How do you know?" Lowery had no intention of making any further moves until he was provided with positive information about the girl's location.

"The stupid whore told me herself!" Andino was almost giddy with excitement as he spoke.

"Explain," Lowery demanded.

"In the past, she has played an online game with her mother. The game app has a chat feature, and they would usually chat back and forth as they played. That account has been dormant for weeks, but I still made sure my computer team continued monitoring it. An hour ago, Cota left a message for her mother in the app chatroom. We were correct. Fraser flew her manager, bodyguard, and assistant to Switzerland with a decoy. Fraser apparently hired an American security company to take Cota to America and hide her."

"America's a big country, priest. Did the girl tell her mother where in America she is?"

"Lake Placid in New York. I had to look it up on Google Earth to find it. It's almost at the Canadian border."

"I know where Lake Placid is. They've held two winter Olympic games there."

"Well, that's where she is. She told her mother she's staying in a house on the lake. How long will it take to get all of your people there?"

"That may not be necessary. Let me make some calls, and I'll get back to you."

"What do you mean, 'that may not be necessary'?" he asked.

"I said I'll call you back. While I'm making calls, you should prepare for a trip."

"What do you mean? What trip?"

"If the girl is in America, there is no way I'm going to

attempt to remove her to Italy. Once we have her, you'll have to do whatever it is you have planned there."

"Impossible! Our deal was that you bring her to me in Rome!" Fabrizio had no desire to travel anywhere, but especially not America. The Americans had a very robust law enforcement apparatus, and he had no intention of spending time in an American prison.

"Well, the deal has changed. If you want me to snatch the girl, you will need to be in America as well. Now stop arguing. I have to make a few calls. I'll get back to you within the hour." Padraig disconnected the call without waiting for the annoying man to respond.

CHAPTER ELEVEN

Belfast, Northern Ireland

Padraig's first call after he disconnected with the troublesome priest was to a former PIRA comrade. The men had run dozens of operations together against their British adversary back at the height of 'the troubles'. Like Lowery, he had no love for the current arrangement between Northern Ireland and the UK.

When the call connected, Lowery said, "Sean, it's Padraig."

"Padraig. It's been a long time."

"That it has, my friend. That it has."

"To what do I owe the pleasure?" A call from Padraig Lowery could mean some much-needed business. It could also mean some serious trouble, which Sean could just as well do without.

"How secure is this line?"

Lowery's legendary sense of security was one of the many things about the man Sean liked. They'd fought side by side against their British oppressors for years, and Lowery's obsession with operational security had saved their arses on more than one occasion.

"As secure as I can make it. With the bloody resources MI6 has these days, I'm being more careful than ever."

Lowery trusted his old comrade-in-arms more than he trusted most people. Sean Flannery had been as passionate and ruthless in the fight against British rule as anyone Lowery had dealt with in the PIRA. The men had planned and pulled off some major attacks on the occupying British forces. Lowery was one of just a few men still alive who knew Flannery was responsible for the kidnapping, torture, and eventual murder of three members of the hated British Special Air Service. He'd fought and bled with Flannery. If he said this line was secure, he'd take him at his word. To a point.

"Do you still have any contacts in North America?"

"Aye. A couple. What area?"

"New York, up near their border with Canada."

Flannery paused as he let Lowery's words sink in. Padraig Lowery had never operated in North America as far as he knew. He also knew Padraig was running a very dangerous para-military group, the Far darrig, and from what he'd heard, his former comrade was getting rich doing it.

"I may have someone, Padraig. Why do you ask?"

"I have a job I'd be willing to cut you in on. I need men to help me snatch a girl hiding in New York."

"Who's the girl, Padraig?"

"Does it matter, Sean?" Lowery never knew Flannery to be skittish before.

"It does if the heat this will draw is more than the job is worth."

"She's an actress. She's somehow pissed off my client, and he wants to teach her a lesson."

"It seems like a lot of work just to teach a girl a lesson," Flannery observed.

"I agree, but the client is obsessed. He is or was some sort of priest, and the girl has really managed to incense him."

"So what is it you need?"

The two former PIRA men talked for another hour. Lowery laid out the framework of a plan, and Flannery played devil's advocate along the way. By the time they'd finished talking, Flannery had agreed to help his old friend for one-third of the total fee Lowery was collecting from his client.

"I need to speak with my client, Sean. I'll get in touch so we can firm things up."

"That sounds fine, Padraig."

Lowery disconnected the call and sat quietly, pondering his next steps. He had to tread carefully. The Brits would be well aware of his involvement by now. He hated them with passion, but he was professional enough to recognize and respect their massive intelligence gathering capabilities. He needed to get himself, Nessa Keever, and the priest into the United States undetected. He couldn't risk trying to bring any more than that. He'd have to rely on Sean Flannery's contacts for the manpower he'd need. First things first. He had to convince his reluctant client of the necessity of him traveling to the U.S. with them.

He called the satellite phone he'd given the priest and waited for the call to connect.

"It's me," he said by way of acknowledgment when the man answered. "Don't say anything until I finish speaking."

"But—"

"I said don't speak until I'm finished," he commanded. "I have a man who can help us. He can arrange for us to travel to Montreal without the authorities knowing about it. Once we're there, he has people who can smuggle us across the border into New York State. You can speak now."

"Who is this person? What is his connection to Canada?"

"That's not your concern. All you need to know is I've trusted this man with my life on numerous occasions and he's never let me down."

"I still don't see why you need me there. Just grab the girl and smuggle her out the same way you get in."

"That won't work. This is the last time I'll tell you this. You're coming with us. We can sneak into the U.S. and grab the girl and get her back to Canada. There's no way I'm going to try to smuggle her back to Europe."

"Fine," Fabrizio reluctantly agreed. He knew arguing with Lowery wouldn't change his mind. It may even cause the man to abandon the entire endeavor, and he didn't want that to happen.

"Good. Now listen closely. It's going to take a couple days for me to arrange things. Meet me in three days in Aberdeen, Scotland. I've got people who can arrange to get us aboard a cargo plane there. I'll have all the details worked out by the time we meet."

Andino's mind was racing. He needed to get himself from Rome to Scotland in three days. This wasn't what he had planned. If The Vulture hadn't failed so miserably, he wouldn't be in this situation. He was almost as terrified of meeting Lowery face-to-face as he was of traveling to the United States. None of that mattered, though. Evora Cota had become an all-consuming obsession for the man. He had to have her. He had to possess her and purify her. Only then could he rid himself of the sinful desires the very thought of her spawned within his heart. Only in purifying her could he purify himself.

The former priest's voice was barely above a whisper as he spoke three little words that would seal the fate of so many people.

"I'll be there."

CHAPTER TWELVE

Lake Placid, New York

It had been almost a week since Evy's spa day, and the stress and anxiety the pampering had helped to relieve was slowly building back up. She had tried to figure out a way to get back into the online game to see if her mother had answered her chatroom message, but Dexter kept a close watch on all of her online activity at the house. None of their frequent outings had offered Evy the same opportunity she had forged for herself at the lodge. She kept sending her mother messages through the methods Dexter had arranged and monitored each day, and each day her mother messaged back, never once letting on that she may have received Evy's covert message.

Each day, she grew a bit more annoyed and ill-tempered.

Evy stood naked and alone in her luxurious bedroom taking a critical look at herself in the full-length mirror that made up the door into her private bathroom. The image staring back did not please her. Though her protectors had kept Evy busy during her weeks of enforced isolation, she had neither the desire nor the drive to take advantage of the full gym located on the ground floor of the home. Both Laura and Dexter had offered to train with her, but she had declined each time.

Now, as she stared at her reflection in the unforgiving mirror, she began to regret the petulance that had made her spurn their attempts to draw her out. Evy had trained long and hard for her role as the heroine, Catia D'Souza, in her show *The Avengstress.* The production company provided her with personal trainers in CrossFit, martial arts, and yoga. She had a nutritionist who prepared and monitored all of her meals to ensure she got the most out of the calories she took in. A personal life coach continually worked with her to keep her mind and spirit as fit as her body. The woman staring back at her from the mirror was a watered-down version of what she had worked so diligently to become. While she still had a figure most women would kill for, gone were her washboard abs. Though her arms and shoulders were still firm and toned, gone were the chiseled muscles she had worked so hard to develop and maintain.

Evy turned her back to the mirror and twisted to look over her shoulder. Her backside was still fit and trim, but there was little sign of the rock-like definition she had grown accustomed to. As she stared in annoyed agitation at her fading physique, she heard a knock at her door.

"Evy, it's Laura. May I come in?"

"Are you alone?" she asked.

"Yes."

"Come in."

Evy made no move to retrieve the cozy robe from where she had dropped it when she began her critical self-assessment. She wasn't at all self-conscious about being naked in front of Laura. She'd lost any pretense of embarrassment about being nude since starting the show. One of the many things that seemed to incense her unknown stalker was the fact that there was so much nudity and sexual content in the show.

She turned from the mirror when Laura entered the room. "What's up? Another pep talk? Or maybe our exulted leader has yet another reason to lecture me?"

"My, my, aren't we a bit of a bitch today?" Laura had learned early on that the best way to deal with Evy's mood swings was to be brutally honest with her. She picked up Evy's discarded robe and held it out toward her.

Evy really liked Laura, and her comment made her laugh. "I'm sorry, Laura. It's not your fault. It's not even Vikstrom's fault. It's me. I was just taking a look at how far out of shape I've allowed myself to get, and I'm embarrassed." She took the robe from Laura and slid it over her shoulders, tying the belt around her waist as they talked.

"First of all, you're not out of shape. You look fantastic.

Secondly, we have tried to get you to work out with us."

"I know. Like I said, it's me." Wanting to change the subject she said, "So, to what do I owe the honor of this visit?"

"There's news. We're going to video conference with Arthur in a half hour, and Christian would like you to be there."

"What's happened?"

"I'm not sure. Christian only said there's been an important development, and Arthur wants to tell us himself. Now get dressed and meet me in the living room."

Fifteen minutes later, Evy came down the massive staircase clad in a white cowl neck sweater that ended at midthigh and a pair of jeans. Her small feet were covered in a pair of fur-lined Bearpaw slippers Laura had purchased for her. As she entered the living room, she saw that Laura and Dexter were already there, while Christian was nowhere to be seen.

"Good afternoon, Evy," Dexter said. "Laura tells me you may have changed your mind about working out with us."

Evy liked Dexter. He was incredibly handsome and very well-built. She thought he must be in his late thirties, but he looked more like a twenty-five-year-old. He was always smiling as if he alone was in on a very funny joke. The thing she liked best about him was that he needled Christian continually. He seemed to be the only person who could get a rise out of the always-serious man.

"Possibly," Evy answered noncommittally. "So what's the big news?"

"No idea," Dex said. "Christian has been on the phone several times over the past hour. He says Arthur has some new information."

As Dex finished speaking, Christian walked into the room. When he saw Evy, he said, "I'm glad you could join us," as he placed a laptop on the coffee table near the fireplace. If he'd noticed Evy's growing sulkiness, he showed no sign. One of his many annoying traits, in Evy's opinion, was her inability to anger him. Just once she wished she had Dexter's talent for getting under his skin.

Before she could fashion an appropriately unpleasant reply, Christian said, "Gather 'round, everyone." He checked his watch before continuing. "Arthur should be logging on any minute now."

As they moved chairs to form a small semi-circle around the computer, Evy heard a quiet chime, and then Arthur Valentine's face appeared on the screen.

"Evy, it's good to see you," he said by way of a greeting.

"You as well, Arthur."

"Good evening, everyone. Let's get right to it. We've identified your mysterious stalker, Evy."

"Is it over?" Evy whispered, hopefully.

"Unfortunately, not yet."

"What's happened, Arthur?" Laura wrapped an arm

around a shocked Evora.

"First of all, it's all thanks to Dexter's hard work. Great job, Dex."

Dexter acknowledged the recognition with a nod of his head.

"How so?" Christian asked.

"Dexter identified the network, or more accurately, the multiple networks, cutouts, and proxies the man was using. The algorithm Dex worked up and sent to Roddy and the British authorities allowed them to finally backtrack and determine where the majority of the online messages had originated."

"So, who is he?"

"His name is Andino Fabrizio. He's a former Roman Catholic priest." As Valentine spoke, the computer screen split into two frames. Arthur's face filled the right half of the screen, while the image of a middle-aged man wearing a Catholic priest's vestment appeared on the left. The man was plain-looking, with thinning brown hair and intense brown eyes.

"I knew it!" Evy shouted. "I knew it had to be one of those deranged religious zealots!"

"Yes and no, Evy. Fabrizio *was* a priest. He left the church and the priesthood several years ago."

"Any idea why, Arthur?" Laura hugged Evy tighter, trying to calm her.

"Apparently, he's so ultra-conservative that even the most conservative members of the clergy and organizations within the church distanced themselves from him. He felt the current pope and Vatican hierarchy were far too progressive and permissive. He's outspoken against many of the reforms being contemplated. He's against anyone from the LGBT community being allowed into the church. He is very vocal in his belief that abortion, no matter the reason, is a sin. He has gone out publicly and decried the many scandals the church has thrown money at to cover up. That includes sexual abuse by priests. He rails about the church's alleged past ties to organized criminal organizations and irregularities in the way the Institute for the Works of Religion, or Vatican Bank, operates, and that just scratches the surface of his conflict with the church."

"Well, the profilers did say there was a high probability he had close ties to the church," Laura pointed out.

"Something doesn't add up, Arthur," Christian said. "The money needed to fund this guy's obsession with Evora has to run into hundreds of thousands of dollars. Where does a priest get that kind of money?"

"That wasn't all that hard to figure out. His father is Macario Fabrizio."

"The Greek shipping magnate?"

"Very good, Dexter." Valentine was surprised that the man recognized the name. "Yes, Macario Fabrizio owns the largest shipping company in the world. He's also heavily invested in real estate and businesses throughout Europe and the Middle East. As Dexter pointed out, Macario is Greek, and he runs his vast empire out of Athens. Andino is his youngest son. While his sibling works in some position within the shipping company, Andino has no interest in the family business. He attended Sapienza University in Rome, where he was a bioengineering and pre-med student. With a year to go before he graduated, he lost interest, and from what we could learn, he became obsessed with the church. He was born and raised as a Catholic. He left the university and attended the Pontifical Roman Major Seminary. When he completed his studies, he was ordained as a priest and eventually went to work at the Vatican. That apparently didn't work out, as his views challenged the church's position on so many issues. He left the church several years ago and fell off the map."

"So his father is a millionaire. Is he financing his son's terror campaign?"

"Multi-billionaire, actually, and no, not exactly. Apparently, on top of everything else, Andino Fabrizio is a legitimate genius. While his father was happy that the kid didn't want any part of the family business, he is the baby of the family, and his mother adores him. His mother is Francesca Andino. She was an actress in B movies in Italy before drawing the attention of Andino's father. She has made sure her baby has always been well financed. Andino took the money his family provided and invested it extremely wisely. He's a multimillionaire in his own right."

"Some much for vows of poverty. Typical hypocrisy of the

Catholic church," Evy snipped. "So has he been arrested?"

"Unfortunately no. I'm sorry, Evy, but they haven't been able to locate him."

"What's been done, Arthur?" Christian asked.

"Authorities in Rome began to investigate Fabrizio as soon as Dexter's algorithm helped identify him. Once they knew who they were looking for, it took some time and serious electronic digging, but they were able to identify numerous electronic banking transactions that connects Fabrizio directly to Le Ombre in Italy and Padraig Lowery's group in Northern Ireland. They've also located numerous properties in and around Rome that he owns. So far, search warrants have been executed at every property they were able to tie to him. No luck. The best they can determine from interviewing his neighbors is that sometime in the past three to four days, he just disappeared."

"No hits on his passport or airline manifests?"

"Nothing yet. They're checking rail lines and bus records as well. The man's a ghost, and it gets worse. Roddy reports that it appears Padraig Lowery has left Switzerland as well. At some point over the past week, the crew conducting surveillance on our decoy in Lucerne has disappeared. Roddy says there have been several unconfirmed reports that Lowery has been seen back in Ireland. They haven't been able to verify that through any reliable sources, though."

"That's not a coincidence, Arthur," Christian said. "We

finally get a line on our stalker, and he and his hired muscle all disappear at the same time. Obviously, they figured out we were using a decoy in Switzerland."

"That would explain Lowery and his people getting out of there, but it doesn't explain why Fabrizio disappeared."

"I agree with Laura. First, the British authorities picked up Nessa Keever and Callum Gilboy, who were conducting surveillance on Evy in London. Then there's the failed attempt to kidnap Evy in Rome, where the Gilboy kid was killed. Lowery and his people had to be aware that we knew they were working for this guy. It makes sense that they'd get out of Switzerland once they discovered our ploy. That doesn't explain Fabrizio's leaving Rome, though. He'd have no way of knowing Dexter would be able to uncover his identity. There'd be no reason for him to disappear."

Valentine turned away to speak with someone off-screen. After a muffled conversation they couldn't quite hear, Arthur turned back to the screen and said, "We have the behavioral analysis folks, Dr. Belmore and Dr. Jawad, reviewing everything we've uncovered so far. They feel there are a couple of possible reasons for Fabrizio to be on the move. One possibility is that he may have become spooked. Between the failed attempt to kidnap Evy in Rome and the resulting deaths and then discovering Roddy and his people in Switzerland were a ruse, he may feel he has lost control of the situation and is moving to someplace he feels safer."

"You said a couple of possibilities, Arthur," Laura pointed out.

"Yes, I did. The second possibility is far more troubling. Dr. Jawad feels there's a possibility Fabrizio believes he's discovered where Evora really is. With everything that's happened, he may want to actually be present the next time Lowery tries to grab her."

"If Lowery is back in Ireland, as Roddy suspects, do we think he's still working for Fabrizio?" Christian asked.

"We do. There was a recent electronic payment from one of Fabrizio's accounts into an account in the Cayman Islands that MI5 has positively linked to Far darrig and Lowery. The transfer happened after Roddy discovered Lowery's people had left Switzerland."

"Shit."

CHAPTER THIRTEEN

Aberdeen, Scotland

"Merda," Andino Fabrizio whispered to himself.

The past few days had been a nightmare for the fastidious man. His normal, orderly world had fallen into chaos. At Padraig Lowery's insistence, he traveled to Leonardo Da Vinci International Airport where he boarded an ITA flight bound for Paris. Fabrizio was wearing what he had come to think of as his 'priest disguise' and was traveling on his still-valid Vatican passport. He knew that there was very little chance any customs or law enforcement agent would interfere with a Catholic priest traveling in Rome.

Fabrizio used the two-hour and fifteen-minute flight to Paris to calm himself and plan. Things were rapidly getting out of hand, and he needed to regain control of the situation. He understood why Lowery didn't want to try to move the Cota girl from the U.S. back to Europe. The difficulty and risks involved would be almost insurmountable. Having Fabrizio with him in the U.S. made the most sense. He didn't like it, but Andino agreed with the man's logic. He would still make the young harlot pay for her insults to the church and for the immoral way she enflamed him. It didn't matter where it happened, just as long as she repented and atoned for her sins.

Fabrizio had learned long ago that wearing the garb of a priest while traveling was always a double-edged sword. While he received preferential treatment from the flight crew, he was also subjected to unwanted interaction with fellow travelers. The flight attendant, a charming, matronly woman, had offered him a vacant seat in first class, which Fabrizio happily accepted. Now, an hour into the flight, Fabrizio feigned exhaustion and closed his eyes as though asleep to avoid the incessant chatter of the lifelong Catholic grandmother he was seated next to.

The flight touched down at Charles De Gaulle Airport without incident, and Fabrizio thanked the flight crew and offered them a blessing as he departed the plane. Once inside the terminal, Fabrizio went to the baggage claim area, where he reclaimed his checked bag. Luggage safely in hand, he joined the queue of passengers waiting to clear customs. When his turn came, Andino stepped up to the customs checkpoint and presented his Vatican passport, doing his best to hide his anxiety as the customs agent scanned the document and waited for verification to appear on his screen. After a short delay and several perfunctory questions, the overworked civil servant stamped the passport, handed it back, and welcomed Fabrizio to France.

After clearing customs, Andino walked out of the airport and hailed a taxi. He settled in for the fifteen-minute drive to the Hyatt Regency Hotel just outside the airport as the cab driver, a recent immigrant from Sudan, chatted away on a cell phone in his native tongue, leaving Fabrizio to his own thoughts.

Not having a reservation for the hotel wasn't an issue. The young woman at the check-in desk went out of her way to accommodate the tired-looking Catholic priest standing before her. Fabrizio paid using a credit card in his own name and allowed a bored-looking teenage bellboy to carry his bag to the room. He tipped the boy far more than necessary before sending him on his way, ensuring the boy would remember him if ever asked.

Fabrizio made sure the door was locked before he began his transformation into a new identity. He stripped off the priest's outfit and hung it neatly in the closet before taking a shower. When he finished his shower, he carefully trimmed his heavy, graying brown beard down to a neat Van Dyke. When he was satisfied with his facial hair, Fabrizio took a carefully folded change of clothes from his bag and quickly put on khaki slacks, a blue oxford button-down shirt, and a navy-blue blazer. He slid his feet into a comfortable pair of worn brown leather high-ankle boots and donned a pair of non-prescription glasses.

From a hidden compartment within his carry-on bag, he withdrew a French passport, driver's license, and several credit cards, all bearing his new identity. He had purchased the fraudulent documents several years earlier from a man who specialized in helping dangerous people disappear. At the time, he had never imagined needing to use the fake persona, but he had taken his father's advice. While he rarely saw eye-to-eye with him, he knew his father was an extremely wise and dangerous man. Macario Fabrizio always preached being prepared for any unexpected complications. He had been the one to introduce Andino to the master forger who had crafted his new identity. The man justified the exorbitant fee he charged because, while the data on the new documents was fraudulent, the documents themselves were not. Through contacts within various governments and several international banks, he was able to provide his clients with legitimate passports, driver's licenses, and credit cards.

Fabrizio now stood in front of the mirror and compared the image staring back at him with the photo on his French passport. The transformation was complete. He was now Claude Du Bois, a French citizen who lived in Paris, La Ville Lumière, the City of Light.

Before leaving the hotel room, he had logged on to a travel

site using a secure VPN and booked a flight on KLM Airlines, departing at eighteen-forty with a short layover in Schiphol, Amsterdam, before arriving in Aberdeen, Scotland at twenty-one-fifty. Once he had arranged passage to Scotland, he logged off and disconnected his secure VPN. He next accessed the internet using the easily-tracked complimentary Wi-Fi provided by the hotel. He booked a flight in his real name to Bangkok, Thailand. In the unlikely event the authorities ever learned his identity and tracked him to Paris, the false trail he'd laid out would lead them to the Orient. The ruse wouldn't work for long, but it would buy him additional time if needed.

With his travel arrangements completed, Fabrizio grabbed his two pieces of luggage and headed for the elevator. He rode the elevator to the second floor, where he got off and took the stairs to the main lobby. He cracked the door slightly and looked around. There was no sign of the bellboy or desk clerk he had dealt with when he arrived. After one last look to be sure no one was watching, he slipped out of the stairwell doorway and headed for the exit at the rear of the hotel. Once outside, he hailed a cab for the return trip to the airport.

At the airport, Fabrizio used his passport to print out a boarding pass at an automated terminal. He took the printed baggage claim tag and placed it on his one checked bag, then rolled the bag to a security station, where he passed the bag to an overwhelmed-looking man who added it to a pile of bags waiting to be run through an X-ray machine.

Fabrizio joined yet another queue, waiting to clear the security checkpoint. As the line slowly wound its way along, Andino felt his cell phone vibrate in his pocket. He could tell by the pattern of the vibrations that it was an alert from his home alarm system. His mind was racing as he pulled the cell phone from his pocket and activated the application for his home security system. After an unbearable fifteen seconds, the system connected, and Fabrizio gasped. His worst nightmare was unfolding. Just as authorities had discovered the surveillance devices he'd installed in Evora Cota's various apartments, the screen again showed members of the Italian Gendarmerie searching an apartment. Only now, it wasn't Evora Cota's apartment. It was Andino Fabrizio's flat overlooking Vatican City in Rome that the authorities had invaded.

The former priest's mind was racing. How could they have discovered his identity? How could they have tracked him down? He'd been so careful. Even the computer hackers he employed didn't know who they were working for.

"Monsieur, s'il vous plaît." The uniformed examiner manning the security checkpoint had to repeat herself three times before Andino tore his eyes from the cell phone when he realized she was speaking to him.

"Désolé," he apologized as he tried to cover the anger and fear coursing through him.

He stepped up to the checkpoint and placed his carry-on on

the conveyor belt before emptying his pockets into the hard plastic tray he was provided. He removed his belt and shoes and walked through the metal detector. Andino was startled when the detector gave off a loud beep, indicating metal had been detected. He began to pat himself down, finding his spare apartment key in his front pocket. Once he surrendered the key, he cleared the screening station without further incident and moved to collect his property. Trying his best to remain calm and not attract attention, he struggled to walk at an unhurried pace through the concourse.

He found an empty departure gate waiting area, took a seat far back away from any prying eyes, and again called up his security system. He watched in silent agony as the authorities systematically tore his flat apart. As he watched, he saw one member of the search team attempt to access his desktop computer. Despite his despair and anger, a small smile appeared on his face as he watched the man working on his computer pull away from the screen and frantically try to stop what was happening. Fabrizio had set up a security protocol within his system that required a facial recognition program to scan his face each time he started his computer. If any face other than his was scanned during the startup, the system contained a self-destruct security measure that completely destroyed all hard drives and any external storage devices attached to the system at the time of the activation.

Andino watched the camera feed for a few more minutes

before disconnecting. He sat quietly for another ten minutes before he felt calm enough to proceed to his departure gate. He disassembled his cell phone and deposited the parts in several trash bins as he walked. Even if the authorities managed to track him to the airport, their search would end there. When he arrived at the gate, he found that the last call to board the aircraft had already been given, and he was the last person in line to present his boarding pass to the gate attendant.

The flight to Schiphol was uneventful, and Fabrizio spent the time deep in thought. Once this was over with—once he had chastised Evora Cota for her sinful and blasphemous attacks on the church and after he punished her for the lustful desires she had given rise to within him—he would have to flee to Greece and the protection of his father. Anger threatened to overwhelm Andino as he realized his life in Rome was over, and it was all because of that blasphemous whore, Evora Cota.

They touched down right on schedule in Amsterdam, and with only an hour and fifteen minutes of layover in the capital of the Netherlands, Fabrizio had to hasten along to make his connecting flight to Aberdeen.

Fabrizio/Du Bois was the last to board the short flight from Schiphol to Aberdeen, and once he was comfortably seated, he ordered a glass of red wine from the flight attendant to help calm his nerves. While the flight attendant went through his preflight safety routine, Fabrizio sipped his overpriced, inferior-grade wine and tried to relax. As he often did when confronted with a serious problem, he allowed his mind to wander. He had discovered over the years that if he just allowed his massive intellect to work without conscious direction from him, he could unravel any Gordian knot.

By the time he landed in Scotland, he was feeling much more confident than he had since first learning he'd have to travel to the United States. First of all, he could not let Lowery know about the authorities raiding his home in Rome. If he learned that the police knew who Fabrizio was, he'd never continue on with the plan. Worse, the violent terrorist might decide it would be best to kill him and dispose of his body where it would never be found. No, he could not let Lowery know what was happening in Rome.

Next, he had to get word to his mother that he would soon need his father's powerful political friends in Greece to protect her youngest child. Once he was done in America, he would take refuge at his family's holiday estate on the island of Skopelos. Even though Greece, the birthplace of democracy, had extradition treaties with both Washington, D.C. and Rome, Macario Fabrizio's powerful friends within the government and court system of Greece would never allow one of his children to be handed over to authorities in the United States or Italy. His father would be furious, but Andino's mother would demand her husband use all of his considerable influence to protect her baby boy.

Feeling far more optimistic than he had when he departed

Amsterdam, Andino's thoughts turned to the terrorist he now found himself tied to. Lowery was a master of tactics, to be sure, and he had the required experience and skill to successfully kidnap the Cota slut, but at the end of the day, he was nothing more than a violent animal. He did not possess Andino's intellect or resources. The man was driven by greed. He'd left his ideals behind on the failed battlefields of Northern Ireland. Now he and his people were nothing more than the modern version of the 'Ten Thousand' legendary mercenaries from his Greek homeland. Lowery was a blunt object—a tool to be used by Fabrizio and discarded when no longer useful.

Fabrizio collected his one checked bag from the luggage carousel and headed for the immigration and customs checkpoint. As he was swept along with passengers from several flights that had all arrived around the same time, he reminded himself that he was now Claude Du Bois. Andino Fabrizio was gone. His naturally arrogant, condescending personality made it easy for Fabrizio to take on the haughty, self-important persona of a Frenchman.

After clearing customs, Fabrizio entered the queue, waiting for a taxi, just as Lowery had instructed. As he waited in line, a small, nondescript white cargo van pulled up, and a woman rolled down the passenger's window.

"Get in, priest," Nessa Keever said by way of greeting. "Padraig is waiting."

The side cargo door slid open, revealing a young man

dressed in blue jeans and a Scottish National Rugby Team jersey perched on the bench seat. The thug motioned impatiently for Fabrizio to toss him his bag and climb in.

"I'd prefer you not refer to me as 'priest'."

If Keever heard him, she didn't acknowledge it as she raised her cell phone to make a call. "We have the priest."

Fabrizio could only assume she was speaking with Lowery. "I asked you not to call me that any longer," he said.

Keever continued to talk on the phone without responding to Fabrizio. "Nothing. The *priest* says he doesn't want us to call him that." She listened for a few seconds and then twisted in her seat and handed the phone to Fabrizio. "He wants to talk with you, *priest*."

Fabrizio just shook his head as he took the phone from the annoying woman's hand. "Hello?"

"Listen carefully to me, priest. It doesn't matter what you do and do not want to be called. You will listen to Nessa and do what she says. This endeavor of yours has already cost me the life of my grandson. We will proceed how I say. Do you understand me, *priest*?"

"I understand." Andino had no choice but to comply with the man for now.

"Good. The woman you are with is Nessa. She is as dangerous as any of my men, so I'd advise you not annoy her any further. She is going to take you to a safe house. I've made arrangements for the two of you to fly out tomorrow morning.

I'll meet you in Montreal."

"What? Wait! I thought we were meeting here in Aberdeen."

"Relax, priest. Everything has been arranged."

"What happens when we get to Montreal?" Andino was confused, and his newly found confidence was once again fading away as the crazy Irishman maintained complete control of the planning.

"Don't worry about that. You just do what Nessa tells you to do, and everything will be fine. Get a good night's sleep, and I'll meet you in Canada tomorrow night."

"Wait, Lowery, I want to know what the plan is." Andino stopped talking when he realized he was speaking to a dead phone line. Lowery had hung up.

"Listen to me, *priest*." Nessa emphasized the last word. The little man annoyed her, and she took a small measure of joy in tormenting him. "Lowery knows that he's doing. I'll get you to the safe house where you can have something to eat and get some sleep. I'll be there with you the entire time. If everything works out, you'll have your little whore in the next few days. Just stop being a pain in the ass."

The ride from the airport took a little over an hour with the driver making numerous turns to ensure they weren't being followed. The stress of the situation coupled with the last-minute travel had worn the man out, and despite his best efforts to remain awake and alert, Andino was sound asleep when they arrived at their destination.

He awoke to someone shaking him.

"Wake up, priest. We're here."

The inside of Fabrizio's eyelids felt like they were lined with sandpaper as he was startled awake. For a moment he forgot where he was and who he was with. "What?" he slurred.

"We're here. Now grab your shit and let's get inside." Nessa held no compassion for the annoying man. He was a job. Nothing more.

Fabrizio looked around as he climbed out of the car with his bag. They were parked behind a small, clapboard house in what looked like a very rundown neighborhood. The moon was completely hidden by heavy cloud cover, and the only light bled into the backyard from the streetlights out front. In the distance, Fabrizio heard a dog start to bark as he walked across an overgrown patch of grass to the porch.

Nessa Keever walked behind him, urging him along. "Come on, priest. This isn't a sightseeing trip. Get inside."

Fabrizio bit back the nasty reply that sprang to his lips. He was in no position to argue. He gripped his bag tighter and climbed the rickety steps to an equally rundown back porch, which had almost as many broken and missing floorboards as it did good ones.

A large, redhaired man opened the door before Fabrizio could reach for the knob. An AK-47 was strapped to his chest and some sort of handgun was secured in a holster at his hip.

"Hurry up and get inside." The man's Irish accent was so heavy, Andino could barely understand him.

Nessa spoke briefly with the hulking man who disappeared further into the house when they finished speaking.

"What is this place?'

"One of Padraig's safe houses. It isn't much, but no one will bother us here. There's food on the stove. Grab something to eat, and then I'll show you where you can get some sleep. Tomorrow's going to be a long day."

"How are we getting to Canada?"

"No questions, priest. Just eat and get some sleep. We have everything all worked out."

The woman's words did nothing to reassure Fabrizio, but having no choice, he did as he was told. He ate what was offered, not knowing when he'd get a chance to eat again. Once he finished the meager meal, he followed Nessa to a small bedroom with two sets of bunk beds pushed against opposite walls. Keever told him she'd wake him when it was time to go, then she closed the door behind her, leaving Fabrizio alone with his thoughts.

CHAPTER FOURTEEN

Lake Placid, New York

The video conference with Valentine had ended a half hour ago, and now the small group sat in front of the fireplace and discussed the new information. To Evy's surprise, the normally tight-lipped Vikstrom spoke openly to her about what it could mean. Evy was brimming with questions, which both Christian and Laura did their best to answer.

"Now that we know who this sick maniac is, can I go home?"

"Not yet, Evy."

"Laura's right, Evy. The authorities still need to track him down and arrest him. On top of that, we don't know how deeply Padraig Lowery and his band of mercenaries are involved. Once Fabrizio is arrested, they may disappear, but there's also the chance he paid Lowery to see whatever deranged plan he has through to the end. There are still too many unanswered questions."

"But can't you just protect me back home?" Evy was desperate for the entire ordeal to be over. She wanted to go home. She wanted to see her mother and sink into the safe haven her family had always provided.

"There's no doubt Fabrizio knows everything about you, your family, and your life back home. Right now our biggest advantage is that he doesn't know where you are." Laura spoke calmly, as she tried to reassure the young actress.

"But Arthur said those behavioral doctors said there's a chance he does know where I am."

"What he said was that behavior analysts believe there is a chance Fabrizio *thinks* he knows where you are," Christian corrected. "I've been thinking about it since the call. We didn't leave any trail behind us for him to follow. We flew on a private charter, which the GIS agent in Italy made sure was not on any flight logs. Add to that the fact that you're using an identity we provided for you that no one knows about but us. Not even Roddy knows the name you traveled under. The methods Dexter has set up so you can keep in touch with your family cannot be tracked back to us here. Dexter is the best in the business. I just can't see how he'd be able to figure out you're here."

As Christian spoke, a horrifying thought crept into Evy's

head. She knew how her deranged stalker could've found out where she was. It was her fault. Her message to her mother. The one time she'd done exactly what all of them had warned her not to do. She'd told her mother right where she was, and in so doing, she may very well have placed them all in danger. Even as the idea filled her mind, Evy wanted to deny it. There was no way the man could know she and her mother played that online game. There was no way he could've seen the message she'd sent to her mother. Even as she tried to convince herself that it wasn't possible, another part of her knew the truth. She'd caused this. This animal may know where she is because she's told him.

Evy knew she should say something. She should pull Laura aside and tell her what she had done. Laura was a woman. She'd understand Evy's need to tell her mother the truth. She certainly couldn't tell Christian. She'd never seen him angry, but she'd seen how easily he handled poor Antonio. He overpowered her big bodyguard with seemingly no effort at all. In truth, Christian frightened the hell out of her. She couldn't tell Dexter, either. The man didn't frighten her the way Christian did, but he was just as intense as Christian was about her following his rules about communicating with her family. She liked Dexter and didn't want him to know she'd intentionally disobeyed him. That brought her back to Laura. Evy couldn't tell the woman she'd lied and tricked her at the lodge. Christian would almost certainly blame Laura for allowing Evy to be out of her sight. She couldn't let that happen. No, she had to keep silent.

"I'm not feeling very well. Please excuse me; I'm going to lie down for a bit."

"What's the matter, Evy?"

"It's okay, Laura. I just need to be alone. All of this is just too much. I'll see you at dinner."

When Evy stood to go back upstairs, Laura moved to comfort her.

"Let her go, Laura," Christian said. "We need to discuss the new developments, and we need to bring Paine and the rest of the team up to speed."

"I'm sure Arthur has already spoken to Steven."

"I agree, but I want to talk with him. We're going to need to change our operational profile."

"How so?"

"We've been keeping the QRF teams on standby. Other than our trip to the lodge, we haven't really used them to advance a location or conduct counter-surveillance on us. We've kept everything low-key to avoid attracting attention. That's going to have to change. From here on out, whatever we do, one of the teams is going to have to advance the location and make sure it's safe, while the second team conducts counter-surveillance and watches our six."

Dexter stood up and said, "I'm going to do a deep dive into this Fabrizio asshole. Give me a couple hours, and I'll have every shred of information there is to find."

"I'm sure Arthur and Roddy have people doing that, Dexter," Laura said.

"Let him work his magic," Christian said. "I'd put Dex up against anyone Arthur or Roddy have working on this."

"Stop. You're gonna make me blush." Dexter added a mocking bow, causing both Christian and Laura to chuckle despite the seriousness of their current situation.

"Okay, let's get Paine and others on the line. It's time to ramp up the operation."

Forty-five minutes later, they ended their video conference with the four members of the QRF teams.

"God, Paine is such an insufferable ass," Christian said.

Laura agreed but tried to spread a little oil in troubled waters. "I know he can be a little irritating, but he's good at what he does."

"Calling that overstuffed asshat 'a little irritating' is like calling a hurricane 'a little rain.' Christ, he's such a pain in the ass. He needs to come to grips with the fact that I'm running this operation, not him."

"I'm not defending him, but Steven has been Arthur's right-hand man since he formed ArVal. Arthur trusts him without question, and Steven has grown used to being in charge."

"I understand that, and I have no issue with people offering their opinion on a plan. It's important to let everyone on the team identify any possible problems they see. What I'm tired of is having to justify every decision I make. Paine has combat operations experience. I get that. He's far more experienced in that area than I am. I have far more experience in protective operations and operating tactically in a civilian environment. He needs to accept that."

"I agree, and so does Arthur. That's why he gave you full control of this operation. Now let's go see if Dexter has dug up anything about Fabrizio we can use."

CHAPTER FIFTEEN

Aberdeen, Scotland

Andino awoke with a start to the sound of a loud pounding on the bedroom door. He hadn't slept well, and what little sleep he did get was filled with dreams of police raiding his home, Keever threatening his manhood with a knife, and Evora Cota mocking and arousing him. Throwing his legs over the side of the bed, Andino tried to rub the sleep from his eyes as he struggled to clear his head. The pounding grew more insistent.

"Wake up, priest. It's time." Nessa Keever's perturbed voice hissed through the hollow, wooden door. "Come on, priest! We've got to go."

Andino was positive that the savage woman would break the door down if he didn't respond.

"I'm up. I'm up. Christ, give me a minute!"

"Hurry up and get moving. Meet me downstairs. We leave in fifteen minutes."

He listened to her heavy footsteps recede down the hallway and then pounded down the rickety wooden steps before he pushed himself upright. He'd slept in his clothes, afraid to undress in the event he had to attempt to flee the house during the night. He shuffled down the filthy hallway to the equally dirty bathroom, where he relieved himself.

He had just splashed a couple of handfuls of icy water on his face, when Keever's unpleasant voice called from the first floor.

"Let's go, priest. We don't have time for you to make yourself pretty."

"I'm coming," he snapped, a little more sharply than he'd planned. Gathering his bags, he descended the staircase, where he found Keever and the armed redheaded thug from the previous evening speaking quietly as they waited for him.

"It's about time, priest. Our flight leaves in an hour."

"Follow me." The redhead motioned for them to follow as he headed for the back door. Once in the backyard, they climbed into the same vehicle that had carried Andino and Keever from the airport to the safe house the previous evening.

Andino stifled a yawn as he looked into the pitch-black night. "What time is it?"

"Three in the mornin'." The ruffian's Irish accent again made it difficult for Andino to understand him.

Andino was confused. He knew very few airports began flight operations before six in the morning. "No airline operates this early," he pointed out.

"The one we're using does. Now sit back and shut up," Keever snapped.

They drove the remainder of the way to Aberdeen International Airport in silence. Andino had about a thousand questions running around in his head, but he didn't bother to ask any of them. He knew Keever wouldn't give him any answers.

From the back seat of the van, Andino saw a large arch consisting of white steel pipes emerge out of the gloomy night. Suspended in the center of the arch was a message board. Welcome, Aberdeen International Airport was written on the left side of the board, while the remaining two-thirds of the board consisted of an electronic message screen with continually changing advertisements and airport messages flashing across the massive display.

They drove by a sign indicating that passenger drop-off was to the right without turning. Two intersections later, they turned right, passing a sign that said Private Charters.

"We're taking a charter flight to Canada?"

"No, we're not."

"So, where are we going?" Andino was growing tired of the surly woman's attitude toward him. He was paying an obscene amount of money for their services. They worked for *him.*

"Stop asking questions, *priest*. Padraig has everything arranged."

Andino sat back and struggled to bite back the angry reply that jumped into his head. He was at their mercy for now. Later, when this was all over and he was safely on his father's estate in Greece, maybe then he'd find a way to make this arrogant bitch pay for her disrespectful attitude.

The small cargo van pulled up to a gate secured by a chain and a large padlock. Beyond the gate, Andino saw a small aircraft hangar lit by several powerful spotlights. There were no markings to indicate who the hangar belonged to. The redhead sounded the vehicle's horn with two short beeps. He waited for several seconds and then held the horn down for one long beep. Shortly after the sound of the horn had faded into the still night, a small door on the side of the hanger opened, and light spilled from the structure into the cloud-covered night. Two men carrying rifles Andino could not identify approached the fence. One of the men drew a key from a jacket pocket, opened the padlock, and unwound the chain securing the fence. As soon as the fence swung open, the second man waved the van through.

"Listen to me carefully, priest. Once we get inside the hangar, you will grab your shit and go directly to the plane parked inside. Don't look around. Don't ask questions. Padraig has paid these people to get us to our next stop. They don't work for Padraig, and they don't like nosey people. Do you understand?"

Andino looked Keever in the eyes as he replied, "I understand."

The woman held his gaze for several seconds, making sure the little turd really understood before she nodded her head and turned to face forward.

The van reached the front of the hanger just as the overhead door finished rising to the top of its tracks. Inside the hanger, Andino saw a small single-engine Cessna Skyhawk sitting by itself in the center of the cavernous space. A single spotlight illuminated the plane, leaving the remainder of the space shrouded in darkness.

"Remember what I said, priest. Grab your bags and go directly to the plane. Don't look around. Don't ask questions."

The van stopped, and both Keever and the redhead got out and approached the men who had unlocked the gate for them. They spoke quietly among themselves as Andino gathered his bags and, without once looking toward the group, went directly to the plane. When he reached the aircraft, a small man wearing a tan flight suit stepped around from the far side of the plane.

"Give me your bags." The man spoke with a barely discernible accent that Andino could not place. Despite the fact that it was the middle of the night, the man had heavily tinted aviator sunglasses perched on top of his head. The arms of the glasses held the man's collar-length, dirty-blond hair back behind his ears. He took Andino's bags and placed them inside the plane, behind the copilot's seat. "Get in back."

Andino quietly climbed into the cramped back seat of the airplane as the man finished the preflight check he was conducting when they had arrived. Andino watched as Keever and the redhead walked toward the plane. When they reached the aircraft, they exchanged a hug, and Keever climbed into the copilot's seat while the big man lumbered back to the van.

"We should be in Edinburgh in twenty minutes," the pilot said as he buckled himself into his seat. "Your flight leaves in a little over an hour."

Keever nodded and took out her phone. "We'll be in the air shortly." She fell silent as she listened to whoever she had called. "The pilot says about twenty minutes." Another pause. "Fine. See you then."

Keever disconnected the call and put the phone back in her pocket. She adjusted her head rest and then leaned back. A few minutes later, Andino could hear the quiet sound of the woman's breathing. She'd fallen asleep without ever speaking with him.

CHAPTER SIXTEEN

Edinburgh, Scotland

The flight from Aberdeen to Edinburgh was bumpy, and Andino was happy when he saw the runway lights out the front window of the plane. The pilot set the plane down without incident, and they taxied to another small hangar, similar to the one they'd just left.

The aircraft came to rest just as a small door on the left side of the hanger opened and two men stepped out. One of the men approached the plane while the other hung back in the shadows.

Keever, who had awakened when the plane's wheels made contact with the runway, turned to Andino, and said, "Grab your shit, *priest*. When we get out, go straight to the hangar."

"How long are we going to be here?"

"Don't ask questions. Just get inside. We'll tell you what to do next."

"We?"

"Jesus Christ, *priest*! Just grab your shit and move your ass. I told you no questions."

Keever climbed out first and then, after admonishing Andino one more time to hurry up, she walked over to the man hidden in the shadows.

The pilot had exited the plane at the same time as Keever did. Now he walked back to the open passenger door and said, "Throw me your bags."

Andino tossed his bags one at a time to the man who quickly set them on the ground.

"Get moving. I want to get back in the air."

Andino climbed out of the plane without responding. He was tired of being ordered around but intelligent enough to realize he was in no position to argue with anyone. He picked up his bags and started toward the hangar but stopped in surprise when he entered. Parked on the concrete floor, a massive Boeing 757 aircraft filled almost the entire available space. The fuselage of the plane was painted a brilliant white. The back third of the plane as well as the vertical and horizontal stabilizers were painted brown with the easily recognized UPS logo painted in yellow. Across the gleaming white fuselage, the words Worldwide Services were emblazed in brown letters.

"Hurry up, priest. We don't have time for you to sightsee."

Keever's irksome voice broke Andino's fixation on the

massive jet. He'd been so surprised by the sight of the huge aircraft that he hadn't heard the nasty woman enter the hangar behind him.

"Get over here," she barked in her grating voice.

Andino looked around and found Keever standing near a row of lockers similar to what you'd find in a health club locker room. The woman had stripped down to her bra and panties by the time Andino joined her at the lockers.

"Stop gawking, priest. Haven't you ever seen a woman's tits before?" She smirked nastily at him as she pulled a brown flight suit from the locker. Before Andino could reply, she continued. "There are clothes in the locker. Now get changed. We have to get moving."

Andino opened the locker and found a flight suit identical to the one Keever was just zipping up. He pulled it and saw UPS stitched in yellow on the left breast. He quickly got undressed and stepped into the one-piece garment. At the bottom of the locker were a pair of black leather boots and a brown UPS baseball-style cap hung from one of the top hooks in the locker. The flight suit and boots were both a size too large for Andino, but he didn't bother saying anything to Keever. She'd just continue to berate him. He stuffed his discarded clothes into one of his bags and closed the locker door. Placing the hat on his head, he turned to follow Keever to the plane.

The one hundred and fifty-five-foot-long aircraft had a wingspan of just under one hundred and twenty-five feet and the vertical stabilizer at the rear of the frame rose almost forty-five feet above the hangar floor. Andino had flown in hundreds of jets over the years, but he'd never stood this close to one before. The sheer size was breathtaking.

"Whenever you're done sightseeing, priest, we can get this show on the road."

Andino saw that Keever had climbed to the top of a set of portable runway stairs that had been pushed up against the giant plane. He looked around the cavernous hangar one last time before joining Keever inside the aircraft.

The inside of the aircraft was filled with pallets of cargo stacked and secured in neat rows almost filling the one hundred and twenty-five feet of available space. Andino didn't see Keever at first, but as he moved through the carefully loaded rows of cargo, he found her seated in one of a half dozen business-class-sized seats.

"Have a seat, priest. The pilot wants to get underway as soon as possible."

The six seats were arranged in a single row with three on each side of a small center aisle. Andino chose the seat across the aisle from the woman.

"Now what?" he asked without thinking.

"Ora andiamo in America e prendiamo la tua piccolo puttana, Signore Du Bois."

Andino almost jumped out of his seat. He hadn't seen or heard the gray-haired man who slowly walked up and took a seat beside him. The man wore a white button-down shirt and black slacks. The shirt had the UPS logo embroidered over a set of gold pilot's wings over the left breast pocket and black shoulder boards with four gold bars, indicating he was the captain in charge of the plane.

Padraig Lowery wasn't a big man. Andino estimated he stood less than two meters tall and weighed around 75 kilograms. Despite his age and average stature, the man radiated power and authority. His green eyes burned with intensity as he stared unblinkingly into Andino's brown eyes, and he spoke in a deep voice used to being obeyed.

Andino tried unsuccessfully to hide his shock at the Irish gangster's sudden appearance. To cover his shock, he said, "So we're finally heading to America so I can punish the blasphemous whore?"

"That is correct, Signore Fabrizio. Or should I call you Monsieur Du Bois?"

"Whatever you prefer, Mr. Lowery."

"I'm sure you have a few questions for me," Lowery said.

As the big jet's two Pratt and Whitney PW2037 Turbofan engines propelled the twenty-two-thousand-pound plane down the runway, Lowery began to explain his plans for getting the group into the United States and obtaining the Cota girl.

CHAPTER SEVENTEEN

Lake Placid, New York

The cargo jet carrying Andino Fabrizio and his small band of mercenaries to North America lumbered down the runway and, with the grace that its massive size belied, lifted smoothly into the predawn sky.

Thirty-four hundred miles away, Christian Vikstrom was lying awake, watching the ceiling fan above his bed slowly spin in the semi-darkness. He'd spent over an hour on the phone with Summer. She'd told him all about her classes and what she was doing at Ithaca College, and he'd told her as much as he felt comfortable with about what he'd been doing. Summer was one of the happiest, most positive people Christian had ever known. She was as intelligent as she was beautiful, and she saw the absolute best in everyone and everything. She was the perfect Yin to Christian's Yang. Where he was constantly vigilant and on guard for the worst in people, Summer was open and carefree.

Summer had grown a little testy as Christian had to continually avoid giving her particulars about where he was and what he'd been doing. She knew he was working a security job for a big company and that he had to keep some things to himself, but she hated not being trusted with the details. Christian thought he had managed to smooth things over with her before they said good night, but he wasn't completely sure. He did know one thing, though. If they were going to have a chance of having a future together, Summer was going to have to understand there would be times he just couldn't discuss what he was working on.

Christian let out a frustrated sigh and shoved that problem to the back of his mind, where he locked it away to be dealt with after his current assignment was completed. Once that potential future problem was tucked securely away, Christian turned his mind to the more pressing issue he had to deal with. Why had Andino Fabrizio fled Italy at the same time Lowery and his people disappeared from Switzerland? Were the doctors with the two behavioral analysis units correct? Had Fabrizio somehow learned where they were hiding Cota? Christian ran the entire operation through his head for the hundredth time. He was sure they'd covered all their bases. The only people outside of the ArVal team who knew where they were keeping Evy hidden were Roddy Fraser and Evy's manager, Alonzo Perez. They hadn't even allowed Evy to tell her parents where she was being taken. Even the authorities in the UK, Italy, and Spain who were working diligently to locate Fabrizio didn't know where they were keeping the young actress. As far as they knew, Roddy had taken the girl to Lucerne, Switzerland to keep her safe.

Christian had gone back and forth with Arthur Valentine and his number two, Steven Paine. Both men were adamant that Fraser would never reveal their location to anyone. Evy's body double, manager, personal assistant, and bodyguard were still in Switzerland under the care of Roddy's people, just to be sure Fabrizio didn't try to get to them to find out where Evy was. Fraser had people keeping close tabs on all of their communications, so they couldn't have told anyone anything that might have aided Fabrizio in his search for the girl.

As Christian continued to work the problem around in his head, he heard a soft knock at the bedroom door. His hand dropped to the Glock 43 he had secured in a holster he'd attached to the bedframe the first night they'd spent at the house. He had complete faith in the high-end security system Dexter had installed on the house and surrounding property, but he was still prepared. There was no perfect security system, and for every newly developed technology that entered the market, there were highly paid experts hard at work figuring out ways to defeat it.

"Yes."

"It's Laura."

Christian quickly grabbed the workout pants he'd dropped on the floor when he climbed into bed and slipped them on.

"Come in." Christian was curious. In the entire time they'd been at the house, this was the first time the former Marine intelligence officer had come to his room.

Laura opened the door just wide enough to slip into the room. Once inside, she pushed the door firmly closed behind her.

Christian was just taking a bottle of water from the small refrigerator next to his bed when Laura came in. "Water?" he asked.

"Sure." Laura chuckled to herself as she took the bottle of water from his hand. Like Christian, she had been lying awake in bed trying to come up with a plausible reason for both Lowery and Fabrizio to disappear around the same time. She knew it was useless trying to fall back to sleep, so she decided to see if Christian was awake so she could bounce some ideas off him. She was still wearing the thin T-shirt and shorts she'd fallen asleep in, and it was obvious she hadn't bothered to put a bra on before she decided to pay Christian a visit. It was equally obvious that Christian was trying valiantly *not* to notice.

"Something wrong?" she asked innocently as Christian struggled to keep his eyes on her face.

"Not at all. What's up?" He finally gave up the battle and turned to gaze out the window at the moon reflecting off the calm waters of Lake Placid.

Laura studied Christian as he stared out the window. She liked him. Probably a little more than she should, considering she was married to Abby and he had a girlfriend. There was no denying that he was handsome and fit, but it was more than that. He was a good person. He treated everyone around him with the same level of respect. He valued every team member's input, and, aside from his ongoing feud with Steven Paine, he rarely lost his temper.

She'd caught the younger man admiring her on a couple of occasions, but it was never in a disrespectful way. It was a glance or a smile, and, if she was being completely honest, she'd done her share of admiring as well.

She pulled her gaze away from Christian and moved to one of the chairs facing the dormant fireplace and sat down, curling her legs up under her and pulling her T-shirt down over them as she made herself comfortable.

Christian stared out the window for a few seconds longer and then joined Laura by the fireplace. "It always amazes me the way women can sit like that," he said as he sat down. "If I tried it, I wouldn't be able to walk for a week after I got up."

"You need to work harder on your flexibility. Yoga will help with that." She laughed as she saw the look in his eyes when she raised her T-shirt just enough for him to see her well-toned legs curled beneath her.

Christian pulled his gaze from Laura's legs. "So what has you up wandering the halls so early?"

"I couldn't sleep. I keep running everything through my mind, and I can't come up with a good reason for Lowery to pull out of Switzerland and Fabrizio to disappear from Italy almost simultaneously."

"I know. I was doing the same thing. I've run through every detail of how we handled the operation so far, and I can't come up with a way they'd know where we are. Lowery eventually discovering that Switzerland was a decoy was expected. He's been in the game for a very long time, and he didn't survive the SAS in Ireland by being lazy or stupid."

"Agreed."

"The issue I'm having is with Fabrizio disappearing at just about the exact same time. The guy's a former priest with no formal intelligence training that we're aware of. How'd he just vanish like that? And why?"

They talked for another hour before Laura finally stood up. "I'm getting a headache," she said. Looking outside, she saw that the sky above Whiteface Mountain off to the east was beginning to lighten. "I'm going to see if Evy is awake yet. Maybe I can get her to join Dex and me for a yoga workout this morning."

"That sounds like an excellent idea. Give me a few minutes, and I'll join you."

CHAPTER EIGHTEEN

Montreal, Canada

Fabrizio was close to a complete breakdown. He'd never felt more out of control of his surroundings than he did right now. The flight from Edinburgh to Montreal had been terrifying. Padraig Lowery was the most intimidating man he'd ever encountered. The calm way the man laid out his plan to kidnap Evora Cota and kill everyone protecting her made Andino's blood run cold. The man was obsessed with avenging the murder of his grandson in Rome, and nothing Andino said could dissuade him.

Murder was not what Andino had planned. All he wanted was to punish the Cota girl for her blasphemous show and the sinful, decadent lifestyle she lived. He needed to free himself from the unholy, lustful thoughts she gave rise to within him.

He didn't want to have any part in killing anyone. He didn't even want the Cota girl dead. He just wanted her to confess her sins and repent. Lowery's reaction to Fabrizio's reluctance to his plan had been all the more horrifying because the man maintained his calm demeanor.

"Understand me, *priest*," he had said. "The men who murdered my grandson are going to die. I don't care what you do with your little whore once we have her, but if you interfere in my plans to kill those men, I will have Nessa gut you like a fish. She'll do it slowly. You'll beg me for death before she finally allows you to meet your God."

One look at Keever's face made it obvious to Andino that the psychopathic woman hoped that she'd be allowed to make good on Lowery's threat.

Once in Montreal, they'd been met by a man Lowery identified as Brandon Flannery. Apparently, Flannery's grandfather was an old PIRA comrade of Lowery's, and he'd arranged for his grandson to assist Lowery in any way he could. Flannery had five hard-looking thugs with him. He assured Lowery that his men had the skills to not only help grab the girl, but they also had the experience to put down anyone protecting her.

Lowery and Flannery talked for a half hour before calling the group together so Flannery could introduce his people.

"Normally, when we smuggle people across the border, the less our cargo knows about us, the better. This situation is a bit different, though. It looks like we're going to be pulling off some serious shit in the States, so it's best if everyone knows their partners." Looking at Keever and Fabrizio, he added, "You two are with Padraig, so I can assume that if you're ever questioned, you know better than to give the authorities anything." Without waiting for any sort of reply, Flannery continued.

"This is Ben Lincoln," he said, laying his hand on the shoulder of the medium-built man at his side. "He was born here in Canada, and he's my second-in-command."

Lincoln was just over five-and-a-half feet tall and lean. His brown hair was pulled back into a ponytail, and his blue eyes never stopped scanning the newcomers. Andino thought he could actually feel violence radiate from the man.

"These two hard arses are Nate and Sammy Boyle. They moved to Canada after they became persons of interest to the authorities in Belfast and London."

To Fabrizio, the two Irishmen looked enough alike to be twins. They both stood a hair under six feet tall and like Lincoln, they looked hard and mean. Their exposed forearms were lined with veins, and their knuckles looked like they'd encountered more than one poor soul's face.

"The big blond"—Flannery pointed to a large man leaning against one of two box trucks parked in the garage—"is Jan Dworak. Jan was a sniper in the Polish army before he was dishonorably discharged for beating the shit out of an officer who didn't show him the respect he felt he deserved."

"The man was a coward and a liar," Dworak said in heavily accented English. "He got what he deserved."

"Last, but definitely not least, is Solomon," Flannery said as he threw his arm around the last member of his crew. "Solomon was a pirate in his homeland of Somalia. He had to flee Africa after his band of cutthroats made the mistake of killing a captive they were holding for ransom. The girl's family had serious political ties within the European Union, and a huge reward was placed on him and the rest of the men involved. Solomon here is the only one who managed to escape when mercenaries tracked them down and slaughtered the rest of his crew."

Solomon was around six feet tall with a shiny, shaved scalp. He wore a white tank top that made his already dark brown skin appear even darker. The man's arms were all wiry muscle, and his right hand rested on a knife sheathed at his right hip.

"It appears the man likes his blades," Padraig commented. "I count three from where I'm standing."

"Six," the pirate corrected as he drew a large blade he had sheathed horizontally behind his back.

"Now *that's* a knife," Ben Lincoln joked in a heavy, fake Australian accent, aka Crocodile Dundee.

"Ah, yes. Solomon is my carver. He's the man I send if I find out someone has loose lips." Flannery had a smile on his lips as he spoke, but the smile didn't extend to his eyes as he looked from Lowery to Keever and finally to Fabrizio with his not-so-subtle warning.

Once Flannery had finished introducing his crew, they split up and climbed into the two box trucks. Sammy Boyle hopped into the driver's seat of a yellow Hino truck with Penske markings. Lincoln would be riding shotgun with Solomon and Dworak hidden behind stacks of used tires in the cargo area.

The second truck was a white Freightliner with North Country Produce painted on the cab doors as well as the sides and overhead door of the box.

"Ben's cousin owns the produce company. He lets me use his trucks to move products to the border," Flannery explained as he climbed into the driver's seat.

Lowery joined him in the cab while Fabrizio, Keever, and Nate Boyle hid behind boxes of produce stacked floor to ceiling in the cargo box.

They'd been traveling down Route 401 for over an hour and a half, when Andino felt the truck begin to slow down.

"Where are we?" he asked.

"Cornwall." Nate Boyle was barely visible in the dark cargo area. "Flannery has a member of the First Nations he works with. He'll get us onto Cornwall Island. From there, we'll take a couple of boats across the river to the U.S."

"We can't just drive across? There must be a bridge." Andino wasn't a big fan of water. He'd never learned to swim, which was ironic since his father owned the biggest shipping fleet in the world.

"Stop with the questions, *priest*. Just do what you're told." Keever had fallen asleep during the drive, and Fabrizio's annoying voice had woken her up.

"I have a right to know what's happening." Fabrizio was scared, and that fear had emboldened him enough to push back against Keever and her constant harassment.

Before Keever could chastise Andino further, Boyle chimed in. "He's right, woman. He has as much right to know what's happening as you do." Before Keever could form a reply, he continued. "Flannery and Lincoln have a member of the local tribe who helps them smuggle shit into the U.S. through the First Nations reservation all the time."

"What does the First Nations thing mean?" Fabrizio had never heard of the term before.

"The Mohawks are members of the Iroquois nation. They're the indigenous people who lived on these lands before the Europeans showed up and stole it from them. In Canada, they're referred to as First Nations. In the United States, they're called Native Americans. I'm confused about the entire thing. There is tribal land that straddles the border between Canada and the U.S., and both nations recognize it as the sovereign territory of the indigenous people. Both countries still have some measure of control over the lands, but it is a lot easier to smuggle stuff across the tribal land than trying to cross at an official port of entry. All the bridges are official entry points and monitored by the CBSA, the Canadian Border Services Agency in Canada, and the CBP, or Customs and Border Protection in America."

"Doesn't the CBSA watch what goes into and out of the tribal land?" Keever was just as curious as Fabrizio. She'd never heard of such a thing in Europe. Since the European Union was formed, citizens of member countries didn't even need a passport to travel between EU countries. Of course, since Brexit had taken effect, those rules had changed, but the idea of a sovereign nation within the borders of existing nations like Canada and the United States sounded extremely complicated.

"They do, but Flannery has CBSA and CBP agents on his payroll. We won't have any trouble crossing onto First Nations land. Flannery's contact within the tribe has arrangements with some of the tribal cops on both sides of the reservation. They're well paid to look the other way when we move things across the border. Once we're on Cornwall Island, we take a couple boats across the St. Lawrence River to tribal land on the U.S. side of the border. Flannery's First Nations contact has someone from the tribe on the U.S. side that will meet us and get us further into the U.S. from there."

"Don't the Americans watch for this kind of thing?" Keever knew it couldn't be as easy as Boyle was making it sound.

"They do. The U.S. Border Patrol as well as the United

States Coast Guard run patrols on the river, trying to interdict smuggling operations, but the people Flannery uses are experts at this shit. We shouldn't have any issues getting into the U.S. If a patrol gets lucky and spots us, we just run back to the Canadian side, where Flannery's native contact makes sure the tribal PD leaves us alone."

"It sounds risky," Fabrizio said.

"Bloody coward," Keever mumbled under her breath.

"It can be. That's half the fun of it. Now quiet down. We're stopping. It could be a CBSA checkpoint."

Fabrizio felt the truck slow and come to a stop. His heart was beating so hard that he was positive Keever and Boyle could hear it.

"If the overhead door opens, keep quiet and stay down as low as you can," whispered Boyle. "If this is a CBSA checkpoint, they normally just do a quick peek inside the vehicle to make sure it's carrying what the driver says it is. They rarely dig through the cargo unless they have information that there may be contraband aboard."

After what seemed like an hour to Fabrizio but was actually just a few minutes, they heard the latch on the overhead door being flipped open. The door rose noisily in its tracks, and bright light flooded the interior of the cargo space.

The welcome sound of Sammy Boyle's voice filled the enclosed space. "Let's go, people. Ryan wants to get across the river as quickly as possible."

"You heard the man. Let's go."

Fabrizio slowly rose from where he'd been hiding and followed Keever and Boyle as they squeezed their way past the stacked crates and boxes of tomatoes, lettuce, and corn. Fabrizio carefully climbed down from the cargo truck and joined Keever and the Boyle brothers. A short distance away, he saw Lowery and Flannery speaking to a huge man wearing a camouflage field jacket and blue jeans.

"Keep quiet and follow me," Boyle said.

"Who are they talking to?"

"Shut your mouth, *priest*. He said to keep quiet and follow along."

Ignoring Keever's angry words, Boyle said, "That's Tyler Jacobs. They call him 'Big T'. He's a full-blooded Mohawk and one mean son-of-a-bitch. Rumor has it that he killed a man with one punch during a bar fight up in northern Quebec. Don't know if it's true or not, but I'd rather not find out."

The moniker definitely fit the man, Andino thought. He stood almost two meters, or six and a half feet tall, and Andino estimated he weighed at least 135 kilograms, or three hundred pounds. As they drew closer to the group, Andino saw that the field jacket the big man was wearing had U.S. ARMY stitched on a strip above the left pocket and the name JACOBS stitched above the right pocket. Jacobs had copper-colored skin and jet-black hair, which he wore pulled into a braided ponytail that hung down between his shoulder blades.

Beyond where the small group stood talking, Andino could see two boats tied to a large dock. Both vessels were Robalo center console fishing boats, with two Yamaha 300 CC engines quietly rumbling away at their stern.

"Come on. Get moving. This isn't a sightseeing tour."

Andino saw that the speaker was Nate's brother, Sammy. He and the group from the lead truck were already climbing aboard the closest of the two boats.

"Let's go before that arsehole brother of mine blows a blood vessel," Nate said.

Fabrizio saw Flannery hand an envelope to Jacobs, and then the group moved to join the rest of the party on the dock. Jacobs, Flannery, and Lowery joined Fabrizio and Keever in the lead boat. While Lincoln joined the Boyle brothers, Solomon and Dworak were in the second boat. Jacobs manned the helm of the first boat, while a subject Fabrizio hadn't previously seen stood behind the wheel of the second. At Jacob's command, both boats slowly motored their way out onto the dark St. Lawrence River.

CHAPTER NINETEEN

St. Lawrence River, near Cornwall, Ontario Canada

The radio on the dash of the center console boat crackled to life, and Jacobs grabbed it. "Go ahead."

"The lookout says the Border Patrol is about to put a boat in the water at the marina, and the Coast Guard is waiting there to meet them."

"Copy."

"Problem?" asked Lowery.

Jacobs eyed Lowery for a couple seconds before responding. "Not a problem. The Border Patrol is getting set to launch a boat and join the Coast Guard on the river."

"And that's not a problem?"

"Not for us. We'll be across the river and on our way inland before they ever reach this spot."

Andino didn't know how long they'd been on the river

when he heard Jacobs radio the second boat. "Keep sharp. We'll be turning into the Raquette River up ahead about a hundred yards." Andino couldn't make out the garbled reply, but it must've satisfied Jacobs because he hung the radio mic up without further discussion.

"How much longer?" Lowery's whispered voice was barely audible above the rumble of the big engines.

"Not long. We're turning into Raquette River up ahead on the right in a couple of minutes. There's a long, narrow island at the mouth of the river. About a quarter mile past the island, my partner owns a small farm. We'll still be on Mohawk land, so we'll be fine."

"How long before we're in the United States?"

"We crossed into U.S. waters about five minutes after we launched."

"You should've told me that." Though Lowery was whispering, there was no hiding the anger in his voice.

Before Jacobs had a chance to respond, the radio crackled to life. "What's up?" he asked into the mic.

"It looks like the Coast Guard didn't wait for the Border Patrol boat. They're about a half mile behind us right now."

"Do we have a problem?"

Jacobs ignored Lowery as he spoke with his man driving the trailing boat. "Do you think they've seen us?"

"No. They're sticking to the main channel, heading east nice and slow."

"Good. We're turning up Raquette River now. Keep the speed down. No need to leave a big wake for the feds to see when they go by."

"Copy that."

"Do we have a problem?" Lowery asked again. This time, there was no mistaking the edge in the man's voice. He apparently didn't like being ignored.

Jacobs met Lowery's hard stare with one of his own before replying. "No problem. The Coast Guard decided not to wait for the CBP boat before it launched. They're a little way behind us heading into the main channel. No need for concern, though. We'll be off the St. Lawrence before they get close." If Jacobs sensed Lowery was annoyed, he didn't show it. His reply was in the same low, confident voice he'd been using ever since they'd hooked up with him.

After turning into the smaller Raquette River, Jacobs slowed the boat slightly. When he saw the confused look on Lowery's face, he said, "We don't want to leave a wake for the Border Patrol guys to see and decide to check out."

The sky had lightened just enough for Andino to be able to see the trailing boat with Jacobs' man at the helm, following them into the smaller tributary. Off the starboard side of the boat, he could just make out the forested shoreline of the island Jacobs had mentioned. Other than the sound of the engines and the water washing along the sides of the boat, there were no other sounds. Andino could see a few lights cutting through the darkness on both sides of the river, but there didn't seem to be any people out at this early hour.

Jacobs began to guide his boat to the southern shoreline, where a large dock with two boats slowly emerged from the darkness. He radioed the second boat. "I'm approaching the dock. Hang back until I call you. Give me a minute to make sure we're good." He gently brought the center console boat alongside the dock with a skill born of numerous clandestine landings in the dead of night.

Andino jumped slightly when a voice from the dock called out.

"Throw me a line."

From the shadows, a man stepped out onto the dock to catch the line Lowery had thrown. Like Jacobs, this man had the coppery skin tone of a Native American and long, dark hair that was pulled back into a long ponytail. The similarity ended there. Where Jacobs was the size of a mountain, this man was barely five-and-a-half feet tall, and Andino estimated he weighed no more than sixty-five kilos, or one hundred and forty-five pounds. After securing the front of the boat to a steel cleat mounted to the dock, he moved toward the rear of the boat, where Flannery was ready to toss him a second line. The small man caught the line with ease and expertly secured the boat to the dock.

"Any issues?" the man asked Jacobs.

"None. CBP is getting ready to launch a boat west of here,

and the Coast Guard has a boat on the river already, but they had no idea we were out there. You have any problems?"

"No, but let's get the other boat in so we can get moving."

Jacobs simply nodded and called his man in the second boat, telling him it was safe to dock.

Once both boats were secured to the dock and everyone had unloaded, Jacobs approached Flannery and shook hands. "You've worked with my cousin Jimmy before," he said, nodding to the man on the dock. "He'll take you from here. Call the number I gave you when you're ready to arrange to get back across, and I'll meet you here."

"Thanks, T. I'll have the rest of your money when we get back."

"You'd better." There was no joking in the man's voice. He was all business. Moving people across the border was dangerous work, and he made an excellent living doing it.

Jimmy walked up to the small group and greeted Brandon Flannery. "Good to see you, man. How was the trip?"

"Uneventful, Jimmy."

"Best kind, eh?" he said with a chuckle. "Let's get going. I have your transportation waiting."

He led the small group to a large, well-maintained pole barn. The building looked brand new. Inside the pole barn, King led them to three SUVs parked just inside the closed overhead door. Along with the three vehicles, the building contained several sleek speedboats on trailers, a half dozen side-by-side ATVs, and at least a dozen four-wheelers. Four snowmobiles sat under nylon covers beside the four-wheelers.

"The smuggling business must be treating you very well, Jimmy," Flannery said as he looked over all the vehicles stored in the barn.

"I ain't complaining, Irish." He took Flannery by the arm and steered him to the three vehicles he had acquired for the job. "These came from the Montreal Airport long-term parking lot. They were all parked yesterday, and Big T's people at the airport made sure their owners boarded their flights, so we're sure no one will be looking for them any time soon." As he spoke, he walked to the back of the first vehicle, a blue 2019 Chevy Blazer, where he raised the cargo hatch. Inside, a canvas tarp hid the contents from view. Once the tarp was removed, Andino could see that the cargo area held four hard-shell Pelican cases. King began to pull the cases out and set them on the floor.

He flipped open the latches on the first case and threw open the top, revealing twelve handguns from several manufacturers. With the weapons were spare high-capacity magazines and hip holsters.

"We couldn't get the same make and model for all the weapons. We've got Sig's, Berretta, Colt, and Glock. They're all forty calibers, though, and I got you five thousand rounds of ammunition."

The next two cases he opened each held two M4-style

tactical rifles with multiple 30-round magazines for each weapon. "I have a buddy working at Fort Drum. They had crates of weapons scheduled to be destroyed. He was able to grab a few cases for us. These M4's are chambered for 5.56 ammunition. I have three thirty-round magazines for each rifle and three thousand rounds of 5.56 ammo."

The final case contained tactical knives, handheld GPS units, binoculars, night vision scopes, and handheld radios. King took one of the radios from the case. "These are older Motorola handheld radios. The tribal cops upgraded their equipment last year, and I was able to get my hands on a bunch of them. I don't know shit about radios, but one of my buddies on the PD says these are pretty good, and they're encrypted, so when you're communicating, only you and your team will be able to pick up the transmissions."

"Excellent," Flannery said. "Let's load up and get out of here."

"Sounds good. It's around seventy-five miles from here to Lake Placid, and barring any problems, we can be there in a little over an hour and a half."

Handguns were handed out to the new arrivals—with everyone except Andino receiving a weapon—along with three extra magazines. The remainder of the weapons and gear were resecured in their cases and tucked back into their hiding places in the vehicles. Next, the team was divided up, and everyone took their assigned spots in the vehicles, King getting behind the wheel of the blue blazer with Flannery in the passenger's seat. Lowery and Fabrizio slid into the back. The second vehicle, a tan 2021 GMC Denali, was driven by Ben Lincoln with Nate Boyle riding shotgun and Nessa Keever in the back. The last vehicle was a 2010 Ford Expedition. Sammy Boyle was assigned to drive with Dworak up front and Solomon in the back.

"Are you planning on joining us during our operation, Mr. King?" Lowery asked.

"Jimmy won't be involved in the actual grab. He's coming along for logistical support," Flannery explained. "He's familiar with the Lake Placid area, and he's hooking us up with a place to sleep. He's also going to make sure we get back to the border after this is all done."

"Big T asked me to come along in the event that things go sideways. My contacts will be able to help us out just in case things go bad and we need to improvise on the fly."

"I see," Lowery said. "So you've been involved in this type of operation before?"

"If you mean kidnapping a person and smuggling them over the border, then yes, I've been a part of something like this before."

When King didn't elaborate, Lowery decided to drop the matter. He didn't like surprises, but he realized he wasn't completely in charge at this point, and he'd need to rely on Flannery's grandson Brandon's best judgment to a point.

Just as King had predicted, it took just over ninety minutes to reach Lake Placid. The three-vehicle convoy entered the small Adirondack village in the early morning hours before the sun had even had a chance to peek out over Whiteface Mountain. They traveled east along State Route 86/Saranac Ave. without realizing they were passing within a mile of where young Evora Cota slept. When they reached Main Street, King turned left and headed around Mirror Lake.

"My cousin hooked us up with the perfect place to work out of. He owns a contracting company, and right now he's working on renovating an old farmhouse into a bed and breakfast. It's outside of town a little bit and sits back off the road on a wooded lot. Nice and quiet. No neighbors."

"Where are the owners?" asked Lowery. He definitely didn't need any surprise visitors right in the middle of their operation.

"Some company bought the place to add to their VRBO properties. My cousin says the management company overseeing the work never actually visits the place. They call in a few times a week from their Manhattan offices to make sure the work is on schedule and to release funds when needed for the project."

"And this cousin of yours . . . Can he be trusted to keep his mouth shut?"

"Absolutely, man. Big T uses him to find spots where he can stash illegals he smuggles through the reservation. He knows better than to run his mouth."

They drove on in silence, with the sound of the windshield wipers clearing a slight mist off the windshield being the only sound in the vehicle. Andino was exhausted from the entire ordeal, and he only partially paid attention to the conversation as he kept nodding off only to awaken when the vehicle hit a rough patch of road or his head hit the window.

King turned off of Mirror Lake Drive onto Northwood Road and followed it until they reached Cobble Hill Road. Cobble Hill Road was a narrow, windy, unlined road in obvious need of paving. Lowery looked out at the street signs excluding commercial vehicles from using the road unless it was for local delivery and warning drivers that the road was windy, and the recommended speed limit was 25 MPH.

"It's not far now. Just to the end of this road, where it meets Route 86."

A few minutes later, King began to slow down as they approached a driveway partially hidden by an overgrowth of trees and bushes. Lowery was certain that if he or one of his people had been driving, they'd have missed the dirt path leading into the heavily wooded area. For the first fifty yards, the narrow, rutted dirt driveway wound through a thick forest of trees and tangles of brush and flowering bushes. King slowly maneuvered the Blazer around as many of the deeper ruts and holes as he could, but the road was in too poor a condition to avoid several spine-jarring bumps as they moved closer to the end. Lowery was rapidly losing patience with their guide when they drove into a small clearing, and he could see the house that was their destination.

The house was enormous and almost completely encased in scaffolding. The white paint of the exterior was cracked and peeling in more spots than Lowery could count, and the front porch was sagging to the point where he wasn't sure how it didn't just collapse. In the front yard was a large, red shipping container with ABBOTTS ADIRONDACK CONTRACTING painted down both sides. The door of the container was secured with an industrial-strength padlock. Lowery saw a portable chop saw and a band saw, along with numerous other pieces of construction equipment scattered around the yard. Parked next to the house was a beat-up white Ram 2500 with the name ABBOTTS ADIRONDACK CONTRACTING painted on the door.

"This place is still under construction," King explained. "My cousin moved all his workers to another job, so we have this place indefinitely. He told me the electricity works fine, as does the furnace. He stocked the refrigerator and pantry with enough food for a couple days, but you'll probably need to do some shopping. There's a Hannaford grocery store on 86. We passed it on the way into town. There are six bedrooms, so you should have plenty of room for your crew."

"Are you staying here with us?"

"No. I'm staying at a rental cottage on the other side of

Placid. We passed the place on the way here. Flannery knows how to contact me if he needs anything. Otherwise, I'll wait to hear from you when it's time to move you and your package back over the border into Canada."

"You're not helping us look for the girl?" Keever asked in surprise.

"No. Big T only hired me to find you a place to stay and get you back to the border once you're done with whatever you have planned."

"Your knowledge of the area could come in handy. I'll pay you extra to assist us in finding and grabbing the girl," Lowery said.

"How much extra?"

Lowery could clearly see the greed on the young smuggler's face.

All three vehicles had come to a stop right in front of the house as Lowery and King reached an agreement on payment for King's continued services. Everyone piled out of the vehicles, tired and needing to stretch their backs and legs after such a long journey.

Lowery looked at the small group and said, "Everyone, get your gear inside and find a place to sleep."

"When do we start looking for the girl?" Fabrizio asked as he walked up to Lowery.

"Patience, priest. We need to get settled first. I want everyone to be rested and ready when we head out."

"What's the plan?"

"Stop with the questions, *priest!*"

Fabrizio hadn't heard Ness Keever approaching, and her abrasive voice caused him to jump.

"Enough, Nessa," Lowery softly admonished the girl. "The priest is not only paying for this job, but he will need to take an active part, so he has the right to know what the plan is."

Keever visibly bristled at Lowery's rebuke, but she held her tongue. Lowery had a fiery temper when crossed, and she didn't want to be the recipient of his anger.

"For now, priest, we are going to get settled and see what provisions our native friends have left for us. I'll send some of the men to the store for whatever supplies we decide we need. We'll eat a good meal, and then I want everyone to get some sleep. We will meet in the morning, where I'll outline my plan."

"And then?"

"And then we go hunting, priest."

Fabrizio was looking Lowery right in the eyes as he spoke, and a chill ran down his spine at the intensity of the man's words.

CHAPTER TWENTY

Lake Placid, New York

Andino didn't know where he was when he woke up. He lay quietly on the bed and listened to the sounds of someone snoring close by. After a few disorienting moments, the events of the past few days came crashing in on him. The claustrophobic ride in the back of the delivery truck was followed by a terrifying ride across a mist-shrouded river in a boat piloted by one of the indigenous people of this land. Then the long ride through night-shrouded mountains.

Andino wasn't tired. He was wide awake and scared. He needed to speak with Lowery and learn what the crazy Irishman had planned. He had tried to question Lowery when they arrived at the house last night, but that evil bitch, Nessa Keever, had intervened. All Lowery would say was that they were going hunting. What the hell did that mean?

The man sharing his room snorted, farted, and settled back to sleep. Andino took that as a sign that he should get up and go find Lowery. He quietly swung his legs around and placed his feet on a chilly hardwood floor. Andino's stomach growled with hunger, and his bowels churned within him. *First things first,* he reasoned. He slowly opened the door to the room he was sharing with one of the men from Flannery's group. He could not recall the man's name. In truth, he couldn't recall more than a handful of the ruffians he had encountered since fleeing Rome and the safety and comfort of his home there. Once in the empty hallway outside the bedroom, he went in search of a toilet to take care of the most urgent of his immediate needs. With nature's call answered, he went in search of Lowery and, hopefully, some food to break his fast.

The smell of brewing coffee led Andino down a narrow flight of stairs to the ground floor. Following his nose, Andino located the kitchen, where he found Lowery, Flannery, King, and Keever seated around a large wooden table. Steaming mugs of coffee sat before each of them, along with plates of eggs, bacon, fried potatoes, and toast.

"I hope I'm not interrupting," Andino said, entering the room.

"Not at all, priest."

Despite his age, Lowery did not look like a man who'd spent the last few days traveling across Europe and then on to North America. He wore a dark green flannel shirt and tan work pants. A shoulder holster secured a large black handgun under his left arm. His green eyes shone like emeralds, and his gray hair was neatly combed.

"Grab some food and coffee from the stove and join us."

Another rumble from his empty stomach reminded Andino how hungry he was, so he moved quickly to take Lowery up on his offer of breakfast. Once he had a plate full of food and a hot mug of coffee in hand, he moved to the table, where he sat next to Lowery.

"You look sick, *priest.*" Nessa Keever could not keep the contempt she felt for the little man out of her voice.

"Nessa," Lowery warned. "I will remind you that we are here to do a job, and the priest is paying us quite well to do it. Now curb your attitude, or I'll do it for you." Lowery's penetrating gaze bore into Keever as he waited for her to respond.

Keever hated the priest, but she respected and feared the man she served. She had no desire to anger him.

"My apologies, Padraig."

Lowery held Keever's stare for another thirty seconds to make sure she was aware that he was tired of her constant poking at their rich client before continuing.

"I want to get started right away," Lowery began. "I have several photos of the girl we are looking for. I will text them to your phones. Make sure all of your men have the photos as well."

"Of course, Padraig," said Flannery.

"We know she is staying in a house right on Lake Placid. She told her mother this. We also know there is a group of Americans guarding her. My hope is that some of the men were in London and/or Rome, and Nessa will be able to identify at least some of them. We'll need to nail down how many are protecting her and how before we can formulate a plan to take her."

"Any idea how many men?" King asked.

"The ignorant girl told her mother there were three people with her at all times. A woman and two men. One of the men is an Asian who once worked for the FBI. She says the other male has a scar running down the side of his face and looks like he walked off the set of the television show, *The Vikings*."

"So just three people protecting her?" The surprise was clear in King's voice.

"No, she says there are a few more close by."

"So we don't have an exact number?"

"No, but it appears most likely there are less than ten people involved, and they're not all together. Once we spot the girl, we should be able to identify anyone protecting her. Nessa has extensive experience in conducting and detecting surveillance."

"True. I spent more hours than I care to remember locating, identifying, and tracking terrorists in the Middle East and the UK. I'll have no trouble identifying her protectors once we locate the girl."

"And how are we going to do that?" asked Andino. "All the girl said was that she was in a big house on the lake. There must be hundreds of houses on the lake here."

"The priest is right," King said. "There are hundreds of houses and camps along the lake. Plus, a lot of people take a look at a map and think Mirror Lake in the middle of town is Lake Placid. The girl could've been confused, and the house could be around the smaller lake."

"What about the resort on the lake? There can't be more than one of those, can there?"

"There are a few places, but the only true resort on Lake Placid where they'd have a spa day is the Whiteface Lodge, and if they spent time there, we may be in luck."

"How so?"

"My cousin Linette works there."

"What's her job there?" Padraig asked.

"I'm not sure. She's some kind of a boss, though. I know her parents are very proud of her. She graduated from Paul Smith's College with a degree in Hotel and Resort Management, and now she makes big money catering to rich pricks at the resort. Maybe she'd know where the girl is staying. If she'd be willing to tell me, that's another matter."

"Why wouldn't she help out her cousin?"

"Her mother, my aunt, is one of the three elected Mohawk tribal chiefs. Her entire family has always looked down on me and my *activities*. Linette and I got along okay, but her parents discouraged her from hanging out with me."

"It can't hurt to ask," Flannery put in. "The worst that can happen is that she doesn't tell you anything."

"No," Lowery said in disagreement. "The worst that can happen is that she somehow lets Cota and her protectors know someone is asking about her. Right now, they have no idea that we know she's somewhere in Lake Placid. If we start asking about her, and they find out, they'll get her out of here as fast as they can."

"I can feel her out. I'll reach out and let her know I'm in town for a few days and see if she wants to meet up. We've done it a few times before, so it won't seem out of the ordinary. We get along pretty well as long as her parents aren't involved."

Flannery looked at Lowery and asked, "What do you think? Is it worth the risk?"

As Lowery was pondering the question, Keever interrupted his thoughts. "It may be our best bet, Padraig. We could scour the town for days and not find the girl. Worse, if her protectors are any good at all, they could spot our people and get the girl out of here without us knowing they've gone."

Lowery mulled over what Keever had said for several more minutes before deciding on a course of action. Keever kept quiet. She'd been with Lowery for a long time now, and she knew the man would look at the problem from every possible angle before making a decision. She'd given him her opinion, and she knew nothing else she said would alter what the legendary PIRA commander decided.

"This is what we're going to do." As Lowery spoke, everyone at the table stopped what they were doing and gave him their undivided attention. "Flannery, divide the men into three-man teams. Give me one of your men, and I'll take Fabrizio with me. You'll take Keever with you. Make sure everyone has copies of the photos of the girl as well as the description of her protectors. Listen to what Keever says. She's had extensive training and real-world experience in conducting surveillance and identifying targets."

"Padraig—" Keever started.

"Not yet, Nessa. I'll take questions after I'm finished." He turned to Jimmy King. "Reach out to your cousin as you suggested. If you think you can get any information on the girl's location without making your cousin suspicious, do it. Don't make it obvious. If she seems dodgy about your questions, then drop it. We got lucky finding out she was here. We might not be so lucky the next time." When he finished speaking, Lowery looked at the group gathered around the table. "Now, I'll go around the table. Any questions or concerns? Flannery, you first."

"We only have three vehicles, and King needs one to hook up with his cousin. That leaves two vehicles to go looking for the girl."

Before Lowery could address the issue, King interrupted. "That's not a problem. I'll make a phone call and have a vehicle here in a couple hours. I won't be able to set anything up with Linette before then anyway."

"Anything else, Flannery?"

"Yes. What do we do if we spot the girl?"

"Excellent question. You notify me, and you keep an eye on her. Under no circumstances does anyone attempt to grab the girl without my order. Am I clear on that?" Once everyone had assured Lowery they understood, he continued. "If she leaves the area, try to follow her without being seen. Keep in mind that we know there are more people protecting her than the three who will probably be with her in public. Once she has been located, we can assess her and come up with a plan of action. It may be to back off and observe until we know where they are bedding down, or it may be to take them as they travel. The circumstances will dictate the action."

"Nessa?"

The intense young woman looked directly at Fabrizio as she spoke. "Why are we bringing the priest with us? He'll just be in the way."

"We're bringing the priest with us because he, better than anyone here, can identify the girl on sight. You know as well as I do that identifying a person from a photograph isn't as easy as they make it seem on television and in the movies."

"He's never done anything like this before. The feckin'

eejit will get us spotted, and we'll lose the girl."

"That's why he'll be with me. I'll make sure he doesn't do anything to compromise the operation." Finally, he looked at Fabrizio and said, "And you, priest. Anything to add?"

Andino had no desire to be involved in the actual hunt for the girl. That's why he hired these criminals. He didn't voice this thought, though. He knew it would be met with derision from the Keever witch, and he feared Lowery might actually assault him. "What are we going to do with the girl once we have her?"

"I was wondering the same thing," said Flannery. "Are we taking her back across the border or not?"

"A lot depends on how we acquire her. My plan right now is to grab her and use King and Flannery's knowledge of the area and local law enforcement to leg it right to the border. Once we're in Canada, Flannery has a place we can hold up. If things are too hot once we have the girl, we may have to come back here and lay low." He turned to Fabrizio. "I don't know what you have planned for the girl, priest, but if it doesn't look feasible to get her into Canada, you may have to do whatever it is you plan to do right here and be done with it."

Fabrizio nodded his head in understanding, though, in truth, he was no longer certain what to do with the girl once he had her.

CHAPTER TWENTY-ONE

Lake Placid, New York

"I want to get out of this house for a while," Evy whined to Laura. "We've been cooped up for days."

The rain that had gripped the region for almost a week was finally passing further east, and in its wake, the clouds were breaking up, sunlight once again warming the beautiful Adirondack village and setting the fall foliage ablaze with colors.

"It wasn't just the rain, Evy. You know that. Christian is being careful. There's still been no word about Fabrizio or Lowery, and that makes us all a bit nervous."

Evora again thought about the message she had secretly sent to her mother. She had spent hours convincing herself that the one simple act of defiance could not have possibly provided the deranged priest with the information he needed to find her.

No one knew about the online game they played, so no one could possibly know about the chatroom message she'd sent. Even as Evy struggled to convince herself she had done nothing wrong, the logical, intelligent part of her brain told her that it was very possible the man had somehow gained access to the chat room information and could already be in Lake Placid watching her.

"Don't you think if the maniac knew I was here, we'd know about it by now?"

"Not necessarily. The man he hired, Padraig Lowery, was once one of the best PIRA Brigade commanders in Ireland. Lowery would know how to travel to America undetected." She didn't want to unnecessarily frighten the girl, but Evy needed to understand the potential danger they faced.

Of the three people protecting her, Evy had grown to like and trust Laura the most. She was one of the most accomplished and impressive women Evy had ever had the opportunity to get to know. She felt comfortable with Laura around and enjoyed their talks. She liked Dexter as well, but she was a bit intimidated by him. He was handsome and fit, to be sure, and he was always respectful and friendly to Evy, but he was also extremely intelligent and observant. Because he was the one responsible for setting up and monitoring Evy's contact with the outside world, she feared he'd be the one to discover her deceit, and this caused her to avoid being alone with the man.

Christian was another story altogether. The intense former

lawman caused a confusing medley of emotions in Evy. He was just as handsome and fit as Dexter but in a more rugged way. Unfortunately, he did not share Dexter's easygoing mannerisms. Christian was always intense and hypervigilant. He rarely relaxed and just enjoyed the moment. At times, he was so demanding and rude that Evy hated him. Other times, when he allowed himself to relax a little and actually smile, she found herself drawn to him.

"I know all of that, Laura. I just want to get out of this house." Evy stood staring into the roaring fire Christian had started earlier in the day to help beat back the damp chill the fall rainstorm had brought with it. "Can't we go into town and walk around the shops?"

Laura looked out the huge sliding glass door at the calm waters of Lake Placid. She knew keeping Evy occupied and happy made the job of protecting her easier, but she wasn't sure she could convince Christian to take her on an outing. In all honesty, she wasn't sure herself that they should take the girl out of the safe house.

"Let me speak with Christian. Maybe we can go for a hike or take the kayaks out again."

"I don't want to hike or kayak anymore! I want to walk around the shops downtown and maybe have dinner in a nice restaurant."

Evy moved past Laura out onto the large deck. The partly cloudy skies allowed shafts of brilliant sunlight to reach down like fingers from Heaven to ignite large sections of the brightly colored trees on nearby Buck Island, causing them to burn with the brilliance of their full fall hues. Again, Evy couldn't help but be impressed by the wonderous display of nature.

Laura had followed Evy out onto the deck, and she too stood silently admiring the amazing display of reds, oranges, and golds in the heavily forested landscape just across the lake. Maybe she could convince Christian that it was important to let Evy get out and see the area. After all, she was their client, not their prisoner.

"I'll talk with Christian." As soon as she spoke the words, she saw Evy's face light up, and she moved to head off the girl's premature enthusiasm. "Don't get your hopes up, though. Christian is in charge of this operation, and he's been adamant about keeping a low profile until they can figure out where Fabrizio and Lowery are."

"You can convince him!" Evy's excitement would not be contained. "I've seen the way you two are together. He'll let us go out if you push him."

"We'll see. For now, just try to relax and enjoy this beautiful day. I'll go have a talk with Christian and Dexter."

Laura left the young actress alone to enjoy the fall scenery while she went in search of her two teammates. She found Dexter right where she expected him to be, seated in a very comfortable-looking chair in front of the elaborate computer system he had set up prior to their arrival. When not working out, eating, or sleeping, Dexter was diligently at work, trying to find a digital footprint out in the ether that would give them a clue as to where Fabrizio and his hired gun had run off to.

"Hey, do you have a second?"

"For you, I have as much time as you need." Dexter flashed her his most infectious smile and let his eyes wander over her athletic frame. He wiggled his eyebrows in an impressive Groucho Marx impression and said, "Hubba, hubba."

Laura couldn't help but laugh. Dexter was well aware that Laura was happily married to ArVal pilot Abby Fuller, but that didn't stop him from flirting with her outrageously at every opportunity. Laura took no offense, as Dexter never went beyond his comical flirting, and he always showed nothing but the utmost respect for Laura and her abilities.

"Careful, lover boy. That kind of talk could be considered sexual harassment."

"Mea culpa. Mea culpa." Dexter raised his hands in mock surrender, once again causing Laura to laugh at his antics. "To what do I owe the pleasure of this visit?"

"I want to talk to Christian about getting Evy out of here for a little while. She's been cooped up for days, and she wants to go downtown and check out the shops and maybe grab dinner somewhere."

"What do you need from me?"

"I need you to back me up when I talk with him."

"You may not need much support," Dexter replied with a

cryptic smile on his face.

"Oh really? Why's that?"

"I was speaking with ole-sourpuss while we worked out this morning, and he mentioned that he thinks Evy is getting antsy and needs to get out. He said he was going to run it by you once he got done speaking with Arthur this morning."

"Well, let's go see ole-sourpuss and see what we can come up with."

Christian had just finished his daily briefing call with Valentine when Laura and Dexter walked into the den that Dexter had set up as their Tactical Operations Center, or TOC.

"Good morning, Laura," he said as he refilled his mug with a freshly brewed pot of coffee. He set the pot back on the coffee maker and blew on the steaming mug he held in his hand. "I just got off a conference call with Arthur and the guys from the Met. Authorities in Rome were finally able to find out where Fabrizio went when he fled Rome. Apparently, when he left the church, they failed to confiscate his Vatican passport. He flew from Rome to Paris using that passport. When Italian authorities first tried to determine where he went, they searched the records for his Italian passport number rather than his name."

"That was sloppy work," observed Laura.

"Possibly. Valentine and Fraser both feel someone in Rome may have been protecting the church, and the failure to check more thoroughly was intentional. Last night, a supervisor was reviewing what has been done so far and realized that whoever did the airline searches never searched Fabrizio's name, so he had it done, and that's when they discovered he flew out using the Vatican passport."

"Where'd he go from Paris?" Dexter asked.

"They have no idea. Authorities reviewed airport security videos from Rome and Paris, and Fabrizio is wearing his priest's vestments in every video they see." He took a sip of coffee before continuing. "They have a video of him getting into a cab at the airport in Paris and traveling to the Hyatt Regency just outside the airport. A video recovered from the hotel shows him checking in. Hotel staff claim that he was gone the next morning, and his priest's clothes were hanging in the closet with his Vatican passport in a pocket. While he was at the hotel, he logged into the internet using their complimentary Wi-Fi and booked a flight to Thailand in his name."

"Hold on," interrupted Dexter. "This genius uses all these high-tech means to spy on Evy and hire mercenaries, and then makes the bonehead move of using an easily traceable Wi-Fi connection to book a flight in his own name? I'm not buying it."

"Neither did the French cops. They checked the manifest for the flight to Bangkok, and Fabrizio never boarded the plane. In fact, there was no record of him boarding any flight from Paris using his own name, and a review of the airport's security footage doesn't show him ever returning to the airport. They checked the security footage from the hotel, and he's never seen again after he checks in and gets on the elevator to his room."

"So he either jumped out of a window or he wore a disguise when he left the hotel," said Laura.

"And we still have no idea where he is now?"

"Correct," Christian confirmed.

"What about Lowery? Any word on him?"

"Cops in Scotland were able to positively confirm he was back in Edinburgh a few days after he was last seen in Switzerland. They also positively identified Nessa Keever as being with him."

"Do they have them under surveillance?"

"No. They have a source who says he may have fled north and is currently laying low in one of the many safe houses Far darrig has all over the region. They're working on confirming that."

"So the bottom line is that we still have no idea where Fabrizio is, and it's just a guess at this point that Lowery is still in Scotland."

"Correct."

"Did you brief Steven yet?" Laura asked.

"Not yet. I'll call him shortly, but I'm sure he's calling Arthur daily to report on our operation here and bitch about how I'm running things."

"No, he's not. I spoke with Arthur about that. He was

calling daily, and Arthur told him this is your operation, and you're the only one he wants to hear from unless there's a major issue."

"I'm glad to hear that. So, what's up? You two looked like you had something on your mind when you walked in."

Laura turned from the painting of a wood duck hanging over the fireplace and said, "I want to get Evy out of the house for a while. She's getting anxious, and keeping her locked up here isn't helping to ease her worries."

"Dexter and I were discussing that this morning. I agree. It's time we got her out. Any ideas on what you'd like to do?"

"She wants to visit the shops downtown, and she'd like to go to dinner at a nice restaurant."

Christian thought it over for a few seconds. "I don't suppose she'd rather go hiking or take a kayak trip around the lake again?"

"I suggested that, and she shot it down. Apparently, she's had just about all of Mother Nature she can stand for now. She really wants to walk around downtown and do some shopping. I'm sure we can find a nice restaurant where we can keep her somewhat secluded."

"Fine. Why don't you ask her to come down and we can discuss how this is going to work. While you're doing that, I'll bring Paine up to speed and tell him to have both teams ready to move this afternoon."

CHAPTER TWENTY-TWO

Lake Placid, New York

Lowery and his band of mercenaries had been in Lake Placid for four days without any sign of Cota or her protectors. Each morning, Lowery divided his forces up and had them fan out around the small village as well as the many tourist sites in the immediate area. He was positive that the people protecting her didn't want to have her out in public for any extended periods. The risk of the girl being recognized in upstate New York was slim, but it wasn't impossible.

Jimmy King had contacted his cousin Linette two days prior and met her at the Black Bear Restaurant on Main Street. When he arrived, he found her enjoying the views on the back deck overlooking Mirror Lake. She was sitting with three people.

"Hey, cuz," he said as he approached the table.

Linette stood up and gave Jimmy a hug. "Pull up a chair and join us," she said, waving him into a seat beside her. "Let me make the introductions." She put her hand on Jimmy's shoulder. "This fine-looking young native man is my cousin, Jimmy King. He runs a smoke shop up near the border."

Jimmy gave the small group an awkward wave and said, "Hi."

"Jimmy, these are coworkers of mine at the lodge. The ladies are Lilli and Rose. They're both massage therapists." She stopped and looked at her cousin. "No massage jokes, you perv." She spoke sternly, but there was a huge smile on her face.

"Linny!" Jimmy protested.

"Just kidding, cuz. The girls get so sick of the lewd comments they get every time someone finds out what they do."

Jimmy reached out and shook both women's hands. Lilli was a petite brunette with light brown eyes and a pert little nose. She was wearing a white peasant top with jeans, and Jimmy thought she was beautiful. Rose was medium build with hair a few shades darker than Lilli. She looked athletic in a pair of yoga pants and a midriff-baring sweater.

"It's a pleasure to meet you both."

"And this is Adam," Linette said, indicating the lone male seated at the table. Adam had his hair shaved so close that

Jimmy could clearly see the dark brown skin on his scalp. He wore a skintight white T-shirt over khaki cargo pants and, despite the bright sunshine, a pair of aviator sunglasses sat perched atop his head. "He works at the spa with us."

"Lucky man," Jimmy observed as Adam stood to shake his hand.

"Damn straight," Lilli joked.

"So what brings you to town?" Linette asked her cousin once the introductions were complete.

Jimmy already had a back story ready, so there was no need to hesitate to come up with a lie. "I'm thinking of opening a cigar shop in Placid. I'm just in town to look at a few possible business fronts."

"Wow. Branching out. I'm happy for you." Linette had always liked Jimmy, even though he was constantly in trouble when they were growing up. Her parents had banned her from associating with him or his immediate family. It had gotten pretty bad.

"Thanks. So how's things at the lodge?"

"Busier than ever," Linette answered. "It's leaf-peeping season. Every rich person from New York City to Montreal is here to look at the trees and be pampered."

"You've never seen so many entitled assholes in your life," Adam added.

Linette had a shocked look on her face. "Adam, knock it off," she chastised. "Those 'entitled A-Holes', as you call them, are the reason we all have decent-paying jobs."

"I know. I just get tired of all the ridiculous demands. Half those people couldn't wipe their own ass without an owner's manual and a YouTube video to show them how."

Jimmy couldn't help but laugh at Adam's colorful description of the lodge guests.

"Don't encourage him, Jimmy. If Jill heard you, Adam, you'd probably get fired."

"Who's Jill?" asked Jimmy.

"She's the executive manager of the lodge," Lilli said. "She's really nice, but Linny's right. If she heard Adam, she'd blow a cork."

"Relax, guys," Rose put in. "Adam knows how to play the game. You have to admit, some of the guests are so used to their money getting them what they want that they treat us like slaves."

They sat and chatted for a while before ordering food. As they ate and continued to share stories about different encounters at the lodge, Jimmy saw his opening.

"Any of you guys ever meet anyone famous?" Though he said it jokingly, he was hoping that someone at the lodge had recognized the Cota girl during her visit.

"Occasionally," said Rose. "It's mostly rich old couples or families with spoiled, rotten little kids, though."

"Shania Twain used to stop in once in a while when she lived here," Linette said.

"Really?" Jimmy had heard that Shania Twain had owned a home in Lake Placid, but he never really believed it.

"Oh yeah. She was very friendly and a big tipper." Rose giggled when she said it.

"Every once in a while, we get a celebrity, but not often, and we always receive a warning not to ask for autographs or to have our pictures taken with them. They've fired a couple people for that kind of stuff."

"Anyone famous staying there lately?"

"Not really," Linette answered.

"Well, there was that one girl," started Rose. "You remember them, Linette. They came in in a group, and the one guy used to work with Tony Alfred or something."

"Oh yeah. Tony had Jill set them up with a full spa day package even though we were booked full that day," remembered Linette.

"That's the group," Rose confirmed. "I think that girl might have been someone famous."

Adam jumped in and said, "I remember talking with Doug Foreman later that day. He said the girl was an actress from Europe. Apparently, some psychopath is threatening her, so she's hiding out here for a while."

"Who's Doug Foreman?" Jimmy tried to keep his voice calm. Could he really be this lucky?

"He's the second in charge of security at the spa," answered Lilli.

"When did he tell you that?" asked Linette.

"The day after they came in, he was talking about how the guy who brought them in used to work with Tony when he was in the state police, and now he runs a security company, protecting celebrities."

"I thought she looked sort of familiar when I was giving her a massage, but I didn't know where I may have seen her."

"Is she staying at the lodge?" Jimmy knew it was too much to ask.

"No, and Doug didn't say where she was staying, but it was definitely off-site."

"Doug shouldn't have told you anything about her, Adam!" Linette was angry. "He works for Tony, and his job is to protect the guests, not gossip about them."

"Take it easy, Linette. It was just talk. No one knows who the girl really is or if the story is even true. Doug could just be trying to impress people with secrets he supposedly knows."

Bingo, Jimmy thought. He tuned out most of the rest of the conversation as he tried to come up with a plan.

When they were finished eating, Jimmy said, "I've got to take off because. . . I have an early meeting tomorrow to look at a storefront over by the Big Slide Brewery."

Linette stood up and gave him a hug. "It was so nice to see you. Keep in touch. Maybe you'll be in town a bit more often if you open up the cigar shop."

"You never know."

Jimmy hurried back to where he had parked his vehicle on Mirror Lake Drive. From where he was parked, Jimmy could clearly see the front door of the Black Bear. He sat back and waited patiently for Linette and her friends to leave the restaurant. When the small group exited, they stood on Main Street for a few minutes, saying their goodbyes before heading off.

Jimmy needed to talk to Adam alone, and he was worried the young spa assistant was riding with one of the girls. His fears were put to rest when Linette and the girls headed south down Main Street, and Adam turned and walked north onto Mirror Lake Drive by himself. As Adam walked past, Jimmy rolled down his window and called out.

"Hey, Adam!"

The young man looked around until he saw Jimmy in the vehicle. "Hey, Jimmy, what's up?"

"Nothing, man. You need a ride?"

"No, I'm good. I rent a place not far from here."

"Come on, hop in. I'll give you a lift."

"No, really, I'm all set. Plus, it's back the other way."

"No worries, bro. I wanted to talk with you for a minute anyway, away from my cousin."

"About what?" Adam asked, his curiosity peaking.

"Get in and I'll tell you. It may even be worth a few bucks for you as long as you can keep your mouth shut."

The mention of money sealed the deal and Adam's fate. He

made decent money working at the lodge and filling in as a part-time bartender at the Blue Line Brewery in Saranac Lake, but the cost of living in Lake Placid was ridiculous. Even the tiny basement efficiency apartment he rented in a house on Stevens Road cost over half of what he made each month. He walked around the front of the gray SUV Jimmy was driving and climbed into the passenger's side.

"What do you need?"

Jimmy pulled out the photos he had of Evora Cota and handed them to Adam. "Is this the girl who you saw at the spa?"

Adam slowly worked his way through the small stack of photos of the girl. There was no doubt about it. It was the same girl. As he realized it was her, he thought back to his conversation with Doug Foreman. The man had said she was here trying to get away from someone who was threatening her. Could Linette's cousin, Jimmy King, be that guy? Adam couldn't imagine how. According to Foreman, the girl was an actress in Europe, and Linette told them Jimmy lived on the Akwesasne reservation up on the Canadian border. But why did Jimmy want to know about her?

"Well?" asked Jimmy. "Is it her or not?"

Adam decided it didn't matter why Jimmy wanted to know. The girl hadn't been back to the spa since that one day and may not even be around anymore. What harm could it do? Plus, he really needed the cash.

"It's her. She was with a really hot broad and two pretty

intense-looking guys."

"What did the two men look like?"

"One was a big blond guy with a scar down his face, and the other guy was Asian. They both looked jacked. Like I said, they seemed pretty intense."

Jimmy couldn't believe his luck. He had arranged to meet his cousin out for a few drinks, hoping she might have seen the girl at the spa, but this kid was much better. He'd just confirmed the people at the lodge were their target and her protectors. Lowery was going to be very pleased.

While Jimmy was congratulating himself on his luck, he had missed what Adam was talking about.

"Hey, man. What's up with you?" he asked his distracted companion. "How much?"

"I'll give you a hundred bucks right now, but I need you to do me a major favor." Jimmy pulled a wad of one hundred dollar bills out of his pocket and peeled the top one off. Handing it to Adam, he said, "First of all, you cannot tell Linette about this." When Adam didn't acknowledge Jimmy's first demand, he grabbed him by the front of the shirt and slammed him into the passenger's door. "Did you fucking hear me?"

Adam was terrified. Jimmy had transformed from Linette's funny, happy-go-lucky cousin, the smoke shop owner, into a violent hood in the blink of an eye. Adam had never even been in a fight in his life, so Jimmy's unprovoked attack rendered the younger man paralyzed with fear.

Jimmy looked at the cowering boy before him and felt nothing but disgust. This kid would never survive in Jimmy's world. He slapped the terrified kid once and said, "Grow up, Adam. Did you hear what I said?"

"I can't tell Linette about this."

"Correct. If you tell Linette, I'll hurt you. You got that?"

"Yes," Adam answered quickly. He'd agree to anything Jimmy said if it meant he could get out of this car and run.

"Good boy," he said, patting Adam on the right cheek. "Now, I want you to do me a favor, and I'll pay you for it. If the girl or any of the people with her come back to the lodge again, you call me and let me know. Can you do that?"

"Yes." His voice was barely above a whisper.

"And who are you going to tell about any of this?" Jimmy gave the kid another hard shove into the passenger's door.

"No one. I swear." Tears rolled down the terrified man's face.

CHAPTER TWENTY-THREE

Lake Placid, New York

After a quick group meeting at the safe house, Christian asked Laura to plan out the shopping portion of the trip while he made arrangements for dinner. He was being very secretive about the location, only saying it was one of the best restaurants in the area.

Laura had fired up her iPad and began to explore the shopping possibilities that Lake Placid had to offer. Once they'd mapped out the 'must-see' stores, they sat down with Christian and Dexter and decided on the most secure way to proceed.

"I know this is tedious, Evy," Christian said when he saw the young actress begin to lose patience with their planning. "But it's the only way we do this. I have to let Paine and the QRF teams know what stores we're going to visit and in what order. They'll have one team advance to each location while the second team follows us as we move."

"Won't it be a little strange if we have someone following behind us all day?" Evy just wanted a normal day out. The thought of all the preparation was taking some of the fun out of it for her.

"You'll never even see them," Laura promised. "They'll stay clear of us so that any potential surveillance doesn't know they're there."

"I'll never understand how politicians and celebrities deal with this all the time."

"You seem to be forgetting something, Evy," Dexter said, with the sly smile Evy recognized as his 'ball-busting' face.

"And what might that be, Dex?"

"You are one of those celebrities."

"No, I'm not. I've never even had a bodyguard until this nut job started threatening me. I would hate to live like this all the time."

Christian and Paine had worked out how the QRF teams were going to operate. Team one would consist of Paine and Durand trailing the group of shoppers. One would follow on foot while the other kept the vehicle close by in the event it was needed. Team two would be Abioye and Altman. As with the first team, team two would have one member physically enter each shop or café just prior to their arrival. The second member had the infinitely more difficult task of keeping their vehicle as close by as possible. Parking in downtown Lake Placid is challenging on a good day, but the current break in the weather after a long stretch of rainy days has made an already difficult situation almost impossible, with tourists and vacationers crowding the streets and shops all along Main Street.

Before they left the house, Christian had called the Mirror Lake Inn and spoke with Abner Thorton. He explained that he was back in town and asked if he could park one vehicle in their parking lot for the day. Thornton gave his permission without hesitation. Anything for his old Cornell University classmate Sven Vikstrom's grandson.

"Okay, folks. Let's mount up." Christian was anxious to get the day started. This would be good to keep Evy's mind off things.

The two-mile drive from the safe house to the Mirror Lake Inn took almost ten minutes due to the heavy traffic. The small group exited the vehicle in the parking lot behind the inn and walked down the long driveway to Mirror Lake Drive. At the end of the driveway, Christian took a quick look around and could see the front end of the Expedition that Paine and Durand were parked in just beyond Interlaken Ave.

Everyone on the team except Evy was wearing a wireless earbud that was synced to both their portable radios and their cell phones.

Christian keyed the radio hidden under his loose-fitting Team USA nylon windbreaker and said, "We are exiting the parking lot and heading west on Mirror Lake Drive."

Paine's voice immediately replied, "Copy that. We've got you."

"This is Jerome. David is proceeding to stop number one to check the store."

There was no sidewalk on the Mirror Lake Inn side of the road, so Christian led the group across the street to the faded red paver sidewalk to avoid walking along the unprotected shoulder of the road. Once they were across the street, Evy stopped to take in the unobstructed view of Mirror Lake.

"It's pretty, but not as spectacular as the view from the house," she observed.

"That's because Mirror Lake is a lot smaller than Lake Placid," Christian explained.

"It's such a beautiful day. I thought there'd be boats out."

"Not on Mirror Lake. No motorized craft. We could go back and get the kayaks so you can explore the lake if you'd like."

"No," Evy quickly replied. "I've had enough kayaking and hiking for a while, thank you very much."

They continued south along Mirror Lake Drive, passing a few people walking their dogs or jogging the 2.75-mile perimeter of the lake. When they reached Main Street, everything changed. Mirror Lake Drive had been relatively quiet, with just a few people traveling on foot. Main Street was a different story. The sidewalks on both sides of the street were crowded with people of every description. Families pushing children in strollers pushed past elderly couples slowly walking along while window shopping. Groups of teenagers maneuvered around bikers dressed in their full leather riding gear despite the unusually warm fall day. Shopkeepers were sweeping their entrances, and beer delivery trucks were fouling up the bumper-to-bumper traffic along the narrow two-lane street.

They walked past Players Sports Bar and Grill and the Top of the Park restaurant, where a group of people stood viewing the menu board posted on the outer wall. When they passed the Black Bear restaurant, Evy laughed at the comical wooden black bear statues sitting outside the entrance. Across the street, an unending line of people were entering and exiting the Dancing Bears restaurant.

"We're approaching Ruthie's Run," Christian reported over the radio.

"Copy that," Jerome responded in his heavy South African accent. "David cleared the store and is moving to location number two."

Christian entered the upscale shop first, with Dexter bringing up the rear of the group. Laura would stay by Evy's side at all times.

"This is just what I needed," Evy said as she and Laura slowly made their way around Ruthie's Run. The small shop catered to high-end vacationers and offered everything from warm, comfy sweaters by Dale of Norway to fox fur boots by Regina.

"It's nice to see you smile." Laura was genuinely happy that Evy was enjoying herself.

"I'm sorry for being so difficult. I'm just tired of the entire thing. Now that they know who he is, why can't they just catch this maniac so I can go back home?"

"First of all, you're not being difficult." Laura laughed quietly. "Well, maybe a bit difficult," she corrected. "But it's totally normal to feel the way you do. This person has violated your personal space. He's threatened you. Any normal person would be angry and frustrated."

Laura stopped talking while a woman and her whiny teenage daughter squeezed by them to get closer to the sweater display they had been blocking. Christian was listening to the conversation between Evy and Laura.

"Second, and more importantly, we can't let you go home until your fan is located and neutralized."

Thirty minutes after entering the store, they walked back out onto Main Street, with both women carrying bags with Ruthie's Run printed on the sides. They were just passing the China City restaurant when Evy saw the Ben and Jerry's sign.

"Let's get an ice cream cone!"

"Evy, we didn't plan to stop there, and David didn't check it out yet." This was what Christian had feared. Evy would get out in public and forget or ignore the plan.

"It's an ice cream shop," she replied as she headed for the front door, with Laura rushing to keep up.

Christian swore and then reported the situation to the advance and follow teams. "Dex, get in there with them. I'll lock down the front entrance."

"On it."

Ten minutes later, the three emerged from the ice cream shop with only Evy carrying a cone.

When they approached Christian, he turned to walk beside Evy and quietly said, "If you pull another stunt like that one, we're heading back to the house. I'm not going to let my people get injured because of a spoiled child. We have a plan. Stick with it."

Evora did her best to look contrite, but she wasn't very convincing.

They proceeded along Main Street, making stops at each spot Evy had requested until they were across the street from the Great Adirondack Brewing Company. Abioye had just reported Altman had cleared the location, so Christian stepped onto Main Street, holding up the already snarled traffic as he waved the rest of the group across.

They sat at a small table overlooking the busy street and ordered several appetizers and a flight of craft beers for Evy to try.

A wall of planter boxes filled with a variety of colorful plants and shrubs provided some privacy from the throngs of people passing by. While Evy enjoyed the flight of craft beers, they talked about the history of Lake Placid and the Olympics that had been held there. Dexter bragged about how the Team USA hockey team defeated the much older and far more experienced team from the USSR during the 1980 Winter Olympics, giving the nation a much-needed morale boost during the height of the Cold War.

"We should have dinner here," Evy suggested as she looked over a menu she had picked up when she and Laura went to the restroom. "The food listed on the menu looks really good."

"I've already made arrangements for dinner tonight."

"So you've said, but you haven't told us where."

"I wanted to make sure we were all set before I told you. I just got off the phone with Tony Alfred at the Whiteface Lodge. He was able to get us a nice table out on their covered deck at the Kanu. It's one of the most exclusive restaurants in town." He checked his watch and added, "If we head back now, we'll have time to get cleaned up and change into more suitable attire before we have to leave for the lodge."

"Then we should get going."

"Okay. Relax for a couple more minutes while I settle the tab."

So far, the day had been a success. Evy was more upbeat and cheerful than she'd been in days, and Christian wanted to keep her that way.

Christian paid the bill and then radioed both QRF teams to let them know they were getting ready to head back to the Mirror Lake Inn to retrieve their vehicle.

He walked back to the patio table and said, "Give me a second to check the street before we head out."

CHAPTER TWENTY-FOUR

Nessa Keever was growing more and more frustrated. They had been searching the tiny village of Lake Placid and the surrounding area for days now, with no sign of the Cota girl or her protectors. There had been a brief period of excitement when Jimmy King came back from meeting his cousin and told everyone about the cousin's co-worker at the lodge who had positively identified Cota and two of her protectors. King said he was certain the kid would call him if Cota or any of the team with her showed up at the lodge again. He said the kid was scared shitless and needed the money King had promised him. That was two days ago, and the initial excitement at the news had faded. Now it was just the drudgery of riding around looking at faces in the crowd.

Today, she was teamed up with Brandon Flannery and Solomon. Because she had been picked up in London and had been in Rome at the scene of the failed kidnapping attempt, Nessa was hidden in the back seat of the tinted-out GMC Denali to prevent anyone protecting Cota from possibly recognizing her. Flannery and Solomon sat up front and chatted non-stop about everything but what they were there to do. Flannery's unending stories of his alleged criminal exploits and sexual conquests, coupled with Solomon's barely understandable English, were just about more than Keever could stand. They were driving slowly down Main Street for the fifth time that day with Keever staring out the side window, trying hopelessly to tune out yet another story of Flannery's sexual exploits, when something caught the former reconnaissance soldier's attention, causing her to sit up straight. Stepping out onto the sidewalk in front of a restaurant called the Great Adirondack Brewing Company was a tall male with blond hair. Nessa didn't need to see the scar on the big man's face to recognize him. She knew him immediately. The last time she'd seen him was when he shot Padraig Lowery's grandson, Callum, dead in Rome.

"Slow down," she ordered Flannery.

"Slow down? If we go any slower, we'll be going backward. I hate the fucking traffic in this town. Bloody tourists ruin everything."

"Look out your window, Flannery. The big blond. That's one of the guys protecting our target."

"Are you sure?" Flannery asked uncertainly. All they had

to go on was a description given to them by the Irishman who'd hired them.

"I'm positive. I saw him in Rome. That's the guy."

As Nessa watched, she saw the man scan the street and then reach up and touch his ear. Nessa knew immediately that he was wearing a wireless earbud to communicate with his team. She'd used a similar kit when she was in the army. Traffic cleared, and Flannery had to move, or he'd draw attention to himself. As their vehicle crawled further along Main Street, Keever looked out the back window of the SUV. She stared in disbelief when she saw Evora Cota join the blond on the sidewalk. With them were the Asian guy and brunette woman they'd been told to look for.

Keever reached for her phone to let Lowery know what was happening.

Back at the house on Cobble Hill Road, Lowery and Fabrizio were sitting at the kitchen table, listening carefully to Jimmy King as he spoke to someone on the phone.

"You're positive?" King said to his caller. "Why did she talk to you about this?" There was another long pause as the caller responded. "What time are their reservations?" Lowery could hear a voice responding to King's questions, but he couldn't make out what was being said. "Listen to me carefully, Adam. Don't ask your girl any more questions. Do you understand?" He paused to allow his caller to indicate he understood. "Good. I don't want her getting suspicious, and you don't want her remembering you being too curious about it." The caller, who Lowery deduced was the kid who worked at the lodge, said something else and then hung up.

"That was the kid from the lodge," King told his two companions at the table.

"I figured as much. What did your friend have to say?" Lowery kept his voice calm, but his heart was racing.

"The kid says that he has a friend who works as a hostess at one of the restaurants at the lodge. The girl was just bitching to Adam that the head of security for the resort just called the restaurant manager and had him move reservations around to accommodate some friends of his."

"Why would she tell your man about it?" Fabrizio asked.

Lowery shot the priest an annoyed look but then turned to King and asked the same question. "Why would this girl tell your new friend about something like this?"

"Apparently, when Cota and her protectors came to the lodge to use the spa, the head of security did the same thing. He threw the whole place into chaos because there were no openings for them, but he insisted King's cousin, the spa manager, move reservations around to accommodate them. This girl is annoyed because it's throwing their schedule off, so she bitched to the one person who would understand."

"And we're positive this is Cota and her people?" Fabrizio found it too convenient; the hostess just happened to talk to the one person Jimmy King had compromised at the resort.

"Adam says the restaurant manager was pissed and told the hostess it was the same people the security chief pulled strings for to get them into the spa on the same day they called."

Before Lowery could ask any more questions, his cell phone vibrated. The caller ID showed only the phone number calling and the words Unknown Caller. Lowery didn't need the caller ID to know it was Keever.

"Yes," he said as he put the phone on speaker so Fabrizio could hear. There was no sense in repeating everything Nessa said.

"We just spotted Cota and her dogs downtown." Nessa had spent years tracking terrorists for the British government. When she left the army, she helped track both law enforcement members and rival criminals for Lowery and the Far darrig organization. She remained calm, and her voice never wavered as she reported what she'd seen on Main Street. "I'm looking at her and her people right now. What do you want me to do?" she asked when she'd finished her report.

"Can you maintain surveillance on them, Nessa?"

"Why not just grab the girl now?" Fabrizio said. His heart was beating so hard that he was having trouble breathing. The little whore was within a few miles of him right now. All he could think about was having her under his control.

"Shut your mouth, *priest*." Lowery never raised his voice. His eyes bored unblinkingly into Fabrizio's, and the smaller man fell silent, cowering at the intensity of the killer's gaze. "You have no idea how these things are done." He stared at Fabrizio for a few more seconds before continuing. "Can you keep them in sight, Nessa?"

"As long as they're downtown, it may be possible. The crowds here are as bad as in London. If they move off Main Street or sit down at a bar or restaurant, it'll be more difficult. I have to remain in the vehicle. I was seen in London, and I'm sure they know I was in Rome. If they see me, they'll flee again, and we'll be back to square one." Nessa was a thinker and a planner. She had proven her worth time and time again.

"I agree. Do the best you can to keep them in sight. I'd like to have a bed-down spot for them, if possible, but avoid being detected at all costs. We just received new information, and I'm working on a way to exploit it."

"What happened?"

"One of the people who works with King's cousin at the resort just called. Cota and her people will be there this evening around 8:00 for dinner. I'm working on a plan to exploit the new information. You finding a possible bed-down spot would help in the event we decide to spring some type of trap as they travel."

"I'll do my best." Padraig detected doubt in Keever's voice. He'd never had reason to doubt her abilities in the past. She had an abundance of real-world experience and never panicked when things got heated.

Lowery took the phone off speaker and stood to move away from Fabrizio. When the priest moved to follow, Lowery stopped him. "Stay here. I need to speak privately with Nessa." Fabrizio looked like he was about to argue, so Lowery pointed back at the table and said, "Sit your arse down, *priest.*"

He walked out onto the back porch of the house before continuing. "What's wrong, Nessa?"

"These men we're working with." She hesitated for just a moment, but Lowery picked up on it. "They are not professionals, Padraig. They worry me. If this turns bad like it did in Rome, I don't believe these men are up to the task." She whispered the last part, as she didn't want Flannery and Solomon to hear her.

"Relax, Nessa. Flannery's a good man. His grandfather was one of the most influential operators in the UK during 'the troubles'. He assured me his grandson is solid."

When Nessa replied, there was little confidence in her voice. "Whatever you say, Padraig. Just know this. These men are not warriors like we're used to. They're criminals. Their loyalty is to money, not each other, and they have no ideology beyond how much money they can make."

"I fear you're right, lass. These men have never had to fight and struggle the way we have. Just do the best you can. One way or another, this thing may come to a head tonight, and we need as much information as we can gather so we can come up with a plan."

CHAPTER TWENTY-FIVE

Once the bill was settled, Christian told Evy and Laura to stay at the table with Dexter for a few seconds while he cleared the street. Once on the sidewalk, he radioed the QRF teams.

"We're heading back toward the vehicle. What are your locations?"

"Paine here. We found a spot to park just in front of the Gap store, just south of your location. I can see you on the sidewalk."

"Copy that. Jerome and Dave?"

"I am parked in the lot on the right as soon as you enter Mirror Lake Drive." Jerome's strong South African accent made it unnecessary to identify himself when he spoke.

"Dave?"

"I'm sitting in The Breakfast Club restaurant across the

street, just north of you, eating lunch. I'm in a window seat looking at you right now."

"I hope you've finished your lunch, Dave. I need you to hoof it back to the Mirror Inn lot and make sure our vehicle is still clear."

"Copy that. I have already paid. I've been nursing a coffee, waiting on you, boss. Heading out now."

"Paine, put Pierre out on foot to trail us from behind while you work your way up Main Street. You can pick him up on Mirror Lake Drive and set up to follow us when we pull out of the parking lot at the inn."

"Got it. Pierre will exit the vehicle when you get a little further up the street."

"Perfect," Christian acknowledged. "Jerome, stay where you are for now. Once Dave has cleared our vehicle, he can rejoin you, and you can advance the route back to the house."

"Copy."

"Once we're back at the house, I want both teams to break off and grab something to eat. Reservations are at 20 hundred and I want to be there by 1945. We'll meet Tony Alfred out back, just like we did when we took Evy to the spa. Make sure you wear something appropriate for the lodge in the event I need anyone else inside with us."

Once everyone had acknowledged their orders, Christian motioned to Dexter and Laura to bring Evy out. They proceeded down the sidewalk back toward the Mirror Lake Inn at a leisurely pace. The two women walked side by side, carrying on an animated conversation, while Christian and Dexter followed closely behind, seemingly at ease but actually conducting counter-surveillance the entire time. Laura encouraged Evy to pause at several storefronts to window shop. In reality, she was allowing her teammates to check the area around them to determine if they were being followed. Reflections in storefront windows were checked without the need to turn around. Did anyone slow when they did or hesitate to walk past them?

"Any sign of a tail?" Christian asked Pierre over the radio.

"Not that I can tell. This traffic is a double-edged sword, though. Someone could be keeping pace with you, using the crowded streets to cover their slow pace."

"Copy that. Just keep your head on a swivel and do the best you can."

The group was stopped in a small courtyard, ostensibly to peer in the windows of the Darrah Cooper Jewelers shop, when Dave Altman reported that he was at the Mirror Lake Inn, and their vehicle was clear.

"I'll keep an eye on your vehicle from inside the rear entrance to the inn until you enter the lot, and then I'll go out the front and hop back in with Jerome."

"Copy that. We're about five minutes away." Christian motioned to Laura to get Evy moving again before radioing Abioye. "Jerome, we're approaching The Dancing Bears on the corner. You should be able to see us anytime now."

"I saw you for most of your walk up the street."

"Dave, we're about to cross Main Street onto Mirror Lake Drive. How's our six look?"

"I'm just passing The Curious Otter now. You're clear."

"Perfect. Wait there for Paine to pick you up. Jerome can keep an eye on us from where he is."

They passed the parking lot where Jerome was parked without looking toward his vehicle.

"Dave, we're coming up the driveway now. Head out the front so you and Jerome can advance the ride back to the house."

"Copy that. Moving now."

CHAPTER TWENTY-SIX

Following Cota and her people up Main Street hadn't been as difficult as Nessa had feared. The slow-moving traffic had helped, and when a small car two places in front of them stopped to wait for another vehicle to leave a parking space, it worked out to their advantage, allowing them to sit stopped in traffic and watch their quarry. Nessa's training and experience paid dividends when her sharp eyes identified a possible trailer slowly walking down the opposite side of the street from Cota's group. The man was doing an admirable job of blending in, but Nessa could tell he was paying too much attention to Cota and her protectors. She used her cell phone to quickly snap a half dozen photos of the man.

"Look sharp. I think we have a tall, white male with long, brown hair trailing the group as a lookout. He's wearing khaki hiking pants and a blue hiking vest."

"I see him," Flannery confirmed. "You see him, Solomon?"

"Yes."

The traffic in front of them cleared just as the girl and her minders crossed the street.

"They're heading up the road along the lake. Drive past them so I can get a few pictures of the group protecting her."

As Flannery made the turn onto Mirror Lake Drive, Nessa was looking out the rear window of the Denali to see if the man she'd identified was following. The man was now standing on the corner, looking back down Main Street, away from Cota's group. A tan Ford Expedition pulled up, and the man jumped into the passenger's side as Nessa rushed to get a picture of the vehicle and its driver.

"We've got a second subject in a large, tan SUV that just picked up the trailing guy." She checked her phone for the pictures she had just taken.

"Get set; we're passing them now," Flannery said.

Nessa looked up in time to see Cota and her group standing on the sidewalk, waiting for a break in traffic to cross the road. She put her phone on video and put it to her ear as she was talking while they passed by. Even though she was wearing sunglasses and a baseball hat and the windows of their Denali were heavily tinted, Nessa could feel the big blond's eyes scrutinizing them as they drove by. *The Viking*, as she'd begun to think of him, appeared to be well-trained and fit. His eyes followed their vehicle for a few seconds as they passed by before dismissing them as a threat and moving on to continue to sweep his surroundings. Nessa let out the breath she didn't realize she'd been holding since the big man first looked their way.

"Keep going down the road. We can't follow them now. He's seen this vehicle. If he sees it behind them right away, he'll know he's being followed."

"He barely glanced at us," Flannery argued. "Your boss wanted us to try to follow them to a bed-down sight."

"Just do what the feck I tell you to do," she snapped. "If you do something to spook them and they take off with the girl, Padraig will make you wish all he did was kill you."

"Listen, you little British bitch, I'm only here because my grandfather asked me to help you out. I don't work for you or that Irish fossil…"

Whatever else Flannery had to say next died on his lips when Nessa reached around the driver's side headrest and laid the blade of her tactical knife along his throat. Solomon shifted in his seat to make a grab for her arm but stopped as Nessa shoved the barrel of her 9-millimeter Beretta in his face.

"Listen to me, you arsehole. Padraig Lowery has put more men in the ground than you could possibly imagine. I don't care who your granddad is; Padraig won't hesitate to kill you if you feck this up. That big blond bastard killed Padraig's grandson, and he plans to cut the man's heart out while he's still alive. Nothing and no one is going to stop him. Do you understand me?"

Flannery tried to nod his head but stopped when the knife at his throat pierced his skin. "Yes," he said. "Whatever you say."

"Good." She kept the knife at Flannery's throat as she turned to Solomon. "How about you? Do you understand?"

"I no care. Kidnap, kill. No difference to me, just so long I get paid." The former Somali pirate's English was barely understandable, but Nessa got his point.

"Good. Now keep driving until I tell you where to go. I have to call Padraig." She pulled up the contact list and chose the only number stored in the phone.

The phone only rang one time before Nessa heard Padraig's gruff voice. "Report."

"We followed them until they left Main Street. After that, we had to break off or risk being seen. I was able to identify two additional men who I believe are working with them. I took photos of the three people with Cota as well as the two additional men I spotted and one vehicle they're using. I'll send them all to you right now."

"Excellent work, Nessa." While her expression never changed, Keever beamed inside. Praise from her mentor was hard-earned and rarely given.

"Any problems?" When Nessa hesitated to reply, Padraig said, "What is it, Nessa?"

"Flannery and his mate had to be brought into line."

"Explain," Lowery ordered.

After Nessa had informed Lowery about the brief standoff in the vehicle, he told her to put Flannery on the phone. Nessa didn't need to hear the conversation. The blood drained from Flannery's face, and "Yes, sir," were the only words he uttered repeatedly. After several minutes, Flannery handed the phone back to Nessa. His hands were shaking so badly that he needed both hands to ensure he didn't drop the phone. "He wants to speak with you."

"You'll have no more problems with that gobshite. Anything else?"

"Did you receive the photos I sent?"

"I did."

"The big blond man?"

"Aye. What about him?"

"Padraig, he's the one who killed Callum."

There was a brief pause as Lowery absorbed what Nessa hod told him. When he spoke again, there was no emotion in his voice.

"Get back to the house. Tonight, we go hunting."

CHAPTER TWENTY-SEVEN

Christian stood in the steaming shower, allowing the scalding hot torrent of water to ease his muscles and clear his mind. He thought about the upcoming evening and went over his operational plan again in his head, looking for anything he may have missed. Seeing no glaring omission in his planning, he turned his mind to his last update from Valentine.

He had called Arthur as soon as they had returned from their excursion downtown, looking for an update on the search for Fabrizio and Lowery. Unfortunately, all Valentine had to report was that none of the authorities in Europe had made any progress in tracking either man. Sources in the U.S. had been just as unsuccessful. There were no records of Fabrizio or Lowery entering the States. Every known alias Lowery had ever used was checked, and photographs of Lowery, Fabrizio, and Nessa Keever, along with all known members of the Far darrig, had been uploaded into the Homeland Security database. So far, there have been no hits at any airport, train station, or harbor.

The absence of information was troubling. Christian knew the lack of any sightings could mean their adversaries had been scared off after the failed attack in Rome. They may all be somewhere in Europe, hiding from the authorities. Unfortunately, it could also mean Lowery had used some of his many contacts within the scattered supporters of the PIRA to sneak into the country. It was a proven fact that there were many people of Irish descent in the U.S. who supported the activities of the PIRA and other anti-British groups in Ireland, both financially and in gathering materials for the fight. Many of the former PIRA members had found homes in the U.S. and Canada after 'the troubles' were declared over, and Lowery could have easily leveraged one of his old comrades-in-arms for help getting into the United States undetected.

Christian turned the water to the coldest setting and forced himself to stand in the frigid flow for a full minute before turning the shower off completely. The artic dousing helped clear his head and rev up his system for the night ahead. As he stepped out of the shower, he heard a tentative knock at his door. He quickly grabbed a towel off the heated copper rack and wrapped it around his waist.

"Come in," he said as he walked into the bedroom.

To Christian's surprise, Evy walked into the room.

"I'm sorry to bother you," she said when she realized Christian had just stepped out of the shower.

"You're not bothering me." Evy turned toward the door as he spoke. "Give me a second to throw on some clothes."

Christian had changed into a pair of workout shorts and a tank top and was sitting on the edge of his bed talking with Evy when there was another knock at the door.

"Holy crap. What is this, Grand Central Station?" Christian said, causing Evy to laugh. "Come in."

Laura and Dexter both did a double take when they saw Evy as they walked into the room.

"Are we interrupting something?" Dexter had a mischievous look in his eye as he looked back and forth between Evy and Christian.

"Not at all," Evy said without a hint of embarrassment for being caught alone with Christian in his bedroom. "I wanted to thank Christian for allowing me to go shopping today and for arranging dinner at the lodge tonight. I know I've been difficult, but I really do appreciate everything all of you are doing."

"You're welcome, Evy." Laura gave the girl a hug. "You're not a pain. It's totally understandable for you to be frustrated." As they broke apart, Laura turned to Christian. "What did Arthur have to say?"

Christian looked around the room with an amused expression. "I was going to hold a briefing downstairs, but since everyone is in my bedroom, we may as well do it now."

After relaying what Arthur had told him, Christian answered the few questions they had as best as he could. He next spent fifteen minutes going over the operational plan for dinner.

"Once we're safely inside the restaurant, I'll have Paine in the security booth with one of Tony Alfred's people keeping an eye on the cameras. Because some high-profile politicians and celebrities regularly stay at the lodge, Tony Alfred had a facial recognition program added to their video surveillance system several years ago. Photos of Lowery, Keever, and Fabrizio have already been uploaded into their system. Durand will stay with one of the vehicles, watching the back entrance where we'll exit, while Jerome and David will stay in their vehicle parked in the main lot out front to monitor traffic coming into the resort. Questions?"

"Looks solid, bro," Dexter said. "What did Paine think?"

"Surprisingly, Steven accepted the plan without argument. I think Valentine crawled down his throat for being such a pain in the ass. He actually made a couple useful suggestions that I've incorporated into the plan."

"Oh, look who's playing nice in the sandbox!" Dexter laughed.

Christian finished the briefing by going over the contingency plans for what to do if anything went wrong at the lodge. "Any more questions?" He paused and looked from face to face. When no one spoke up, he said, "Well then, get the heck out of my room and go make yourselves pretty for this evening's festivities." He paused, looking at Dexter, and added, "Dex, just do the best you can. We don't expect too much."

"Don't encourage him," Dexter lamented when Evy and Laura laughed at Christian's joke.

CHAPTER TWENTY-EIGHT

"Nessa, go get the priest for me, please."

Keever walked across the living room to the bottom of the staircase to the second level and hollered, "Priest, get your arse down here!"

When there was no reply from upstairs, Keever climbed the steep staircase, mumbling under her breath about what she'd like to do to the worthless shite if Lowery would just let her. As she reached the top of the stairs, Fabrizio stepped out of the bathroom, still toweling off his head from the shower he had just taken.

"Didn't you hear me, priest?" Nessa shoved the terrified man up against the wall. Her face was so close to his that her spittle moistened his face as she continued to berate him. "When I call you, you answer, you worthless feck!"

"I was in the shower," Fabrizio argued in defense.

"I don't give a shite, *priest!*" She looked the scrawny, pathetic excuse for a man over and said, "Get dressed and get your arse downstairs. Padraig wants to talk with you." When she finished speaking, she pulled Fabrizio close to her and then slammed him into the wall one last time. "Be quick, priest. Don't make me come back to get you again."

Fabrizio stood still until the horrid woman had walked back down the stairs before he moved. He rubbed the back of his head and checked his hand for blood. When his hand came back blood-free, he turned and looked at the perfectly round indentation his head had left in the drywall.

"Capste sten kolasi gaimeni porni!" he muttered in his native Greek. *"Burn in hell, you fucking whore."*

He rushed to his room and quickly dressed in a pair of tan slacks and a flannel shirt before hurrying downstairs.

When Fabrizio walked into the kitchen five minutes later, he found Lowery seated at the table with a laptop open in front of him.

"Tell that bitch to keep her hands off of me!" Fabrizio pointed at Keever as he spoke.

"You piece of shite!" she hollered, advancing toward him before being waived off by Lowery.

"Nessa, take a walk and cool down."

When the angry woman hesitated, Lowery raised his voice a little and repeated the order. With one last glare at the priest, she turned and stormed out of the house, slamming the door as she left.

"She does not like you, priest," Lowery observed with a wry smile.

"I don't care what that bitch likes."

"I do not like you, priest."

Andino had no idea how to respond to that, so he chose the wisest course of action and remained silent.

"Sit down," Lowery ordered, indicating the chair directly to his left. Fabrizio quickly moved to comply, hoping not to draw the man's ire. "Things have changed."

"What do you mean?" Fabrizio was confused.

"I mean, the plan has changed."

"In what way?" Fabrizio feared the Irish terrorist was going to end the operation and flee without grabbing the Cota girl for him. He couldn't allow that to happen. They'd finally located the blasphemous harlot. She had to be punished!

"If you don't obtain the girl, I won't pay you!" Fabrizio knew the only hold he had over Lowery was the huge payday he would earn once he obtained the girl and delivered her to him.

"Don't speak again unless I ask you a question." He silently stared at Andino, waiting for an acknowledgment of his order. "Did you hear me, priest?"

"I heard you." He was growing tired of being threatened by these thugs, but Fabrizio needed the Irishman if he wanted the girl, so, for now, he would continue to comply.

"As you are aware, we know where the woman will be this evening."

"Having dinner at—" He stopped speaking when Lowery held up his hand.

"I told you not to speak again unless I asked you a question, priest," he warned. "As I was saying, we know where the woman will be this evening, and now, thanks to Nessa, we have photographs of some of the people protecting her. Even though Nessa and her team were not able to follow them back to wherever they are hiding for fear of being spotted, we do know they appeared to head in the direction of the Whiteface Lodge. We also know that they have used the spa at the lodge at least once in the past, and tonight they will be dining there." He paused to make sure Andino was listening, then continued.

"King's source at the lodge has confirmed that they are not guests there, so we will need to either take her at the lodge or trail them from the lodge to wherever they are keeping her. Trying to trail them may be difficult at best. Nessa observed them employing surveillance detection strategies when they were in town, so we know they are professionals and are staying alert. Tonight, we will set up a very loose surveillance of the only road that leads into the Whiteface Lodge. Hopefully, we can get a better sense of where they are keeping the girl. I would prefer we find where they are staying and assault that location in the early morning hours. A mobile assault as they travel will only be done as a last resort. We do not have the manpower for it. As that moron in Italy so perfectly demonstrated, there are a great many variables, and too many things can go wrong with an attempt while they are in transit."

Fabrizio, not wanting to further annoy Lowery by speaking, simply nodded his understanding.

"Now for the change of plans." As Lowery spoke, he turned the laptop that sat in front of him toward Fabrizio. "I need you to release the remainder of the payment to me." He saw that Fabrizio was about to protest and raised his hand to cut him off. "Also, I know from talking with that Italian scum, L'Avvoltoio, that you were very clever with your arrangements to pay him. For instance, I am aware that the bulk of what you promised the man is still awaiting your release authorization before being transferred into his account. Now that L'Avvoltoio is dead, and his entire organization is being systematically dismantled as a result of the Italian authorities declaring them a domestic terror organization, you can transfer those funds to me."

"That wasn't our deal!" Fabrizio protested.

"First of all, I did not ask you a question." He glared at the little man, daring him to continue. The Greek remained silent. "Second, we did not have an agreement. Your deal was with L'Avvoltoio. He hired me to assist him. Now he's gone, and I'm all you have. So, again, the plan has changed. You will authorize the money you had arranged to go to L'Avvoltoio to be released to the accounts listed on this pad." He pushed a yellow legal pad toward Fabrizio. On the pad were five different account numbers and routing information. "None of these are the accounts you initially sent money to when I took over for The Vulture. I have reason to believe that account may have been compromised." He nodded at Fabrizio and said, "You may ask questions now."

"If I release any money to you, what guarantee do I have that you'll complete the job and obtain Cota for me?"

"There is no *if,* priest. You *will* release the funds, and you will also transfer the remainder of what we agreed upon when I took over this job. As for a guarantee, you have my word that I'll bring the girl to you." He nudged the laptop closer to Andino before continuing. "Now, priest, transfer the money as outlined on that pad. Do it now." To emphasize his point, Lowery drew a large, black handgun from his waistband and laid it on the table. His finger was on the trigger, and the barrel was pointed directly at Fabrizio's heart.

Seeing no alternative and fearing Lowery would kill him if he refused to cooperate, Fabrizio did as he was told. He arranged for all of the money he had agreed to pay L'Avvoltoio to go into Lowery's accounts.

"It's done," he said in a flat, emotionless voice.

"Now you will transfer the remainder of the money you agreed to pay me to the accounts on the back side of that paper. Place an equal amount into each account. Once I've verified the funds have been transferred and are available to me, I will explain what will happen tonight."

Andino again followed the instructions outlined on the paper. As soon as Fabrizio informed him the transfer was complete, Lowery went into each account to verify the priest wasn't lying to him.

"Very good, priest. Perhaps you're not as foolish as Nessa thinks you are."

Had he known the elaborate double cross Fabrizio had just put in place with the allegedly transferred money, Lowery would've killed the man immediately.

"Now what happens?" Fabrizio asked.

"As I said, I had to change the original plan. I have discussed this with King. No matter how we grab the girl tonight, it is going to cause an immediate response from law enforcement. King informs me that because we are so close to the border, federal agents from the U.S. Border Patrol and Homeland Security would almost certainly become involved to assist local law enforcement with any response once we've kidnapped the girl and killed the men protecting her."

"What do you mean 'killed the men protecting her?' I didn't hire you to kill anyone."

"Understand me, priest." Lowery leaned into the man, his green eyes boring into Fabrizio's brown ones. "The men protecting this girl are responsible for my grandson's murder. In fact, Nessa has identified the man who pulled the trigger and ended Callum's life. I will get the girl for you because I said I would, but I am going to kill the man who killed my grandson."

"What happens once we have the girl?" It was plain from the look on Andino's face and the frightened tremble in his voice that the man was out of his depth in the current situation, and he was regretting ever becoming involved with Lowery.

"King spoke with Tyler Jacobs in Canada. They believe our best bet is to bring the girl back here once we have her. From here, we will split up into three groups. Both men have years of experience smuggling people across the border, and they agree that a group as large as ours will have no chance of getting by the police and making it to the border. Especially when we'll have a kidnapped girl with us. Three smaller groups heading for three different points to cross the border will have the best chance. King has already decided on the best way to divide our group once we're back here."

"And when we get to Canada?"

"That's the next change. Once we get to Canada, we will not regroup. We will each have to make our way back to Europe. Jacob says he'll take you wherever you wish, for an additional fee, of course."

To Lowery's surprise, Fabrizio did not protest when he was informed he would be on his own once he was in Canada. Had his mind not been so preoccupied with the operation ahead, Lowery would've sensed the double cross Fabrizio was planning.

CHAPTER TWENTY-NINE

Andino sat alone in the back seat of the Chevy Blazer, which he occupied with Lowery and the Irish kid, Sammy. He quietly contemplated the latest developments and the subsequent change in plans, and he decided it was a sign from God. The Lord was telling Andino that his path was the righteous one and he was destined to succeed. He would possess Evora Cota so that he could cleanse her of her evil ways and purify the stain of desire she had caused to mar his soul. There could be no other explanation. It was Divine will. He was God's instrument on Earth.

His thoughts soon turned to his hired guns. Lowery and that hideous troll, Nessa Keever, had seriously underestimated him. By allowing Andino to use a computer to force him to transfer the money to Lowery's accounts, it afforded the brilliant man the ability to place a key code on each transfer. When Lowery or any of his people attempted to access those funds, an access code would be requested. When they attempted to use the codes Andino had provided, the accounts would lock, and the funds would immediately be sent back to Andino's account. From there, they would be moved into dozens of accounts in several countries with draconian banking privacy laws. Andino would have the girl, while Lowery and his minions would be left penniless and hunted by authorities on both sides of the Atlantic.

Lowery thought Fabrizio would balk at being left on his own once they were back in Canada, but nothing could have been further from the truth. Andino had actually been working tirelessly to come up with a way to get free of Lowery once over the border. He would offer the native, Tyler Jacobs, an obscene amount of money to get him to Ottawa. Once he reached Ottawa, he would be home free.

When he first realized that he would have to travel to Canada, and then into the U.S., Andino reached out to his mother. While his father had little use for him, Andino's mother doted over her 'baby' and could never deny him any request. He asked her to ensure that his father would be prepared to leverage his almost limitless political influence in Greece to help get him home. Once in Canada, he would reach out to his father and have him arrange for the Greek embassy in Ottawa to offer him refuge and arrange to get him out of Canada and back to Greece. Once in Greece, the politicians Macario Fabrizio owned would ensure that any attempt to have his son extradited to any country to face charges for the crimes he had committed would be met with a flat rejection. Extradition treaty be damned. The shipping magnate would never stand for the embarrassment to his family name to have one of his sons tried as a common criminal.

Now that Andino had had time to consider everything rationally, he found that his current situation was as good as he could have hoped for. He sat silently and marveled at the aged Irish terrorist's ability to calmly plan the kidnapping and killing of his fellow human beings with no apparent remorse whatsoever. With any luck, Lowery and his bitch would be killed trying to avenge his worthless grandson's murder, thus removing any possible future threat from the deranged man and his insane witch.

While Fabrizio contemplated his next moves alone in the back seat, Lowery sat in the front seat next to Sammy Boyle, fine-tuning his operational plan. Jimmy King's information that Cota would be having dinner at Whiteface Lodge was a Godsend for more than one reason. Not only would they know where the girl was going to be and when, but there was only one road, Whiteface Inn Lane, into the facility from the main highway. This allowed Lowery to set up his teams to provide them with the best chance of spotting the girl when she arrived and identifying the vehicles they were using so they could follow them when they departed.

Lowery had once again teamed Nessa Keever with Brandon Flannery and Solomon. They were currently sitting in their GMC Denali to the west of Whiteface Inn Lane, parked behind the Kinney's drug store. Their position afforded them a clear view of the road. After Keever's earlier display of violence, both men sat silently, not wanting to anger the crazy woman again.

Lowery had placed the Expedition carrying Ben Lincoln, Nate Boyle, and Jan Dworak just east of Whiteface Inn Lane in the parking lot of the Pirates Cove Adventure Golf facility. The three men took turns using a pair of binoculars to watch Whiteface Inn Lane.

King suggested to Lowery that he be allowed to go into the lodge and hang out at the bar. He said he'd drank there a few times before, and he could always ask his cousin Linette to join him to give him better cover. Lowery was hesitant to agree at first. He feared King could somehow compromise the mission. Lowery finally agreed after King convinced him he would remain low-key and be in a position to alert them as soon as Cota and her team prepared to depart.

As often happens in these types of operations, fate intervened in favor of Lowery and his plan. Lowery ordered Boyle to park the Blazer in the back corner of the Quality Inn Hotel overlooking the intersection of Palisades Road and Saranac Avenue. The career tactician had unknowingly placed himself in the exact location Cota's team would travel past when they left the safe house en route to the lodge.

CHAPTER THIRTY

Laura was just slipping her feet into a pair of Columbia hiking shoes when Evy knocked on her open door.

"I hope I'm not bothering you."

"Not at all. What's on your mind?"

Evy was still battling about telling Laura about sending the message to her mother. The more she bonded with the woman, the more she liked and respected her. It was because of this that she couldn't bring herself to admit to Laura how she'd deceived her and possibly endangered all of their lives.

"Not much," she lied. "I just wanted to say thanks again for putting up with me."

"That's not necessary, Evy. We all know how hard this has been for you. All things considered, I think you're holding up very well. I haven't heard Christian complain about you one time in the past couple of hours." She waited for Evy to join her in a laugh at the joke, and when she didn't, Laura asked, "Are you sure everything's okay?"

"I'm fine. I'm just tired of it all. I really want to go home and see my mother." Her eyes began to tear up as she spoke, and she couldn't be sure if it was because of the strain of the situation or the guilt over her deception.

Laura walked over and wrapped her arms around the girl. After a few minutes, she gently pushed Evy away and looked over her choice of outfit for the evening. Where Laura and the men would be sporting clothes suited for the outdoor activities favored by many of the guests at the lodge, Evy had dressed for the 'wow' factor. The ivory sweater dress she wore clung to her shapely figure, accentuating the curves concealed beneath. The off-the-shoulder design of the dress left Evy's tanned, well-toned shoulders on full display, and a pair of dark brown knee-high lace-up combat boots completed the ensemble. Evy wore her thick brown hair loose with the chestnut locks framing her face, highlighting her piercing jade green eyes.

"You look beautiful this evening."

Evy smiled at the compliment as she took in Laura's violet Columbia PFG shirt and form-fitting gray capri hiking pants.

"Did I overdo it?" she asked after seeing Laura's more practical outfit.

"Not at all, Evy. Unfortunately, the rest of us need to dress so that we can conceal our weapons and be ready to act if there's a threat." She saw Evy's face darken at the mention of a possible threat and rushed on to reassure her. "Not that we're expecting any problems, Evy. We have no reason to believe Fabrizio or his hired thugs even suspect you're in the U.S. We've all been trained to always be ready, just in case." Attempting to break the tension she had inadvertently created, she added, "Not to mention, that outfit will ensure everyone's paying attention to you and ignoring the rest of us. Just the way we like it."

Five minutes later, the two women walked into the living room, where Dexter was busy at work on his laptop. Through the sliding glass doors, Evy could see Christian on the deck speaking with someone on his cell phone.

When Dexter looked up and saw Evy, he said, "Wow. Someone sure does clean up nicely." He waggled his eyebrows in Groucho Marx fashion, causing Evy to laugh out loud.

"Down boy," Laura laughed. "What're you working on?"

"Just trying to figure out where Evy's tormentors have gotten off to."

"Any luck?"

"Not really. I must be missing something. Don't you two worry your beautiful heads about it, though. I will figure it out!"

Evy desperately wanted to change the subject. "Who's Christian talking to?"

"He was on the phone with Paine." Dexter looked at Laura and added, "I have never known a man whose name better suited him."

"Be nice, Dex."

"Oh, I was being nice for Evy's sake. Anyway, now I believe he's speaking with his lady friend."

A few minutes later, Christian joined the group in the living room. "You look amazing, Evy."

"Thank you. I feel a bit overdressed with all of you dressed like you've been out exploring all day."

"Nonsense," Dexter said. "You add some class to the rag-tag bunch of barbarians."

"Shall we head to the lodge?" suggested Laura.

"Absolutely." Evy's enthusiasm was a welcome change for her three guardians.

Christian led them into the garage, where he got behind the wheel of the Jeep, and Laura climbed into the passenger's seat. Dexter opened the back door and assisted Evy in getting in before he walked around the back of the vehicle and got in next to her.

"Let the teams know we're heading out," Christian told Laura.

Once Laura had notified both QRF teams of their departure from the house and received confirmation that they were all set, she placed the radio mic back in its clip and reached down to ensure the Daniel Defense MK18 tactical rifle was secured next to her seat. "Be prepared" was more than just a Boy Scout motto.

Upon receiving Laura's call, Abioye told Altman to head for the lodge so that they could make sure it was safe to proceed with the evening's festivities.

Paine had positioned the Expedition he and Durand were in on a dirt road that led to a trailhead parking lot just off Peninsula Way Road. He had a clear line of sight up the road that the Jeep was traveling on. Once the Jeep traveled past their position, he fell in behind, providing both counter-surveillance and protection.

Christian kept their speed just under the 30-mile-per-hour posted limit and split his time between watching the road ahead and checking the driveways and small dirt turn-offs along the way for any potential threats.

Dexter carried on a pleasant conversation with Evy while surreptitiously keeping a watchful eye out the side and rear windows, constantly scanning for anything suspicious.

When they reached the intersection with Saranac Avenue, Christian radioed Paine. "We've got a line of cars coming both ways. Sit tight."

"Copy."

CHAPTER THIRTY-ONE

Peninsula Trails was a narrow, paved road that ran adjacent to the Quality Inn parking lot and ended at the intersection with Saranac Avenue. A left-hand curve brought the road directly toward the Quality Inn parking lot for about fifty yards before curving right again back toward Saranac Avenue. As Lowery watched, a green Jeep Grand Cherokee followed by a tan Ford Expedition rounded the far curve and traveled straight toward Lowery's position. Lowery sat up a bit straighter when he realized the Expedition matched the photo of the vehicle Keever had observed providing overwatch for Cota's group on Main Street earlier in the day. Lowery quickly raised a pair of small binoculars he had been holding to his eyes. Despite years of deadly combat and dozens of violent operations against highly trained adversaries, Lowery's heartbeat quickened when he looked through the front window of the Jeep and saw the man in the driver's seat. The blond hair and scarred face confirmed the man captured in the lens of the binoculars was the same man who Nessa Keever had witnessed murder his grandson.

When the Jeep entered the second curve, the heavily tinted side windows caused Lowery to lose sight of the man Keever had taken to referring to as *The Viking*. Lowery next moved his binoculars to the tan Expedition, which was once again shadowing Cota's protectors. Through the windshield of the big SUV, Lowery easily identified one of the men Nessa had photographed earlier.

When Lowery was deciding where to position his people for tonight's operation, he had done a Google Earth search of the target area. From that search, Lowery knew Peninsula Trails became Peninsula Way Road just around the bend and led to a series of roads that twisted and turned their way through large, opulent homes along the shores of Lake Placid. Lowery thought back to the message Cota had sent to her mother. The stupid girl, thinking the chatroom in the game app was safe from monitoring, had told her mother she was being kept in a beautiful home on the shore of Lake Placid. *Could it be that easy?* he asked himself.

Both Boyle and Fabrizio had noticed Lowery's reaction.

"What's going on?" asked Fabrizio.

"Silence, priest!" Lowery hissed. As he watched the two vehicles stop for traffic at the intersection, he called the two surveillance teams on the radio. "Be alert. There will be two vehicles heading your way in a few seconds. The first vehicle is a green Jeep Grand Cherokee. The blond subject who was with Cota when Nessa observed them on Main Street is driving that vehicle. The second vehicle is being driven by one of the men Nessa identified earlier, helping to protect the girl."

Lowery waited for the two teams to acknowledge his message before he took out his phone and called Jimmy King. "Be prepared. It appears the girl and her lapdogs are headed your way. Are you all set?"

King confirmed that he was currently at the lodge, walking the grounds. Once his cousin Linette showed up, he'd move into the bar area of the Kanu, where he could keep his eye on their target.

Just a couple of minutes after Lowery watched the two-vehicle convoy turn onto Saranac Avenue, Ben Lincoln radioed that the target had just passed Pirates Cove heading west.

Less than a minute later, Keever announced that the target vehicles had just turned onto Whiteface Inn Lane.

"What now?" Fabrizio wanted to know.

"Now we wait."

Lowery's otherworldly calm unnerved him.

CHAPTER THIRTY-TWO

The evening had been everything Evy had hoped for. The food was delicious, and the atmosphere was a wonderful combination of sophistication and informality that she'd never experienced before. Dexter had treated her like they were on a date and personally made sure she was enjoying the evening. As Laura had predicted, Evy's outfit drew the attention of most of the men in the room as well as a fair number of the women.

From the moment they arrived at the resort, they were treated like royalty. Tony Alfred, the head of security for the lodge, had met them at the rear entrance just as he did when they arrived for their spa day. He had one of his people park the Jeep and show Paine where he could position the Expedition. When they entered the lodge, they were met by Jill Jimenez, the resort's executive manager. Jimenez explained that they had a full house in the Kanu restaurant for the evening, but they were welcome to wander around and enjoy the lodge until their table was ready.

Alfred led the group on a short tour of the majestic Adirondack lodge before taking them to a small bar in the Peak 47 restaurant. The bartender was taking their drink order when Laura recognized Linette King, the lodge's spa manager, seated next to a young man at the far end of the bar.

"Excuse me for a minute," Laura said to the group as she moved down the bar to say hello.

Evy watched with trepidation, praying Linette wouldn't mention Evy having cut her massage a half-hour short during their previous visit.

Jimmy watched with barely concealed dismay as the woman with Cota approached where he sat with Linette at the bar. He kept reassuring himself that there was no way the woman could possibly know about his involvement with the crazy Irishman in trying to locate the girl.

Linette was busy speaking with the bartender and didn't see Laura approaching until she was standing next to her. "Hi there," she said in surprise when she looked up and recognized Laura.

"Hi, Linette. I hope I'm not intruding. I just wanted to say hello and thank you again for the wonderful spa day we had."

"You're not disturbing me at all, and there's no need to thank me. It was my pleasure. I actually just got off work and was about to head home when my cousin Jimmy showed up and asked me to have a drink with him." She turned and nodded toward King. "Jimmy, this is Laura. Laura, my cousin, Jimmy King."

Laura offered her hand and said, "It's nice to meet you, Jimmy."

Jimmy did his best to hide his nervousness as he stood to shake Laura's hand. "Yeah. It's really nice to meet you."

Laura chatted with Linette for a few minutes, thanking her again before returning to her seat next to Evy. They had just finished their drinks when Tony told them their table was ready.

Jimmy watched as the group left the bar and headed for dinner. He waited ten minutes and then suggested he and Linette move to the patio just outside the Kanu restaurant and enjoy the beautiful fall evening.

Linette balked at first, knowing the restaurant was booked to capacity and hating to impose on the Matre'd to get them a table. Jimmy persisted, and Linette finally gave in. Jimmy was a wild child and always in trouble, but Linette had always liked having him around. He never had the opportunities she'd been lucky to have, and if sitting on the patio of the Kanu watching the rich people party made him happy, she'd play along.

Evy pushed her empty dessert plate away. "This place is amazing, and the food was delicious."

"I'm glad you enjoyed it." Christian flashed a rare smile at her.

"It was perfect," she proclaimed, causing her tablemates to smile at her enthusiasm. "What's next?" Evy was enjoying the evening and didn't want it to end.

"Well, I have a little surprise for you. Let me go settle the bill so we can get out of here."

Evy looked at Laura for some hint of what the surprise might be, but she just shrugged her shoulders and told Evy she'd have to wait to see.

Christian texted Tony Alfred and let him know they were ready to leave. During the five minutes it took Alfred to arrive to escort them back to their vehicle, Evy tried unsuccessfully to get Christian to tell her what they were doing next.

"You may as well just wait and see, Evy," Dexter said. "Christian was a fed, and those jerks take their secrets seriously."

The statement, coupled with the pained look on Christian's face and the sly grin on Dexter's, caused Evy to laugh out loud.

"Please don't encourage him," Christian said, making Evy laugh even harder.

Tony Alfred and three of his well-dressed security team escorted them back to their waiting vehicle. As they were walking through the hallways filled with Adirondack décor, Christian called Abioye and told him to advance to the next location.

By the time they reached the rear entrance, one of Tony's

people had the Jeep parked in the small traffic circle with the engine running and the doors open.

"Thank you again for the hospitality," Christian said as he shook Alfred's hand.

"No worries, my friend. You and your friends are welcome back any time."

Once everyone was safely in the Jeep, Christian radioed Paine. "We're ready to move. Are you all set?"

"We're good to go," Paine responded.

CHAPTER THIRTY-THREE

"They're heading for the back exit right now."

This was Jimmy's third call to Lowery since he arrived at the lodge. The first call was to inform him he had spotted their targets, and the second was to tell him about the encounter with the woman at the bar. Lowery hadn't been happy about one of Cota's people having seen King, but there was nothing he could do about that now.

"Where are you?" Lowery asked.

"I'm heading out a different exit. There's only one road in and out, so there's no sense following them when we know where they'll be going."

Lowery relaxed a little bit. Maybe the young Native had more common sense than he'd shown thus far. "Let me know once you're in your vehicle."

"Now what?" Fabrizio was again just a spectator as events

around him unfolded out of his control.

"Keep quiet and listen. Maybe you'll learn something."

Fabrizio fell silent at the rebuke. *Fuck you!* thought the former man of God. *Soon you'll learn something. . . if you're still alive.*

"Everyone get ready," Lowery said over the radio. "King says they're preparing to leave. If they turn right, I want Nessa's team to take the lead. Lincoln, fall in behind and move up when Nessa tells you. If they turn left, I want Lincoln's team to take the lead, and Nessa can move up when needed."

Keever and Lincoln acknowledged their orders.

"King, you need to stay out of sight now that they've seen you."

Ten minutes later, Keever radioed, "We've got them. They're stopped at the stop sign at Whiteface Inn Lane and Saranac Ave."

"Here we go, people. Look sharp," Lowery responded.

"They just turned left onto Saranac Ave., heading toward Main Street."

"They're passing our location now," Lincoln reported a few seconds later. Two vehicles separated Lincoln from their target when he pulled out of the Pirate's Cove parking lot onto Saranac Avenue.

"We're about a half dozen cars behind Lincoln," Nessa radioed.

Lowery was still sitting in the Quality Inn parking lot,

trying to watch for their targets. A heavy cloud cover had rolled in over the past couple of hours, causing it to be even darker than normal, and Lowery didn't see the Jeep until it was passing by him.

"Be advised, they just passed Peninsula Trails. They are not heading back the way they came out."

"They just turned right at Hillcrest Ave." Nate Boyle was using the navigation app on his phone to keep track of their location while Lincoln concentrated on driving. "From the looks of the map, this is a residential neighborhood. Not sure where they're going, but we can't stay behind them for too long without being made."

Lowery knew exactly what they were doing. He'd done the same thing himself on many occasions. *They're good,* he thought to himself.

"They're running a surveillance detection route. I'm looking at the nav map now. You should be approaching Elm Street. Take a right there and then left on Grand Ave. and parallel them. Nessa, move up when Lincoln turns. If they go straight, Hillcrest passes by the Crown Plaza Hotel, and Grandview empties into the hotel parking lot. They may be heading there."

Again, both teams acknowledged Lowery's orders.

Once Lincoln had turned onto Elm Street, Nessa told Flannery to move up but to stay a block behind the Expedition. There were no vehicles between the big SUV and their vehicle, and she didn't want to be spotted.

"I can see the hotel up ahead. Lincoln, can you get to that lot ahead of us and pick them up? I'd rather not follow them into the lot if that's their destination."

"Got it."

Lincoln sped up and reached the parking lot just as Keever radioed to let everyone know the Jeep and Expedition had continued past the hotel parking lot onto Olympic Drive.

"Hurry up and get in behind us," Nessa ordered. "The navigation map shows this street ends at Main Street. I need you to pick them up when they turn."

CHAPTER THIRTY-FOUR

"Come on, just a hint," Evy pleaded with Christian.

"Just sit back and relax, Evy. You'll find out soon enough. It'll be worth the wait. I promise."

Christian's refusal to let her in on the secret that apparently everyone else knew was driving Evy crazy.

When they had turned off the main road and started driving down darkened back streets, Evy noticed her three protectors seemed to become even more alert than normal if that was even possible.

"What's the matter?" she asked Dexter.

"Nothing, Evy. Christian is just taking the scenic route."

"Scenic route? It's dark out. I can't see anything through these tinted windows."

"Everything is fine, Evy," Laura said to reassure the girl. "We're taking a shortcut around the downtown traffic."

Evy was an intelligent young woman, and she'd been

paying attention to her team of protectors from the very beginning. A troubling thought entered her mind. "Are we being followed?" She fought to conceal the fear that suddenly coursed through her body.

Christian's eyes met hers in the rearview mirror. "No, Evy. No one's following us. We're just being careful. Now sit back and relax. We'll be there in a few minutes."

"Where is 'there?'" she asked.

"You'll see," was all the infuriating man would say.

A few minutes later, they drove past the Crown Plaza Hotel. Looking out the front window of the Jeep, Evy marveled at the beautiful view of Mirror Lake and the surrounding area. Even in the dark, the view from Olympic Drive overlooking the small Adirondack village was amazing.

There was one vehicle ahead of them when they came to a stop at the intersection of Olympic Drive and Main Street. On their right was a beautiful wood and stone building that housed the Olympic Conference Center and the Visitor's Bureau. On their left was a large public parking lot.

The vehicle ahead of them had just turned left onto Main Street, and Christian was waiting for a break in traffic when Paine's voice came over the radio.

"Be advised, we may have company."

"What do you have?" Laura asked.

"When we came out of the lodge onto Saranac Avenue, a black Expedition pulled out of the miniature golf course behind us. When we turned onto Hillcrest, that vehicle followed. It turned off when we were on Hillcrest. That same vehicle just came racing down the hill, and it's sitting three vehicles behind us right now."

"You're sure it's the same vehicle?" Laura asked.

"Ninety-five percent sure."

Christian may not have liked Paine, but he respected the man's experience and training. If Paine said he was ninety-five percent sure, then, in reality, he was one hundred percent sure.

Christian took the radio mic from Laura. "Jerome, did you copy Paine's transmission? We may have company."

Abioye and Altman had left the lodge parking lot as soon as Christian had Evy safely inside the building. They'd grabbed some excellent barbecued ribs at Smoke Signals and then proceeded to the parking lot of the Lake Placid Marina and Boat Tours on Mirror Lake Drive. Christian had planned to end Evy's night out with a surprise boat ride around Lake Placid so she could see all of the huge camps lit up at night. Their job as the advance team was to make sure it was safe to bring Evy to the marina. When the rest of the team arrived, they would wait for the boat to depart, and then Altman would take the Jeep Christian was leaving and follow Abioye back to the safe house. They would secure the boat house and wait for Christian and company to arrive.

"We copied. We're at the marina. What do you want us to do?"

"Stay where you are for now. We're not positive we're being followed, but I'm going to run an SDR to be sure. Be ready if we need assistance."

"Copy. We're standing by."

CHAPTER THIRTY-FIVE

"These eejits are fecking worthless, Padraig," Nessa said into her cell phone. "They've no clue how to follow someone without being spotted." She didn't care that her companions could hear every word she said. Both men in the vehicle feared her. She could see it in their eyes.

Neither man was pleased with being referred to as an idiot by their crazy female partner, but neither of them had the courage to say anything to her. She was bad enough, but her boss, Lowery, was a whole other level of scary. If Flannery's grandfather was to be believed, the man had killed more British soldiers during 'the troubles' in Northern Ireland than any other member of the PIRA.

"Calm down, girl, and tell me what's going on."

"We trailed them for several back streets down to Main Street. We're sitting two vehicles behind them, waiting to see which way they turn. Those morons in the other vehicle just came flying down the hill behind us and damned near hit us. If the people protecting the girl are any good at all, they probably know we're following them."

"Just relax, Nessa. Have they done anything to indicate they know you're there?"

"They ran a surveillance detection route, but that was to be expected. The problem is that it may have worked for them!" Keever was so disgusted with the amateurs they'd been forced to work with in both Italy and now the U.S., she could barely conceal her anger.

"So you're not positive you've been spotted?"

Keever hesitated. She felt in her gut that her inept associates had messed up and caused them to be seen by Cota's guardians. "No, I can't be positive," she reluctantly admitted.

"Then stay with them and keep me posted. We won't get another chance like this, Nessa."

Was there a subtle threat in Lowery's last words, or was she being paranoid? The man was a legend. His tactical genius had been displayed time and again against the vastly superior British forces arrayed against him. No matter the odds, Padraig Lowery always prevailed.

As she tried to ponder the meaning behind Padraig's last words, the Jeep turned right onto Main Street, followed closely by the tan Expedition.

Nessa grabbed the radio and said, "Lincoln, once we make this turn, we are going to pull to the curb. You need to take the eye. Try to keep a vehicle or two between you and them if possible."

"Got it." Lincoln, like the others, was growing to hate the woman, but he also feared both her and her menacing boss.

Lincoln watched as the green Jeep Grand Cherokee, followed closely by the tan Ford Expedition, turned right onto Main Street. Flannery followed the two vehicles around the corner and pulled to the curb in front of the Olympic Center building to allow Lincoln to pass them in his black Expedition. Once Lincoln had passed them, Nessa told Flannery to let a few vehicles pass and then pull back out and be ready to take over the surveillance when needed.

Traffic on Main Street in Lake Placid was normally heavy, and this evening was no exception. Lincoln was able to allow a couple of vehicles to pull out of parking spaces along the street and create a mobile buffer between his vehicle and the target.

"They're signaling to turn left onto Mirror Lake Drive."

There was a small Subaru Cross Trek and a Ford F-150 pickup truck between Lincoln's vehicle and the tan Expedition as it prepared to turn.

Nessa had a bad feeling. She grabbed the radio and said, "Keep going beyond the turn. We'll follow them. Get turned around and get back behind us as quickly as you can."

CHAPTER THIRTY-SIX

Christian turned right onto Main Street, with Paine following close behind.

"They made the turn with us," Paine reported.

"Copy. Can you tell if they're alone?"

"I can't be sure. Next turn, I'll drop back and force them to close up to make the turn if they are following us. If they have help, I should be able to identify it."

As they approached Mirror Lake Drive, Paine slowed and allowed a fifty-foot space to develop between his vehicle and the Jeep.

Christian knew there was a Mobile gas station at the corner of Main Street and Mirror Lake Drive. One very effective method Christian liked to use to determine if you're being followed was to drive through the parking lot of a gas station or convenience store and keep going out of a different exit without stopping. Driving through the lot that way serves no legitimate purpose, so if anyone else follows you into and back out of the lot, then it's a pretty good bet you're being followed. Unfortunately, the Mobile station had a small parking lot, which was partially taken up by the center island and its two gas pumps. As Christian approached the intersection, he could see that the parking lot was too full to be able to drive straight through quickly, and he didn't want to run the risk of being boxed in with no quick way out with a potential enemy at his back. Having been forced to abandon his plan to use the parking lot to identify any possible tails, he turned left onto Mirror Lake Drive.

On the corner opposite the mobile station sits the North Elba Town Hall building. Along with various village offices, the three-story brick building houses the Lake Placid Police Department. Christian counted four black-and-white Lake Placid PD vehicles parked in the parking lot behind the building as he drove past. He briefly considered reaching out to Valentine's friend, the chief of police, for assistance but decided against it. Not yet. He still wasn't certain they were being followed.

As Christian made the left-hand turn onto Mirror Lake Drive, Paine kept a close eye on the Expedition behind them. When the vehicle slowed to maintain its distance from Paine's vehicle, he was positive they were being followed, but when he made the turn onto Mirror Lake Drive, the big SUV drove straight past, continuing along Main Street. Paine was so locked in on the black Expedition that he failed to take note of the tan GMC Denali that turned onto Mirror Lake Drive a few seconds after he did.

"I'm not sure, but I think we may be clear. The Expedition kept going straight on Main Street."

"Copy that."

Evy had remained quiet from the time Paine reported they might have company until he said they were clear. "What's happening?" Her voice shook from the tension that was building inside of her. "Are we being followed?"

"It doesn't look like it, Evy," Laura said in a calm, quiet voice. "Steven thought someone might be following us, but that vehicle has moved on."

"How can he be sure? How does he know? That Fabrizio freak may be out there." Evy was slowly becoming hysterical. The weeks of fear and uncertainty were finally starting to get to the young girl.

"Relax, Evy." Dexter tried to put an arm around the girl to draw her into a hug, but she resisted and pushed him away.

"No! He's out there somewhere. Him and the men he's hired to get me!" Tears streamed down her face and into her mouth as she ranted. "It's my fault. I did this!"

"This isn't your fault, Evy." Laura desperately wanted to calm the girl down. "You didn't do anything wrong. The man is sick, and you're the unfortunate fixation of his sickness."

"It doesn't matter! He's here! Don't you understand? I

know he's here. No place is safe!"

"Evy, there's no way he knows where you are. We've gone over this."

"Yes, he does!" she screamed over Christian's words. "He knows I'm here, and it's my fault!"

Something in the tone of the girl's voice caused Christian to pause. "Evy, what do you mean it's your fault?"

"Evy, please, it's not—"

"Laura, let her talk," Christian ordered. "Evy, what did you mean?"

Evy tried to sink deeper into her leather seat. She wanted to just disappear and be anywhere but where she was. She had to tell them, but she didn't know how. How could she tell Laura she'd betrayed her trust and done the one thing they'd forbidden her to do?

Laura gave Christian a look, just daring him to try to silence her again. "Evy, what did you do? Why is this your fault?"

Evy sat quietly and stared straight ahead. Although her eyes were locked on Christian's in the rearview mirror, he could tell the girl wasn't looking at him.

"I told him where we are," she whispered.

There were a few seconds of stunned silence as all three of them tried to understand what the young actress was saying.

"What do you mean you told him where we are?" Despite the shock she felt at Evy's words, Laura kept her voice as calm and soothing as she could.

"The day we were at the spa, I sent a message to my mother. I told her everything, and somehow that deranged freak saw the message."

Evy went on and explained to Laura and Dexter what she had done, but Christian wasn't listening. He was planning. He grabbed the radio and called the two QRF units.

"Be advised. It appears our location may have been compromised. I don't know if the vehicle Paine saw was following us or not, but there is a chance our stalker knows where we are. We stick to the ops plan for tonight." He paused to allow the teams to acknowledge his message, then continued. "Jerome, is the marina clear?"

"All clear. The boat is set to go, and Altman checked with the marina manager. No one has been anywhere near the boat since we docked it earlier today."

"Copy that. We're about five minutes from your location." Once he updated Jerome, Christian keyed the mic again. "Paine, drop off to about 75 yards and keep a buffer between us and anyone coming up from behind."

"Roger that."

CHAPTER THIRTY-SEVEN

Keever ordered Boyle to keep enough distance between them and the tan Expedition they were trailing to avoid detection. From her place in the back seat, she could occasionally see the vehicle as it passed beneath the streetlights, which were placed at regular intervals along the dark, two-lane road. Just beyond the big SUV, she could just make out the taillights of the Jeep carrying Evora Cota.

So much bullshit for one sick man's obsession with a woman. Nessa kept that thought to herself. She took out her cell phone and hit redial. Lowery answered immediately.

"Report."

"We are currently about fifty yards behind them on Mirror Lake Drive."

"Do you still believe they know they're being followed?"

"I honestly don't know, Padraig. I had the other team continue on Main Street when the target vehicles turned onto

Mirror Lake Drive, and we remained far enough away from them that we shouldn't register as a threat. Other than conducting an SDR, they haven't given any indication that they know we're here."

"And your earlier concern?" Was that doubt she heard in her mentor's voice? She couldn't be sure.

"It was the way these wankers operate. They have no idea how to conduct surveillance. I was afraid that their actions may have drawn the attention of our target."

"And now you're not sure?" Again, Nessa thought she detected something hidden beneath Lowery's words.

"No, Padraig. I can't be sure," she reluctantly admitted.

"This may very well be my only chance to kill the man who murdered my grandson, Nessa. Do not do anything to jeopardize that." Though Lowery never raised his voice, the intensity of his desire to kill the big blond protecting Cota was clear.

"I understand, Padraig."

"I hope for your sake that you do."

There it was. There was no mistaking it this time. The threat was real. If Keever messed up and caused Lowery to miss his chance to avenge his worthless shite of a grandson, she would pay dearly for it.

Nessa had been sitting in silence for several minutes, pondering Lowery's threat, when she heard Lincoln on the radio.

"We're coming up behind you now. What's the plan?"

"We continue to follow them at a distance. Lowery still wants to try to determine where they are staying. He would rather hit them there than try to take them on the road."

"Got it."

CHAPTER THIRTY-EIGHT

Jimmy King had done exactly as Lowery had ordered when he departed the lodge. He made himself scarce. Lowery didn't want to take any chance that the woman traveling with the Cota girl would see him and recognize him from the bar in the Kanu restaurant.

After a few seconds of indecision, Jimmy had decided the best place to stay out of sight but still be close by in the event Lowery needed him was the Lake Placid Marina and Boat Tours parking lot. The marina and gift shop were closed, and the last lake tour had ended hours ago. He could park in the back of the parking lot down by the lake where there would be little chance anyone would accidentally stumble across him.

King drove all the way down to the docks and backed his vehicle into a parking space under a towering white pine tree. In the space to his left was a boat trailer with a large party barge secured in its cradle. To his right was a white Ford F250 heavy-duty pickup truck with the Lake Placid Marina and Boat Tours logo emblazoned on its door. The small SUV King was driving was completely hidden in the dark space between the larger vehicles.

For the second time that evening, fate, luck, or whatever cosmic force one believed in intervened in the game and placed Jimmy King in the perfect spot to see where Cota's protectors were taking her.

King was sitting quietly in his vehicle, listening to the progress of the people following Cota on the tactical radio Lowery had provided him when the sound of tires traveling over the blacktop of the single roadway leading into the marina drew his attention.

"Crap," he muttered to himself. Did one of those rich, nosey assholes that live in the condos along Harbor Lane see him pull in and call the cops to check and make sure he wasn't breaking into the marina offices? King thought briefly about starting the vehicle and trying to sneak out of the lot with his lights off but abandoned that plan as headlights played over the lot in front of him.

King watched a black Chevy Tahoe drive past his location and park down near the docks. Interior lights came on inside the vehicle as two men stepped out and began looking around the parking lot. The driver of the vehicle was a black dude with a buzz cut. The guy who got out of the passenger's side was a tall white guy with long hair. Even from as far away as King was, he could tell both men were fit. King slid down in the driver's seat so he could just see over the dash. Even though Jimmy knew there was no way either man could see him sitting in his vehicle across the parking lot, when their eyes passed over his location, he shivered.

After spending several minutes checking the lot, both men walked out onto the dock and climbed aboard a party barge that was tied securely to the mooring cleats, rocking gently in the waves.

What the hell? It wasn't unusual for people to take a boat out on the lake at night, but normally it was either someone who lived on one of the lake's three islands heading home, or fishermen hoping the quiet of the night might make hooking a nice-sized trout a little easier. These two were not dressed for fishing, and after walking around the boat for a few minutes, they both walked back to their vehicle, where they stood talking quietly and looking back toward the marina entrance like they were waiting for something.

Jimmy had been too preoccupied with the two newcomers to pay attention to what was happening on the radio. He was still trying to figure out what the men were doing on the dock at this hour when radio transmissions between the two vehicles following Cota caught his attention.

"They're signaling to turn left onto Mirror Lake Drive." King recognized Ben Lincoln's voice over the radio.

"Keep going beyond the turn. We'll follow them. Get turned around and get back behind us as quickly as you can." King had no trouble identifying the second voice, either. It was that evil bitch, Nessa Keever.

Jimmy spent a fair amount of time in Lake Placid, and he knew there were several side roads that ran off Mirror Lake Drive that led to rental camps and condos. Could it be possible that Cota was being hidden in one of those?

Jimmy continued to watch the two men near the docks as he monitored the radio.

"We're coming up behind you now. What's the plan?" It was Lincoln again.

"We continue to follow them at a distance. Lowery still wants to try to determine where they are staying. He would rather hit them there than try to take them on the road."

The radio remained silent for several minutes before King heard a transmission from Keever that sent a jolt of fear through his body.

"They're turning into the Lake Placid Marina."

"Oh shit," King whispered to himself.

CHAPTER THIRTY-NINE

"Jerome, we're three minutes from your location. How's the marina look?" Christian asked over the radio.

The former South African Special Forces soldier took one last look around the dark marina parking lot before responding. "The parking lot is quiet, and we have the boat running. You're clear to proceed."

"Copy that. Prepare to cover our arrival." Christian keyed the mic again and said, "Paine, did you copy that?"

"I copied. The marina is clear, and you're good to go."

"When we pull into the marina, the road winds around to the left and then down to the docks. As soon as we pull in, there's a small parking area alongside one of the buildings off to the right. It's where boaters can wash their boats off after they exit the lake. Pull in there and see if anyone tries to follow us down to the docks."

"Got it," Paine responded.

"Alright, Evy, listen to me." Christian spoke quietly and calmly, hoping to help reassure the frightened girl. There'd be time to deal with what she had done later. For now, they needed her to be quiet and move quickly. "When we reach the dock, Laura and Dex are going to escort you to the boat. Jerome and David have already made sure the area is safe, and they'll be covering our arrival."

Evy started to speak, but Christian stopped her. "No questions." His firm tone silenced Evy immediately. "Once we get back to the house, we can discuss what's happened. For right now, just follow directions, and everything will be alright. Do you understand?"

"Are we being followed?" Evy couldn't help it. She needed to know.

Laura cut Christian off before he could reply. "Evy, it doesn't look like anyone was following us after all. Christian is just being cautious. Because of what you've told us, we now have to consider the possibility that Fabrizio knows where we are. Please, just do as Christian asks and move quickly and quietly. There'll be time later on to sort things out."

Christian slowed as they approached the entrance to the marina. "We're pulling into the marina now."

"Copy that," Jerome replied.

A minute later, Jerome and David watched as the green Jeep Grand Cherokee Christian was driving pulled up next to their Tahoe and came to a stop. Laura got out and opened the rear passenger door for Evy. As the girl stepped out, Dexter joined them, and all three went directly to the waiting boat.

Christian made sure Evy was safely on board the party barge before turning to Jerome and David. "Good work, guys. As soon as we clear the dock, head for the house. Paine and Durand are going to secure the boathouse. I want you two there to escort us from there to the house."

"You don't want anyone out in front of the house keeping an eye on the road?" Altman had been a member of the U.S. Marine's Force Recon and a member of the CIA's para-military branch before being poached from his job by Arthur Valentine. His experience was in combat and tactics, not protection.

"No. We have cameras and alarms to monitor the exterior. The only thing putting men out front would accomplish would be to announce to anyone looking that we're guarding the place."

Altman accepted Christian's explanation without further comment.

"What about the Jeep?" Abioye asked, nodding toward the vehicle.

"Leave it here with the keys inside the gas tank door. I want it here in the event we have to use the boat to evacuate Evy from the house."

"So what happened?" Abioye was curious.

"Fabrizio may know where we are. No more questions for

right now. I'll bring everyone up to speed once we have Evy securely back in the house."

When he finished giving Abioye and Altman their orders, he took a long look around the marina parking lot and docks before hustling over and climbing aboard the boat.

Like everything else Doctor Matas did, he'd gone top of the line when he purchased his party barge. The 27.5-foot Regency 250 LE3 was a combination of sophisticated luxury and maximum power. The 350L Verado V10 motor could propel the spacious boat through the water at over 70 miles per hour.

Dexter untied the mooring lines, and Christian slowly backed the boat away from the dock. Once clear of the dock, he pushed the throttle forward and turned the boat out into the dark waters of Lake Placid.

"Well, Evy, it's not quite what I had in mind, but. . . surprise! We're taking a boat ride."

CHAPTER FORTY

Jimmy King couldn't believe his eyes. As he watched, a green Jeep Grand Cherokee pulled up next to the Tahoe. When the door opened and the driver stepped out, Jimmy immediately recognized the man Nessa Keever had nicknamed *The Viking*. The big man approached the black guy from the first vehicle and shook his hand. He gestured toward the boat and then back at the Jeep. As he spoke, King got the second shock of the night. Walking away from the Jeep were three people. He recognized Laura Knight from the bar at the lodge. He was surprised to see Knight carrying what appeared to be a tactical rifle. Walking with Knight was an Asian guy with shoulder-length black hair pulled back into a ponytail. He looked just as fit as the two guys who'd arrived earlier. Between Knight and the Asian guy walked Evora Cota. He recognized her from the pictures Lowery had supplied them with. Cota and her escorts climbed aboard the party barge that the first two guys had checked out when they arrived. *The Viking* spoke with the two men for a few minutes before jogging down to the boat.

Jimmy knew he needed to call Lowery, but he didn't want to move around inside his vehicle and risk being seen, so he just sat quietly and watched as the party barge slowly backed away from the dock with *The Viking* driving. Once clear of the dock, the boat turned and headed slowly out onto the lake.

The first two guys who had arrived waited until the boat had cleared the dock and moved off into the lake before climbing back into the Tahoe and driving off toward the marina exit. King waited several minutes to make sure they were actually gone before he reached for his cell phone and called Lowery. The phone rang just once before disconnecting. King looked at the screen in surprise before thumbing the redial button. Again, the phone rang just once before disconnecting. King stared at the phone in frustration for several seconds before he decided to send a text message.

Call me back right now! Very important! he typed.

He hit the send button and waited. It didn't take long before his phone began to vibrate.

"What do you want?" Lowery's soft, menacing voice caused King to hesitate. "Well?"

"They're at the marina."

"I am aware of this."

"I'm at the marina," King said.

There was a brief pause before Lowery replied, "Why are

you at the marina?"

King quickly explained to Lowery how he ended up at the marina when Cota and her people arrived.

"And you are certain they could not see you?"

"I'm hidden in the shadow of a huge pine tree between a boat on a trailer and a big heavy-duty pickup. There's no way they could see me."

"So they have left by boat, and we've lost them."

"Not exactly," King replied.

"Explain." For the first time, King heard something other than extreme confidence in Lowery's voice. He heard confusion.

As he was talking with Lowery, King had retrieved a pair of battered binoculars from his backpack.

"I am watching them cross the lake. They're heading straight for the shore north of the marina."

"One of the islands?" Lowery pulled a Google Earth image of Lake Placid up on a tablet.

"No. It looks like they may be heading for Sand Point."

"Sand Point?" Lowery's confusion was clear.

"Sorry, I forgot you're not familiar with the area. Sand Point is out at the end of the peninsula."

A smile crept slowly across Lowery's face in the dark vehicle. "Can Sand Point be reached from Peninsula Trails Road?"

"Yeah. Peninsula Trails Road becomes Peninsula Way

Road and winds all the way out to the end of the peninsula."

"I assume there are big camps along the shoreline?"

"Million-dollar places," King confirmed. "Why?"

"Don't worry about why. Keep your eye on that boat for as long as you can. Call me back when they land or if you lose sight of them." Lowery hung up without waiting for King to reply.

"You're welcome, asshole," King whispered into the phone.

Jimmy set his cell phone down and retrieved his binoculars. The party barge's running lights made it easy for him to follow the boat's progress across the dark lake. Jimmy was surprised when bright lights suddenly came on as the boat neared the tip of Sand Point. He trained his binoculars on the light source and could just make out a dock and boathouse. From that distance, he couldn't tell if there were any people on the dock. He moved his binoculars back to the boat and watched as it slowly approached the well-lit dock. Jimmy kept watching the dock until both the party barge's running lights and the dock lights shut off. A smile slowly spread across his face as he called Lowery to report what he'd seen.

CHAPTER FORTY-ONE

"Good work, Jimmy-boy. Good work. Keep an eye on that dock, lad. Let me know if there's any movement."

A smile slowly spread across Padraig Lowery's weathered face. *I've got you now, you bastard. You're going to pay for Callum. I swear to God, you're going to pay.* Lowery allowed himself a few moments to thank God and ask him for His continued blessings before he called Keever.

"Where are you?"

"We're getting set up on Mirror Lake Drive. They drove into the marina, and the following vehicle set up just inside the entrance to watch for any tails. We had to go by. If they come back out, we'll see them and be ready to follow. But Padraig..." Nessa hesitated, fearing the man's response. "If they took a boat, we've lost them."

"They did take a boat, Nessa," he told his discouraged-sounding underling. "But no, we have not lost them." He explained what King had observed and told her to get herself and the rest of the group back to the safe house.

"So now what's the plan?" Fabrizio had been silent for so long that Lowery had almost forgotten the bothersome little priest was even in the vehicle with him.

"Now we regroup. Then we go get your whore for you, and I get to kill the scum who murdered my grandson. Now, no more questions, *priest*. Let me think."

From where Sammy Boyle sat in the driver's seat, he could see the annoying little priest's face in the rearview mirror. From the look on the man's face, Boyle could tell he was struggling desperately to obey Lowery and not ask any more questions. He was hoping the man lost his inner battle. There was no doubt in Boyle's mind that the Irishman would kill the priest if he continued to annoy him. Hell, the little man was so annoying that Sammy would offer to do the job for him. For a price, of course.

They were the first team to arrive back at the house, and Lowery wasted no time exiting the vehicle and hurrying inside. The priest took his time getting out of the vehicle, then wandered off toward the wood line, muttering to himself. Sammy leaned against the back of the Blazer and waited for the rest of the guys to arrive. He had no desire to be alone in the house with Lowery. Sammy was no stranger to violence, and he'd dished out his share of beatings during the time he and his brother had been working for Brandon Flannery. He definitely was not afraid to get his hands dirty, but Lowery was a whole different level of bad. Violence seemed to emanate from the man.

Ten minutes after Sammy had pulled into the driveway, the Expedition carrying his brother Nate pulled in, followed by Flannery in the GMC five minutes later. While Flannery's men greeted each other and traded tales of their evening so far, Nessa Keever ignored the lot and went directly into the house.

Fifteen minutes after the last vehicle arrived, Lowery had the entire group gathered around the dining room table. He looked each person in the eyes, trying to assess their level of commitment before proceeding.

Fabrizio was hanging back by the doorway to the kitchen. He wore a stoic look, like a man who finally realized he was being swept out to sea and there was nothing he could do to fight the tide.

"Priest, get your worthless arse over here." Keever made no attempt to hide her hatred of the man.

"I can hear just fine from here."

Lowery placed a hand on Keever's shoulder, restraining her as she moved to confront Fabrizio.

"Come over here, priest. I wouldn't want you to miss anything." Lowery's contempt for Fabrizio was just as apparent as Keever's hatred.

Seeing nothing to gain by continuing to argue with the man, Andino walked over and stood between Solomon and Dworak.

Flannery was looking around the room and realized one person was missing. "Where's King?"

"I just got off the phone with Mr. King," Lowery said. "He called to inform me that he knows a spot where he can keep a closer watch over the boathouse where Cota was taken. He will keep us informed of any movement. Now, no more questions until I'm done talking. Is that understood?" Lowery looked at each person gathered around the table until every one of them acknowledged what he'd said. "Good. Now, the first issue. Flannery, we need a boat."

"Not a problem," he assured Lowery. "Even this late in the year, there are dozens of boats with long-term docking spaces at the marina. The boat owners are required to leave a set of keys with the marina office in the event of an emergency where the boats would have to be moved. Breaking into the office and grabbing a set of keys won't be a problem."

"Good. That was my one concern. I was hoping you could take care of that. Now, we will split into three teams. Team one will be Flannery, Nathan, and Solomon. You will steal a boat at the marina." Lowery looked at Solomon and said, "You were a pirate, correct? I assume you've stolen your share of boats?"

"A pirate, yes. I steal many boats," he confirmed in his barely intelligible English.

"Good. That may come in handy. Flannery, take the GMC. You'll park it as close to the docks as possible and leave the keys on top of the driver's side rear tire."

When Flannery started to speak, Lowery held up a hand, stopping him. "Hold all questions until I'm done."

"Team two will be Lincoln and Nessa. You'll take the Expedition. Team three will be Sammy and Dworak. Sammy, you'll drive the Blazer. Fabrizio and I will be with you."

Lowery turned the laptop on the table around so that everyone could see. On the screen, he had a Google Earth satellite image covering the area they would be operating in.

"King saw Cota's security team take her by boat across Lake Placid and dock at a boathouse at Sand Point." Lowery used a pen to point to the spot where King had observed the boat land. "We know from an intercepted message that Cota sent to her mother that she is being kept in a beautiful mansion on Lake Placid, and she can see other camps across the lake from where she is. That description matches the house on the property where the boathouse is."

Lowery pointed to a spot on the shore just off Ruisseaumont Way. "Jimmy King is currently here. He reports there has been no activity since he saw them take Cota to the house."

"And if we hit this house and the girl isn't there?" asked Flannery. "All we have to go on is the message you intercepted, and that description matches dozens of houses on Lake Placid."

When Nessa appeared to be ready to respond, Lowery held up his hand, silencing her. "An excellent point, Brandon. Your grandfather would be proud of you." Lowery looked around the room before he said, "If the girl is not there, then we are done. Word will get out about the house being assaulted, and the girl's security team will move her again." He looked directly at Fabrizio as he emphasized his next words. "At that point, it will be over." Assured that Fabrizio wasn't going to interrupt, he continued. "Team one, you will take the boat across the lake and then hug the shoreline as you approach the boathouse. You will hold up right here." Lowery pointed to a spot along the shore. "You will have the cover of these trees. Wait there for me to call you on the radio and tell you to move in. When you move, tie the boat to the dock and proceed along the tree line to the south side of the house. Questions?"

"Will we be using the boat to leave?"

"Possibly. That's why I want it secured at the dock. Depending on how this goes, we may need the boat. Team two, you will drive out to Point-O-View Way." He again pointed to where he wanted them to stop. "Work your way through the woods until you can see the house and hold there until I order the strike. Team three will stop on Roland Way. There is a house just before the target house." Lowery pointed to the map as he explained everything. "We will park here and move through this small, wooded area to this row of trees. Once we are in position, I will give the order for all three teams to assault the house. We have enough weapons and small explosives to gain entry, even if they have fortified the doors. Once inside, we have two distinct missions." He looked at Fabrizio, expecting an argument, but to his surprise, the priest remained silent.

"First, we locate the girl." Lowery replaced the Google Earth image with the photo of Evora Cota. "She's the reason we are here." Lowery looked into Fabrizio's eyes as he continued. "I have decided the *priest* will pay an additional one hundred thousand dollars to whoever finds the girl and secures her." Again, to Lowery's surprise, the little man did not respond.

Lowery pressed a button, and Cota's face was replaced with one of the pictures of Christian Vikstrom that Keever had taken earlier in the day. "This man is in charge of the people protecting the girl. He won't be hard to find. He must die. Is that understood? I want this man dead."

"Are you bringing the priest on the assault with you?" Keever asked.

"No, the *priest* stays with the vehicle."

"I'm coming with you," Fabrizio argued.

"No, you're not, *priest*. You have no experience with this type of work."

"Nonetheless. I'm coming along. I will take control of the girl for the ride back to the house."

Lowery gained a small measure of respect for the man. Finally, he wanted to take direct action.

"Fine, *priest*, have it your way but know this. If you are

wounded or become separated from the team and can't make it to the extraction point, you will be left behind and the girl with you."

"I understand," Fabrizio said.

"Once we have the girl, we'll have to assess the best way out. If we can get back to our vehicles, I'd prefer that, but if we're cut off, we will take the boat back across the lake. That's why I want the GMC left there. If we get separated, we may have to split up and use both the boat and the vehicles to get out."

For the next twenty minutes, he allowed the team to ask questions. Lowery showed why so many called him a tactical genius. Even on short notice and with limited information, the man prepared a plan of attack with a high probability of success.

"Alright, get your gear ready and make sure no one leaves anything behind that the authorities can use to identify you. I'll check with King once more for an update, and then we go."

CHAPTER FORTY-TWO

Christian went into high gear as soon as they had Evy safely inside the house.

"I'm going to give Valentine a call and let him know what's happened. Laura, once Paine has the boathouse secured, have him leave Durand there and come up to the house."

"Got it."

"Dex, is there any way to tell if Fabrizio knows about the game app Evy and her mother use? Can we determine if he saw the message Evy sent?"

"Possibly. If he's as good as he seems, he may have buried any type of notification he had set up to monitor the account."

"Do your best." Christian turned to Evy and said, "Evy, is there anything else you haven't told us?"

Both Laura and Dexter paused to hear Evy's reply before handling the tasks Christian had given them.

"No. That's it." Evora spoke in a whisper and never looked

up. Her long hair fell over her face, making it impossible to see the mixed expressions of fear and guilt she wore.

"Maybe we should notify Valentine's buddy, the chief of police," Dexter suggested.

"Not yet. I want to talk with Valentine first. I also want to see what you can dig up. I don't want to involve the local cops unless we're certain we've been compromised."

Christian's conversation with Valentine lasted twenty minutes before the men hung up. The team had all gathered next to Dexter so Christian could fill them in on what Valentine had said.

"Dex, have you been able to find anything?"

"No. I can't find it anywhere in the settings. Since we've had Evy with us, there's just the one message she sent. It doesn't appear that her mother has accessed the app in months, and she's the only person other than Evy that appears in the app's activity log."

"So the bottom line is that we cannot rule out the possibility that Fabrizio, or someone he hired to keep watch on Evy, may have accessed that app and knows where we are."

"That's correct." Christian could tell Dexter was disappointed and angry with himself for not being able to provide a more definitive answer.

"What did Arthur say, Christian?" Laura asked.

"He's concerned, obviously. He wants us to move Evy, but since we are not certain we were followed today, he wants us to take our time and find a good spot to secure her."

"He believes moving her is the best option?" Laura asked.

Christian could tell from Laura's demeanor and tone of voice that she blamed herself for allowing Evy to slip away and contact her mother. Christian would've liked to reassure her, but part of him also felt Laura shared some of the culpability for what had transpired. It had been her responsibility to watch the girl and make sure she followed the rules they'd established, and she'd failed to do that.

"He does. He left it up to us where we go, but he didn't rule out taking her back to Europe someplace."

"What'd Arthur say about calling the Lake Placid police chief?" Paine asked.

"He's going to do it. He'll explain that we've developed intelligence that someone may try to grab Evy. Valentine's going to ask him to increase his patrol activity in the area." He looked around. "Okay. Everyone, get your stuff together and get some rest. I'm going to spend the remainder of tonight deciding on a new safe house. Laura, once I find a location, I'll need you to arrange accommodations for everyone."

"I'll have one of the men relieve Durand in a couple hours so he can get some rest as well," Paine said.

Evy sat quietly, staring into the fire Dexter had started as soon as they were back at the house. The flickering flames cast ever-changing shadows over her face as she struggled with the guilt she felt for having betrayed the trust of the people protecting her. She needed to atone for what she'd done, but the young actress didn't know how.

"I'm so sorry," she began, only to have Christian cut her off.

"Now's not the time, Evy. We need to concentrate on where we go from here. We'll have time later to discuss what happened."

Evy fell silent as she contemplated the man. When she first met Christian, she thought he was exactly what she'd always considered to be a typical arrogant American male: full of himself and believing his opinion was more important than anyone else's. Now, after weeks together, she realized she had been wrong. He was gruff and stern, and he definitely did have his fair share of arrogance, but that wasn't what defined him. He had been unwaveringly respectful to Evy, and he'd done his best to keep her informed about what was happening every step of the way. Evy realized that, even on that first day when he'd dealt so severely with Antonio, everything he did was for the purpose of keeping her safe. While her opinion of America and its incessant meddling hadn't changed, her opinion of the Americans working so hard and risking so much to protect her had.

Laura sat next to Evy on the couch and wrapped her right arm around her. "Come on, Evy. You need to try to get a few hours' sleep. If we find a spot to move to, we may be on the road all day tomorrow."

Evy didn't move at first. She just kept staring into the flames. After a few minutes, she leaned slowly toward Laura, placing her head on her shoulder. "I'm so sorry," she whispered too quietly for Christian to hear.

Laura felt the girl's warm tears on her arm. "It's okay, Evy. Everything will work out."

Christian watched Laura lead Evy up the stairs and disappear down the hallway before continuing. He picked up the radio and said, "I want one man on each team to get something to eat and grab some sleep. I want one person at the boathouse and one watching the backyard. Switch out with your partner every four hours. Dexter and Laura will take turns monitoring the security system. I'm going to work on a new safe house. I'd like to be out of here by tomorrow— midafternoon at the latest."

CHAPTER FORTY-THREE

"Has there been any movement?"

"It looks like they've got a guy posted on the boathouse dock. Lights were going on and off inside the house for a little while, but the entire place has been dark for the last half hour." King held the cell phone he was speaking to Lowery on in his left hand. In his right hand, he held the binoculars he was using to keep track of the boathouse across the lake.

"Keep watching and call me the second you see any movement. We'll be departing here shortly."

Once Lowery finished checking with King for an update, he asked Nessa to call the men back into the dining room. He was taking a cup of coffee out of the microwave when Nessa walked into the kitchen.

"The men are ready, Padraig."

Lowery thought he detected a trace of excitement in the

girl's voice. He was glad he hadn't killed her in Rome after she had let Callum die. He would need her skills tonight.

Lowery walked into the dining room carrying his steaming cup of coffee. He stood quietly, looking from face to face, trying to determine if these men he had hired would have the courage to face what was coming. For one fleeting moment, he allowed himself to wish that he had a dozen of his old comrades-in-arms from the PIRA to pull off tonight's operation. Even as the thought crossed his mind, Padraig realized it was a waste of time. Fate had provided him with what he had. These men would either be up to the task, or they wouldn't. The only one he trusted fully was Nessa Keever, and she'd already let him down once.

"Does anyone have any questions about their assignment?" He paused for a few seconds, and when no one spoke, he continued. "Each of you came highly recommended, and you're being paid very well for this job. Jimmy King has been watching our targets since they left the dock. From what we can tell, we will have them outnumbered. We don't believe they're aware we're here, so we'll also have the element of surprise on our side." He held up a photo of Evora. "As I have already said, this is our primary target. She is not to be harmed. If she is, the person responsible will regret being born." He paused to allow his warning to set in. "Everyone else protecting her is fair game." He replaced Cota's photo with Vikstrom's.

"This…Man…Must…Die." Lowery emphasized each

word. "I would prefer to be the one who kills him, but he must not survive the night. I have already placed a one-hundred-thousand-dollar bounty on the girl for whoever finds and captures her. Our benefactor, the *priest*"—He pointed to the far wall where Fabrizio stood with his arms folded over his chest and an unreadable expression on his face—"will be paying that fee." He smiled condescendingly at the Greek before continuing. "I am now placing a one-hundred-thousand-dollar bounty on *The Viking's* head. I will be paying that bounty personally."

Flannery's men couldn't believe their ears. They'd already been promised a huge payday just for helping the crazy Irish terrorist kidnap the girl. Now they were being offered the opportunity to make more money in one night than most of them had made in years. They cheered at Lowery's words and began boasting among themselves about who would find the girl and kill her protector.

Lowery allowed the men to continue firing each other up for several minutes. Then he shouted, "Enough!"

When the boisterous group didn't quiet down, Nessa Keever pointed her tactical rifle at the ceiling and pulled the trigger three times. "Shut your pieholes!" she bellowed as the men ducked for cover at the sound of gunfire.

Lowery looked at the startled faces staring at Keever. "Now that I have your attention once again, are there any questions?"

Not one person spoke, and Lowery hoped it was because

they all understood their assignment and not because they were terrified of Nessa and her rifle.

"Good. Now load up the vehicles. I want team one on the way in ten minutes. The rest of us will leave twenty minutes after that. That should give you enough time to secure a boat and be halfway across the lake."

When the men didn't move out quickly enough for her liking, Keever shouted, "You heard the man! Get your arses moving!"

Fabrizio stood quietly in the doorway separating the kitchen from the dining room, where Lowery was currently outlining his plan for the assault. When Lowery reminded the men that Fabrizio would be the one paying the one-hundred-thousand-dollar bounty on Evora Cota, he fumed silently. He knew that if he reacted to the taunt, Keever would make his life miserable, so he just waited and listened.

Fabrizio turned to the kitchen, only half listening to Lowery as he spoke. His attention was drawn to the cell phone Lowery had left on the kitchen table, and a very dangerous plan took root in the brilliant man's head. Lowery wasn't paying any attention to him, and Keever was hanging onto every word her mentor was saying. Moving quickly to avoid being seen, Andino grabbed Lowery's cell phone, praying the paranoid man hadn't locked it. He tapped the screen and almost let out a shout of joy when the factory default screen saver opened up. He opened the phone app and then the Recent Calls function.

He knew that the last person Lowery had spoken to was King, just before starting the meeting. He quickly memorized the last phone number listed and set the phone back down on the table.

He was walking back to the hallway toward the dining room when Keever entered the kitchen. She gave Fabrizio a suspicious look. "What the fuck are you doing, *priest?*" It amazed Andino how much hatred and loathing the evil woman could put into that one word.

"I was looking for a couple bottles of water to bring with me." He hoped the lie didn't sound as transparent to Keever as it did to him.

"Never mind that. If you want your little whore, you'd better get moving. Padraig wants to leave shortly. If you aren't there, maybe I'll just kill the little bitch and save us all the trouble of getting her and you back over the border."

Andino knew any response he gave would just draw further vitriolic raving from the girl, so he brushed past her and hurried to the bedroom where he had left his backpack. Before shutting the door, he checked the hallway to ensure it was clear. He dug his cell phone out of the bottom of the pack and, using the number he had memorized from Lowery's phone, he called Jimmy King. He had to dial the number three times before the smuggler answered.

"Who is this?"

"Mr. King, please listen. This is Andino Fabrizio, *the priest*. I have an offer for you."

CHAPTER FORTY-FOUR

Peninsula Road

Lake Placid, New York

"Any idea what this is all about?" Officer Lisa Baker asked her partner, Officer Teddy Fernsby.

Fernsby was busy blowing on a cup of piping hot coffee he'd picked up at Stewart's, trying to cool it down enough to take a sip. "All Seargent Francis said when he called was that some rich friend of Chief Nilsen is renting that huge mansion that some plastic surgeon built out on Sand Point. Apparently, whoever is renting the place is worried about security, and the chief's buddy asked him if we could keep an eye on it."

"Must be nice. Armed security for the rich and shameless, all at the taxpayer's expense."

"Get used to it. Lots of rich, pampered, entitled people in this town."

Theodore "Teddy" Fernsby joined the Lake Placid Police Department after serving four years as a military police officer in the U.S. Army. Born and raised in Saranac Lake, the thirty-five-year-old was just starting his twelfth year with the department. With a wife and two small children at home and a third on the way, he welcomed any opportunity to work a little overtime.

Lisa Baker grew up in Lake George and joined the PD shortly after earning an associate degree in Criminal Justice: Police Science from Adirondack Community College. Baker was happy at Lake Placid PD, but her ultimate dream was to work for the FBI in their Cyber Crimes division. The ambitious twenty-four-year-old was hard at work completing her four-year degree in Cyber Security online at the State University of New York in Albany. While she enjoyed working for the PD, she grew tired of the routine nature of the work. The majority of her workday consisted of barking dog complaints, domestic disputes, and DWI arrests. She longed to work on big investigations involving international bad guys. With her tuition bills piling up, she too took advantage of any opportunity to work overtime when it was offered.

The two police officers were currently sitting in their black-and-white Ford Explorer tucked back into a heavily wooded area where Peninsula Road split off from Peninsula Way. There were no streetlights, and the trees surrounding the vehicle cut off any illumination the moon might have provided, leaving the area outside the patrol vehicle as black as pitch. The police radio occasionally came to life with a state trooper calling in a traffic stop or the hourly status check from the dispatch center.

Baker was reaching to change the radio station from the classic rock of WKOL to WIRY and some country tunes out of Plattsburgh when the headlights of a vehicle traveling along Peninsula Way lit up the woods around them. The two officers watched as two SUVs drove slowly past the Peninsula Road split continuing along Peninsula Way.

Baker looked over at Fernsby, where he sat behind the steering wheel. "Should we check them out?"

"Might as well. That's what they're paying us overtime for."

He put the Explorer in drive, slowly pulled out of their wooded hiding place, and followed the two vehicles down the road. If the lighting had been better, Fernsby would've held off turning on his headlights until he was right behind the vehicles ahead. Unfortunately, the darkness around them made it necessary to turn on the lights just to see the road.

When they were about fifty feet from the trailing vehicle, Fernsby activated the vehicle's emergency lights. Rather than pulling to the side of the road the way a vehicle normally would when being pulled over by the police, the two vehicles in front of him came to a stop in the middle of the narrow road.

"What the hell's wrong with these guys?" Wealthy people never ceased to amaze Baker.

"No idea. They're probably lost," Fernsby replied.

Baker reached for the radio to call in the stop as Fernsby opened the door and stepped out of the patrol vehicle. He tried to shine his flashlight into the SUV as he approached, but he couldn't make out any occupants through the dirty rear window. Fernsby was five feet from the back of the vehicle when he heard a twig snap off to his right. Before he could react, he felt a hand grip his chin and pull his head back. The tactical knife Nessa Keever slid into Officer Fernsby's throat was so sharp that he never felt the blade. One second, he was alive, and the next, he was dead. Keever held the officer tightly against her, watching the life drain from his eyes before letting his dead body slide to the ground.

Baker was busy with the radio and didn't see her partner fall. She was waiting for dispatch to respond to her call when something struck the passenger's window. Startled, she looked up just as Lincoln fired a single round from a suppressed Springfield Armory Hellcat Micro-Compact 9mm through the window, striking Officer Baker just below her right eye. Lincoln opened up the passenger door and fired two more rounds into Baker's head, just to be sure.

"Help me with this guy," Keever called quietly.

Lincoln helped Keever drag Fernsby's body back to the patrol vehicle, where they struggled to stuff the dead body into the back seat. Once they had the body inside the patrol vehicle, Lincoln got in the driver's seat and backed it off the road and into the woods, then shut off the engine.

"Let's get moving. Someone is going to miss these two before very long."

CHAPTER FORTY-FIVE

Lowery barely had time to react to the emergency lights that activated behind their vehicle when he heard Nessa Keever's voice over the radio.

"Sit tight. We'll take care of this."

Lowery was startled when, a few seconds later, he saw two shadowy forms move past his window, heading toward the stopped police vehicle behind them. He craned his neck to see what was happening, but the glare of the police vehicle's emergency lights prevented him from seeing anything. After several seconds, Lowery heard a gunshot, followed by silence. Several seconds later, two more gunshots pierced the quiet night. Three minutes later, Keever knocked on their window.

"We took care of them, but we need to get moving. It won't take them very long to miss those two, and when they do, Lincoln says we'll have cops swarming in from all over the region."

"Wait!" Lowery ordered. Once again, fate seemed to be intervening to ensure Lowery's plan of vengeance succeeded. "We have just been provided the perfect way to breach their security."

"I don't understand, Padraig." Keever's confusion was obvious.

"What's going on?" Lincoln asked as he stepped up beside Keever. "We need to move!"

"Listen to me," Lowery commanded. "Doesn't it strike either of you as odd that a police car with two officers just happened to be hiding out in the woods of a quiet, affluent neighborhood? Wouldn't they be of more value out patrolling downtown where there are bars and restaurants and people partying at this time of night? The only logical explanation is that our targets have the police watching out for them."

Lincoln thought it over and said, "It makes sense. So what do you want to do?"

"I want Nessa and Boyle to put on the police officer's uniforms. Dworak, the priest, and I will get into your vehicle. Stash this vehicle in the woods. When we are ready, Nessa and Boyle will pull into the driveway in the police vehicle and knock on the door. When they open the door, we strike."

Keever and Boyle quickly stripped the two police officers out of their uniforms. While they put the uniforms on, Lincoln moved the bodies of Officers Fernsby and Baker into the rear cargo area of the patrol vehicle.

Fabrizio was amazed at how quickly everything had fallen apart. *Dear God, these savages just murdered two police officers and show no sign of remorse! What have I gotten myself into?*

Lowery came up with the new plan, and in less time than Fabrizio would've believed possible, he ordered them to proceed.

They had just started moving toward their target again when Flannery's voice came over the radio. "We're in position around the bend from the dock."

"Stand by," Lowery answered. "We were delayed, but we'll be in position in five minutes. There has been a slight change in plans." He explained what had happened.

"Copy that." Even over the radio, Flannery's voice sounded strained to Fabrizio.

Sammy turned the patrol vehicle right onto Sand Point Way and turned his headlights off. Lincoln extinguished his headlights and followed close behind. The ambient light from the moon filtering through the leaves of the trees provided just enough illumination to allow Sammy to guide the patrol vehicle along the wooded roadway to the driveway of the last house before the target house. A bend in the road and a stand of trees provided more than enough cover to hide them from anyone inside.

Sammy slowly pulled the vehicle onto the shoulder of the narrow lane, allowing the vehicle to drift to a stop without touching the brakes, thus eliminating the chance of a sentry at the target location seeing his brake lights.

The moon was providing just enough light inside the vehicle for Lowery to be able to see Fabrizio. Even in the darkness, the fear the little man felt was clearly displayed on his face.

"Are you ready, *priest?*"

Fabrizio swallowed and took a deep breath, trying to will his fear away. "I'm ready." His voice cracked as he spoke, and the whites of his wide, open eyes were clearly visible. Lowery chuckled quietly at the little man's obvious terror.

"Flannery, we are in position. Bring the boat around but be alert. They may have left someone on the dock."

Before Flannery could reply, King's voice came over the radio, confirming Lowery's suspicion. "There is one guy at the very end of the dock closest to the water. From where he is, he'll hear you before you can see the dock, and you'll be in his line of sight as soon as you round the bend."

There was a brief pause, and Flannery called out, "Stand by Lowery; I have an idea. Give me five minutes before you move in."

CHAPTER FORTY-SIX

"Solomon, take the wheel."

Flannery moved aside to allow the pirate to take over control of the boat. He picked up his rifle from where it had been stowed for the boat ride across the lake and climbed over the side into the cold, thigh-deep water.

"Give me a couple minutes to work my way along the shoreline. I'm going to try to take the guy out quietly, but if you hear a gunshot, haul ass and get to the dock," Flannery said.

"Sounds good," Boyle replied.

Once Flannery was on his way, Boyle called Lowery on the radio to relay the plan.

The trees around the point came right down to the shore, and Flannery found himself wading through the frigid waters of the lake for the entire trek. By the time he reached the bend, his feet and legs were numb, and the jeans he was wearing felt like they weighed fifty pounds, making each step even more difficult. As he slowly rounded the point, moving as quietly as he could while slogging through the frigid water, the dock attached to the boathouse came into view. He stopped moving and watched the dock ahead, but he couldn't see the guard. Flannery wanted to call King on the radio to see if he still saw the guard, but he didn't want to take a chance of alerting the man if he was close enough to hear.

Flannery slowly crept closer to the dock, alternating his attention between the dock and the rock-strewn shallows. He took each step slowly, careful to avoid tripping on the uneven surface. When he was about twenty yards from the dock, he finally spotted the sentry. The man was seated in an Adirondack chair tucked back under the eaves of the boathouse. If Flannery hadn't already known the man was there, he never would have seen him. He stopped moving and watched the guard for any sign that he'd heard Flannery approaching in the water. When the guard didn't stir from his chair after almost a minute, Flannery felt confident he hadn't been detected, so he slowly started moving forward again.

When Flannery was within ten yards of the dock, he left the lake and worked his way into the narrow strip of trees that separated the large yard from the water. Careful to remain within the line of trees to avoid being seen from the house, Flannery snaked his way between the trees until he reached the last one in line. There, he found a small gravel path that led to a single step to the deck. He strained to try to see if the guard had moved, but from where he crouched, he couldn't see him. He reached back and swung the rifle around from where he had it slung down his back. Flannery brought the barrel up and slowly peaked his head out. Only twenty feet away, sat a large black man facing out toward the middle of the lake. Resting against the man's chair was a black tactical rifle. Flannery wasn't a *gun guy*, so he had no idea what type of weapon it was. All that mattered was that whatever type it was, it could kill him.

He stepped up onto the deck, keeping his rifle trained on the back of the man's head the entire time. As he inched his way toward the guard, Flannery realized how big the man was. He needed to end this guy quickly. There was no way he could match strength with a man that size.

Swinging his rifle around so that it once again hung from its sling down the middle of his back, Flannery used his right hand to draw his ten-inch tactical knife from the sheath on his belt. Flannery was three feet from the man when he stepped down softly on a loose deck board. He froze when the weakened board squeaked under his foot.

The big man began to turn in his chair. "You're early, Paine."

Flannery didn't hesitate. When Pierre Durand's eyes met his, Flannery launched himself at the much larger man. The shock of seeing the unknown subject sneaking up behind him caused Durand to freeze for less than a second, and that slight hesitation was all Flannery needed. He thrust his knife into the side of

Durand's exposed neck before the former member of the French GIGN could react to the threat. Flannery put all of his weight behind the strike, causing the sharp blade to slice into Durand's spine as it passed completely through his throat.

Flannery slammed into the bigger man, his momentum causing the chair Durand was sitting in to tip over, toppling both men into the lake. Flannery's knife had become wedged in Durand's spine and was torn from his grip as they fell. He fought to reach the surface of the water, panicking as he struggled to bring his rifle around from where it hung down his back to confront the man he had just stabbed. Water poured off his face, partially blinding him and making it difficult to see the red dot in the holographic sight mounted to his rifle. He kept the weapon pointed in front of him with his right hand while he used his left to wipe the water away from his eyes. Once he had cleared his vision, he saw the big man floating face down just feet away from him, the blade of his knife jutting upward from the man's neck toward the night sky.

The adrenaline from the life-or-death encounter he had just survived caused Flannery to suffer the phenomenon known as auditory exclusion. Flannery was so focused on the threat in front of him that he never heard the boat approaching from behind. He was standing waist-deep in the lake, trying to control his breathing, when he realized the boat carrying Solomon and Boyle was pulling quietly up to the dock.

Solomon jumped into the water and assisted Flannery in

climbing up onto the dock, while Boyle tied the boat up. The three men gathered their weapons and moved from the exposed dock into the trees lining the lake shore.

"We're at the boathouse," Flannery radioed.

CHAPTER FORTY-SEVEN

Lowery sat in the back seat of the Blazer, with Fabrizio seated next to him. The little man seemed to be in a state of shock and said nothing as events began to unfold.

"Wait until they reach the house and activate their emergency lights before you pull in," he ordered.

Lowery planned to wait until Keever and Boyle knocked on the front door of the house before he ordered the men from the boat to break cover. He didn't want them to trigger any alarms until it was too late for the defenders to react. The element of surprise, when the two fake cops began the assault from inside the safe house, should be enough to overcome the men inside and guarantee their success.

A gravel driveway ran from the roadway to the massive, dark brown house. Accent lights spaced evenly along the driveway and sidewalk to the house revealed the two-stall garage that dominated the left side of the structure. To the right of the garage was a large porch with wooden columns that reached two stories to an angled roof. A steel door with an ornate stained-glass window was surrounded by a wall of windows that reached from the porch to the eaves of the roof twenty feet overhead. Boyle activated the emergency lights as soon as he pulled into the driveway, parking the vehicle as close to the front door as possible to help obscure Lincoln's vehicle when he pulled in behind the patrol vehicle.

Keever mounted the large porch first, with Boyle staying three feet behind her and off to her left. She knocked on the door, then rang the doorbell and stepped back to see if the occupants would be foolish enough to open the door and compromise their security.

When he saw Keever knock on the front door, Lowery radioed to the rest of his men.

"Everyone move in!"

Lincoln and Dworak exited the Blazer and raced to join the bogus cops at the front door, while the three men on the dock broke from the cover of the trees and began to sprint across the lawn toward the expansive back deck.

CHAPTER FORTY-EIGHT

Things had finally settled down inside the safe house, and Christian was taking advantage of the peace and quiet to search online for a new place to keep Evy safe.

Dexter was in the small office just off the living room they had designated as the TOC, or Tactical Operations Center, dozing quietly in front of his computer monitors.

Laura was upstairs, trying to convince Evy to get some rest. Once she had confessed to sending the unauthorized message to her mother, the young girl had become nearly inconsolable. They needed Evy calm and ready to move when the time came, and that job had fallen to Laura.

Abioye and Paine were in a small den located off the main entrance foyer, trying to get a few hours of sleep so they could relieve the others. They needed to be on their A-game when Christian finally decided where they were going to take Evy.

Altman was seated in a small alcove inside the front door with a clear view of the driveway and front yard.

The first inkling Christian had that they were in trouble was when David Altman stood from his place near the front door, saying, "The cops just pulled in. What the hell is wrong with these clowns running their emergency lights? They may as well send up flares, telling everyone we're here. Morons."

Christian looked up from the computer to see strobing red lights shining through the windows of the main entrance and reflecting off the interior walls. Before he could ask Altman what was going on, Dexter came running into the room, shouting.

"We've got trouble. There are three armed men coming across the backyard from the boathouse!"

Christian heard the doorbell ring and looked past Dexter to where Altman was reaching for the doorknob.

"Don't open that—"

But it was too late. When Altman opened the door to greet the uniformed police officers on the porch, Nessa Keever shoved her Beretta through the opening and shot him twice in the face. Altman's body hadn't even hit the floor before Keever and Boyle forced their way into the house.

"Laura, get Evy out of here!" Christian yelled up the stairs.

Christian's Glock 43 had been resting on the table next to the computer when Dexter appeared in the room, shouting his warning. He grabbed the weapon just as Boyle saw him and began to swing his tactical rifle in Christian's direction. Christian didn't let the police uniform slow his response to the attack. He extended his handgun toward the threat and pulled the trigger. With Boyle only twenty feet away, Christian didn't need to use his sights. He pointed the weapon at the center of the fake cop's body and pulled the trigger three times. The first shot struck Boyle in the chest, causing the man to spin slightly to his left. Christian's next two shots hit Boyle in the neck and face, dropping him instantly.

Christian dove into the kitchen and slid behind the center island when Keever opened fire on his position. He knew the island would not stop incoming rounds for long. If he didn't move, he'd die. He low-crawled toward the edge of the island, trying to give himself a better angle to engage his attacker.

Nessa Keever pushed deeper into the room, with Lincoln and Dworak following closely behind, searching for targets. Keever stepped over Sammy Boyle's lifeless body and slowly worked her way toward the center island where she had last seen *The Viking.*

Steven Paine and Jerome Abioye had been sleeping in the den when the first shots were fired. Both men were instantly awake and reaching for their weapons without hesitation. Years of combat experience allowed them to flow from napping into full battle mode in seconds. Paine watched as a woman wearing a Lake Placid PD uniform stepped over the prone body of a man wearing the same uniform. Paine fired off a quick round from his MP7 without aiming. The 4.6 mm x 30 mm round slammed into the marble top of the island and broke off a large chunk. He may have missed the attacker, but his round served its purpose. The fake cop flinched when the round struck the island and then turned to try to locate the threat, giving Christian time to find better cover.

Paine was congratulating himself on drawing the woman's attention away from Christian when a searing pain caused his left leg to buckle, dropping him to the floor. Paine had been so intent on the woman that he'd made the rookie mistake of falling victim to tunnel vision. He'd failed to identify the two additional shooters who had followed the fake cops into the house and nearly paid for it with his life.

Seeing Paine fall, Abioye grabbed his teammate by the collar of his shirt and dragged him back into the den, just as Dworak opened fire on the downed man. Five rounds struck the spot where Paine had been just seconds before. Abioye had almost reached the far side of the room with Paine in tow when two 7.62 x 39 mm rounds fired from Dworak's AK-47 slammed into his chest, piercing his heart and killing him instantly. Paine rolled behind a large leather sofa and pressed himself as tightly to the floor as he could.

Dexter had dived back into the TOC when the shooting started to retrieve his weapon. Now he carefully peeked around the door frame and saw two men firing tactical rifles into the living room. He couldn't see what they were shooting at, but the living room was the last place he'd seen Paine and Abioye.

In his years with the FBI, the only time Dexter fired his duty weapon was at the academy and during the mandatory twice-yearly firearms qualification. Now, with his teammates' lives depending on him, he fell back on his training. As he knelt down, using the door frame as cover, he slowed his breathing and prepared to join the firefight. Dex placed the front sight of his Glock 22 on the side of the shooter closest to him and pulled the trigger. The Speer 40 caliber Smith and Wesson 180 grain Gold Dot Hollow Point round left the barrel of his weapon traveling 1025 feet per second. At the close range from which Dexter fired the round, there was no perceived time between when he pulled the trigger and when Jan Dworak's head erupted in a red mist of blood, bone, and brain matter.

Lincoln saw Dworak fall and turned to see where the shot had come from, giving Paine time to get back into the fight. The pain from the leg wound, coupled with being dazed from hitting his head when he fell, interfered with his accuracy. He fired three rounds at Lincoln. Two rounds flew harmlessly past the man, while the third grazed his arm, causing him to fall back toward the front door.

Christian used the confusion of the firefight to work his way to the bottom of the staircase. He crouched, hidden in the shadow of the wooden banister, as he tried to figure out his next move. He had to get to Evy and Laura and get them out of there, but he couldn't do that while he was pinned down on the ground floor.

Movement in the kitchen drew his attention when he saw the woman wearing the Lake Placid police uniform come into view.

He recognized Nessa Keever from the photographs Roddy Fraser had provided. Gun shots drew her attention back toward the front door, allowing Christian to quickly climb the stairs.

When he reached the second floor, he slowly approached the closed door to Evy's bedroom. He flattened himself on the floor off to the right-hand side of the door. He knew Laura would be prepared to defend Evy with her life, and he didn't want to accidentally get shot trying to get into the room.

He reached out and knocked on the door, quickly withdrawing his hand and quietly saying, "Laura, it's me, Christian." He waited a couple seconds before moving to a squatting position and knocking again. "Laura, it's me, Christian." Checking behind him to make sure no one was sneaking up the stairs, he reached for the doorknob and tried to turn it. The door was locked. "Laura, it's Christian. Open the door." He thought he heard movement from inside the room just before he heard the lock being disengaged. The door swung open a crack.

"Quick, get inside," Laura whispered. Once Christian was through the door, she quickly relocked it. "Thank God," she said, giving Christian a brief hug. "What happened?"

"I'll explain later. We have armed men inside and out. We need to get Evy out of here." Christian looked around for Evy as he spoke. Not seeing her, he asked, "Where is she?"

"I'm right here." Evy stepped from the large walk-in closet and rushed to embrace Christian. "What's happening? It's him, isn't it?"

Christian was amazed at how calm the girl was. "I honestly don't know, Evy. I saw the woman that followed us in London, so it's a safe bet Lowery is nearby. As for Fabrizio? I have no clue."

"What do you want to do?" Laura asked.

"What do we have for weapons up here?"

"I have my Glock 23 with three extra magazines with me, and there are two MP7s with three magazines in the bedroom down the hall."

"All I've got is my 43 with two spare mags," Christian said.

Christian was angry. Despite the security system Dexter had installed, they'd been taken completely off guard. Somehow, Lowery had made his way to the states undetected with a small group of mercenaries and taken them by surprise. The brazen assault on the house had almost overwhelmed them. Almost. He and Laura were still alive. Christian didn't know about the others, but he knew Dex well enough to know his best friend wasn't that easy to kill. There were still occasional shots coming from downstairs, so some of the good guys were still in the fight.

"What are we going to do?" Evy's calm façade was beginning to crumble.

"We need to get down the hall and retrieve the MP5s. Then we need to make our way down to the garage and out of here."

"What about the others?" Tears rolled down the frightened girl's cheeks.

"Evy, this is what we were paid to do. Protect you. The others will keep fighting to give us a chance to get you out of here." Laura spoke calmly as she hugged the girl. "Now put on your hiking shoes and grab your backpack. We have to move."

Christian turned off the lights in the room before crawling to the window overlooking the backyard and the lake. From where he was, he couldn't see any of the men Dexter had said were coming across from the boathouse.

"Okay, listen to me. We're going to go down the hall to the other bedroom. From there, if it's clear, we're going to climb down and get into the garage through the side door."

"I'm so sorry…" Evy began.

"Not now, Evy." Christian took the girl's face in his hands and looked her in the eyes. "What's done is done. Now we concentrate on getting you out of here. Got it?" He waited for Evy to nod her head before continuing. "You need to do what we tell you and move fast if you want to get out of this. Do you understand?" Again, he waited for Evy to acknowledge what he said. "Good. Now get ready to go. I'm going to check the hallway and make sure it's clear to move."

Christian walked softly to the door, trying to muffle his footsteps from the hostile force on the ground floor. He unlocked the door and slowly turned the doorknob, then pushed the door open just enough to see the top of the staircase.

"It looks clear. Laura, take Evy down to the other room. I'll bring up the rear."

Laura led Evy out into the empty hallway and hurried her off to the right. Christian stepped out behind the two women and was just preparing to follow them when he heard footsteps coming up the stairs.

CHAPTER FORTY-NINE

Lincoln leaned against the wall just inside the front door. The bullet that grazed his right arm hadn't done much damage, but it was painful just the same. From where he stood, he could see Keever using the island in the kitchen for cover as she tried to get a shot at whoever was still alive and firing from the den. Until they neutralized that gunman, they couldn't move on to search for the girl or the guy Lowery wanted dead.

A noise behind Lincoln caused him to turn toward the front door to engage whoever was coming up behind.

"Hold your fire. I'm coming in."

Lincoln immediately recognized Lowery's rough Irish brogue and shifted his aim away from the door. Lowery carefully entered the house, holding a Bushmaster AR 15 across his chest. The rifle was fitted with an Aimpoint Carbine Optic Red Dot Reflex sight. There was a thirty-round magazine of AAC 300 Blackout 125 grain FMJ ammunition firmly seated in the magazine well of the rifle, and Lowery had an addition of three thirty-round magazines stuffed in the pockets of his tactical pants.

"Hug the wall. There's at least one shooter left alive on this floor."

Lowery acknowledged the warning with a nod before calling out to Keever. "Nessa, what do you have?"

From where she crouched down behind the kitchen island, Keever replied, "One shooter is in the front room. He's wounded, but he's alive and alert."

"And the man who killed Callum?"

"He was in the dining room when I came in, but he took off when we started shooting. I haven't seen the girl yet."

"I want Callum's killer, Nessa. The girl doesn't matter until he's dead."

Keever shook her head in frustration. Even dead, that worthless wanker was still causing problems. "I understand, Padraig."

"We have to hurry, Nessa. Someone has probably already called the police because of the gunfire."

Brandon Flannery and the men from the boat had just reached the back deck when the shooting started. He led them up the stairs to the huge deck, but, unable to determine who was shooting inside, they were forced to take cover and wait. Now that the shooting had stopped, he took his radio from where it was secured in a pouch on the load-bearing vest he wore and keyed the microphone.

"This is Flannery. We're at the back door."

"Come inside but stay low. There's a shooter in the room directly across from the back door."

When Flannery tried to open the door, it was locked. He nodded at Solomon, and the wiry pirate picked up one of the Adirondack chairs from the deck. Then, with strength belied by his wiry size, he launched it through the glass of the French doors.

The three men entered the house through the shattered doorway and were moving to take cover when Keever saw Paine pop into view, taking aim at the newcomers with his rifle. She was bringing her weapon up when a shot rang out, and Solomon fell to the floor with a perfectly round hole dotting his bald forehead and his blood rapidly spreading out around him.

Flannery and Boyle scrambled to find cover as Keever fired round after round into the den, forcing Paine to retreat behind cover once again.

Nate Boyle had dived into the kitchen to avoid Paine's gunfire. He rolled behind the center island and aimed back into the entryway. As he swept his rifle sights across the room, looking for a threat, he spotted his fallen brother. Sammy had fallen facedown with his head turned toward the kitchen when Christian shot him. Nate found himself staring into the lifeless, unseeing eyes of his baby brother. A piercing, inarticulate scream rose from the stricken man as he sought to release the anguish he felt. Tears streamed down his face as he silently vowed vengeance.

The sound of a door closing drew Nate's attention to the stairway off to his right. It had come from the top of the stairs. He didn't bother telling the others; he just started up the stairs on his own. No one—not even the Irishman or his crazy bitch—was going to stop him from getting revenge for his murdered brother.

Lowery had been in too many gun battles to remember, and he immediately took control of the turmoil around him.

"We don't have much time. We need to kill the scum who murdered Callum and find the girl. Nessa, where is the shooter?"

"He's in the room on your right. He's off to the left, behind some furniture. I can't get an angle without exposing myself."

Lowery moved to the right side of the entrance into the small room and leaned against the wall. He grabbed Lincoln by his wounded arm and pulled him close.

"When I tell you to, I want you to run across the room toward that doorway on the far side. Don't look around, and don't hesitate. Nessa will take out the shooter when he reveals himself."

Lincoln winced in pain as he yanked his arm away from the man. "You must be insane! You want to use me as bait? Fuck that. I'm out of here."

Lowery pushed the younger man against the wall and placed the barrel of his rifle against the startled man's chest. "You will run across the room as I told you to, or you will die right here. The choice is yours."

Lincoln stared into the Lowery's eyes and knew the man wasn't bluffing. "Okay! Okay! Jesus Christ, put the gun down!"

Lowery never took the weapon or his eyes off Lincoln as he gestured to Keever. The two had worked together long enough for the woman to understand what Lowery wanted without him calling out and revealing his plans to the man hidden in the room. He was going to send Lincoln across the entrance to the room to hopefully entice the shooter to expose himself to take a shot. If the man left his cover, Nessa would be ready to take him out.

"Get ready to run in three…two…one… Go!"

When Lowery said "go," he shoved Lincoln out into the open. The scared man didn't need any further coaxing to move. He took two steps when a shot rang out to his right. Lincoln flinched and continued to run, waiting for the searing pain from the bullet that never came.

Paine was peeking out around the huge leather sofa he'd taken refuge behind just as a man flashed across the entrance to the room. He rolled out slightly and took a quick shot that went wide of its mark. As he tried to scoot back behind the sofa, he was struck by two rounds. The first round entered his right shoulder, destroying the joint completely. The second round struck his right side, passing completely through his body. The energy transferred into his body when the rounds struck and knocked him unconscious.

A loud shout full of pain informed Keever that she'd hit her mark. She dove back behind the cover and replaced the almost-spent magazine in her weapon with a full one before leaning back out just far enough to peer into the den. From where she knelt, she could see Paine's motionless form lying partially hidden behind the big sofa.

"He's down!" she yelled out.

"Good. Now find them. Kill the man and bring the girl to me."

Keever moved across the room, picking up Dworak's fallen AK 47 and two spare magazines before joining Lincoln, where he stood pressing his back against the wall just outside of the room she'd seen the Asian guy duck into after shooting Dworak.

"When I say go, we enter the room. You go left, and I'll wrap around to the right."

Lincoln knew better than to argue. He just nodded his head and began praying for God to get him out of this madness alive.

Keever gave Lincoln a shove and shouted, "GO!"

They entered the room, sweeping their weapons back and forth as they each emptied a magazine into the walls and furniture. Dexter's computer was reduced to a pile of smoldering electronics when the shooting stopped. A search of the room came up empty, but Keever found an open window leading to the backyard.

"He's gone!" she shouted to Lowery.

"Never mind him. Get out here so we can clear the rest of

the house."

The small group reassembled in the living room, waiting for Lowery's instructions. When Lowery realized they were missing a man, he glared at Flannery and said, "Where's Boyle?"

"The last time I saw him, he was heading up the stairs."

Lowery was angry, but he realized there was nothing he could do about it. They didn't have long before the police began to swarm the area, and they needed to be gone before they arrived.

"Search the house quickly. We don't have much time."

CHAPTER FIFTY

Christian quickly crossed the hall and hid behind a large, mounted black bear standing on its hind legs. He waited silently as a man slowly appeared, sneaking quietly up the staircase. When the man reached the second floor, Christian saw that he wore a look of barely restrained rage on his face and clutched an M4-style tactical rifle in his hands. He stood at the top of the stairs, looking down the hallway that Laura and Evy had just run down, before stepping up to the closed bedroom door. Christian had to take this guy out as quietly as possible. He didn't want the man firing his weapon and drawing the attention of his buddy downstairs.

With the man's attention focused on the bedroom door, Christian began to step out from behind the bear mount. He inched closer to the man, and when he raised his foot to kick the bedroom door, Christian saw his chance and pounced.

Something seemed to alert the man to the danger behind him

because as Christian pounced, the man ducked low and swung his rifle around. Christian was able to grab the rifle's handguard and deflect the barrel of the weapon down and away from him before the man pulled the trigger, sending a .556 round sizzling out the barrel of the rifle, where it plowed a shallow groove in Christian's right hip before ending its short journey in the leg of the stuffed bear. Christian realized that if he lost control of his hold on the rifle, he was as good as dead. Rather than draw away from the weapon as instinct dictated, Christian stepped into his attacker, pinning the rifle between them with the barrel pointing toward the ceiling.

Boyle pulled his head back, and Christian realized he was about to be on the receiving end of a headbutt. As Boyle's head shot forward, Christian turned his face to the right and raised his left shoulder, partially deflecting the blow. Boyle's forehead skipped painfully off Christian's left shoulder and into his cheek. The blow was painful, but it failed to incapacitate him. Boyle didn't wait to see the result of his strike. He shoved Christian back far enough to gain the leverage to turn his right hip into Christian's pelvis and, using the rifle as a fulcrum, threw him over his hip. When Christian hit the floor, Boyle was able to tear the weapon from his grip. Before he could bring the rifle around, Christian rotated to his right hip and whipped his left leg around in a desperate round kick.

Boyle staggered as he completed the hip toss and was just regaining his balance when Chrisian's round kick tore the rifle from his grip and sent it sailing back down the staircase. Boyle stepped back and drew a Cold Steel combat knife from a sheath attached to his belt. He let out a frustrated scream as he moved toward Christian.

Christian allowed the momentum of his round kick to carry him around and away from Boyle. He planted his hands on the floor and pushed himself to his feet, only to stagger to his right due to the pain from the gunshot wound. Boyle took advantage of his adversary's misstep by closing in and swiping his blade horizontally toward Christian's midsection.

Christian had studied knife fighting as part of his martial arts training. He'd also taken lessons from a SOG buddy in the Marshals Service who was a master instructor. The one thing that had always been hammered home during his training was one simple truth. If you're in a knife fight, you're going to get cut. The trick was to minimize the damage so you could stay in the fight.

With no time to avoid Boyle's sweeping attack, Christian raised his left arm, his palm toward his own face, and blocked the blade with the outside of his forearm as it passed by. The blade cut deep into Christian's arm. The cut stung like hell, but it was better than having his guts spill out onto the hardwood floor.

Seeing the bloody trail the strike had left on Christian's arm seemed to embolden Boyle, and he stepped in for a backhand swipe. Christian stepped into the attack, using his right hand to painfully block Boyle's elbow while delivering a left palm strike to the man's face. Boyle rotated his head as he moved to his right, mitigating the effectiveness of the strike, and countered by driving his blade directly at Christian's midsection. Christian turned his body slightly to the left, trapping Boyle's right wrist with his right hand as the blade passed harmlessly by his body. The force of the strike caused Boyle to stagger forward, allowing Christian to tighten his one-handed grip on the man's wrist and pull the man further off balance. When Boyle attempted to pull his arm back, Christian stepped forward and used his left forearm to deliver a hammer strike to Boyle's elbow. The blow ruptured tendons and ligaments in the overextended joint and allowed Christian to use his right hand to bend the weapon back toward the man. With his elbow destroyed and his momentum working against him, Boyle could do nothing to prevent Christian from driving the blade deep into his body just below his right collarbone. Christian released his grip on Boyle's wrist and drove a right-hand palm strike to the back of the hilt, driving the knife deeper.

The pain was unimaginable, and Boyle began to sag when Christian stepped in close, wrapping his right arm under the stricken man's left armpit and swiveling his hips around to draw Boyle across his body into a Harai Goshi judo throw. Boyle sailed over Christian's right hip back down the stairs he had just climbed up. He crashed violently into the banister on the landing below and lay in a broken and bloody heap.

Christian fell to his knees as he completed the judo throw. He placed his hands on the ground in front of him and gasped for air. Blood flowed freely from the knife wound on his left forearm, and the bullet wound to his right hip throbbed. He looked down the staircase to where his unmoving opponent lay. Christian knew he had to move. The shooting had stopped, and he could hear people talking on the first floor. It would only be a matter of minutes before they regrouped and followed their fallen comrade up to the second floor. He had to reach Evy and Laura and get them out of the house.

As Christian struggled to gather himself, he felt something vibrating on his left hip. It took him a couple of seconds to realize it was his cell phone.

He grabbed the phone and saw that it was Dexter. "Dex, are you okay? Where are you?"

"I'm fine. I slipped out a window in the TOC. I'm working my way around the back side of the house right now. Where are you?"

"Second floor. Laura and Evy are in the back bedroom waiting for me. We need a way out of here, Dex."

"I think I have one. Listen. Whoever these guys are, they're not trained very well. They're all inside right now. They didn't leave anyone outside to cover the perimeter. I'm at the southeast corner of the house, and there's no one in the backyard. Can you get out a window on the north side of the house?"

Christian had begun to move down the hall as he said, "We can."

"Good. I'm going to work my way down to the boathouse. You and Laura take Evy out the north side of the house and into the woods. Get down to the water, and I'll swing the boat around and pick you up."

Christian disconnected the call and, moving as fast as his wounds would allow, headed for the back bedroom. When he got to the room, the door was closed and locked. Once again, he laid prone on the floor and knocked.

"Laura," he called softly.

The door cracked open. "Get in here. Quick." As soon as Christian was through the door, Laura resecured it.

Christian walked over to where Evy sat on the king-sized bed. The young girl's head was down, and her brown hair fell across her face. Christian gently lifted her chin, looking into her tear-stained eyes.

"Are you okay?"

Evy nodded and leaned against him. He could feel her sob. "All my fault," she whispered.

"Never mind us. What the hell happened to you?" Laura asked as she took in Christian's bloody hip and arm.

"No time. We have to go." He crossed to the window on the north side of the bedroom. Being careful not to disturb the curtain, he peeked outside.

Laura grabbed Christian's left arm and turned it over to examine the cut. "We aren't going anywhere until I get this bleeding stopped. You won't make it another hundred yards before you pass out from blood loss." She let his arm go and moved to his hip wound. "Christ. Evy, grab me two of those pillowcases."

"We don't have time for this, Laura. They'll be up here any second, and we have to be gone."

"As soon as I stop the bleeding."

Christian knew arguing with her would just prolong things and waste time they didn't have. "Fine but make it fast. Dexter is going to wait for us."

"What about the others?" Evy asked as she handed the pillowcases to Laura.

"I'm not sure, Evy. I saw Abioye and Altman go down. Paine was wounded but still fighting."

"We can't leave them."

"We have to, Evy. You're what matters. Paine and the others would agree. It's what we do."

"He's right, Evy. We have to get you out of here."

When Laura finished putting the pressure bandage on Christian's arm, she said, "I can't do much with the hip. It's a deep gouge, but at least it isn't bleeding too much."

"That's fine. Grab the weapons. We have to go." He moved to the window again and checked outside. Still no sign of anyone.

"From the sound of things, they're coming up the stairs," Laura reported.

Christian opened the window and pulled the screen into the room. He took a quick peek around one more time before motioning for Evy and Laura to join him.

"Evy, Laura is going to go out first. I'll lower you down as far as I can, and Laura will help guide you to the ground."

"I'll be fine. I did a lot of my own stunt work during the filming. I can make it by myself."

Christian looked into the girl's eyes and saw the fear he expected, but he also saw something else. He saw determination.

"Fine. Laura will still go first. You can hang down and drop. It isn't that far. As soon as you are both on the ground, move into the trees. I'll be right behind you."

"What's the plan, Christian?"

"Dexter is working his way to the boathouse. We're going to make our way to the shoreline north of here, and he's going to pick us up."

"And then?"

"One thing at a time. Out of the house first. Once we make it to the boat, we can decide what to do next."

"What about calling the police chief?"

"Two of the people who attacked the house are wearing police uniforms. I'm not taking any chances. Now let's get out of here."

CHAPTER FIFTY-ONE

"Don't you fecking move, *priest*," had been Lowery's last warning before disappearing into the house to join the gun battle raging inside.

Well, fuck you, Fabrizio thought. *I'm not sitting here and waiting to get shot or arrested!*

Fabrizio took his cell phone from where he had it hidden in his waistband and called King. When the smuggler answered, he said, "It's time, Jimmy. Meet me like we planned."

Once the man confirmed where they were to meet, Fabrizio hung up the phone. He knew that if either Lowery or that crazy bitch, Keever, spotted him trying to leave, he was a dead man, but he didn't care. He had to chance it. He briefly thought about how close he was to having the Cota girl. He looked at the house before him and realized this was as close as he'd ever been to her. It didn't matter, though. If he stayed, he'd either be shot dead or arrested. Lowery and his band of killers had murdered two police officers. There'd be nothing anyone—not even his mega-rich, mega-powerful father—could do to save him at that point. No, it would be far better if he made his way to the political safety his father could provide. He would find another way to get to the girl. He had money, and he had time. As long as he could make it out of his current situation, he was confident he'd find a way. The girl would pay. He'd see to it.

Sliding behind the wheel, Fabrizio shifted the vehicle into reverse and slowly backed out of the driveway. He kept the headlights off until he was around the curve on Roland Way and out of sight of the house. As he drove along Peninsula Way, he noticed there were lights on in far more homes than when they'd passed by on their way in. The gun battle appeared to have woken the entire neighborhood. Fabrizio sped up. He had to reach the main road before the police swarmed into the area, cutting off his only avenue of escape.

He reached Route 86/Saranac Avenue without incident and turned west toward Saranac Lake, praying that Jimmy King kept his end of the bargain.

CHAPTER FIFTY-TWO

Dexter crouched silently in the shrubbery outside the window on the south side of the house. He had seen both Altman and Abioye fall. He had no idea what had happened to Steven Paine, but the attackers had kept shooting, so the former Delta Force man must have been giving them hell. He hated leaving anyone behind, but their mission was simple. Keep Evy safe. He couldn't help Christian do that if he was dead.

The gunfire inside the house suddenly stopped. Dexter figured Paine was either dead or wounded so badly he couldn't continue to fight. Dexter had to hurry. Christian should already have the women out of the house and moving toward the shoreline, but he still had to make it to the boathouse, get the boat started, and back out into the lake without drawing the attention of the men inside.

Thick landscaping ran all the way to the back corner of the

house, and Dexter used it for cover as he crawled to a spot where he could see most of the backyard. He scanned the open expanse, looking for anyone who'd been left behind to cut off any attempts to flee to the boat. When he didn't see anyone, he quickly dashed to a stand of pine trees surrounding an outdoor fire pit. He waited, hidden among the pines, to see if he'd been observed. After thirty seconds of silence, he moved across the lawn into the trees that lined the shore, then silently worked his way to the boathouse and climbed up onto the deck. He paused at the door to listen for anyone hidden inside. Once he was reasonably certain there was no one waiting in the boathouse, he opened the door and slipped in. The moonlight shining through the open overhead door facing the lake provided just enough light for Dexter to see. The pontoon boat rocked gently where it sat, tied off to the slip. He climbed aboard and set about getting ready to launch. He untied the lines at the bow and stern before starting the engine. Dr. Matas had maintained the boat well, and it started without an issue. Dexter slowly backed the boat away from the dock and into the lake. As the bow cleared the boathouse, Dexter saw a body floating partially submerged near the exposed dock. Dexter turned the boat and started along the shoreline without a backward glance at Durand's body. There'd be time to mourn later.

A cold wind had picked up, bringing with it a heavy cloud cover. What little moonlight there was reflected off whitecaps on the agitated lake.

Dexter was about fifty yards from the boathouse when he saw Christian wading out into the lake to flag him down. Laura followed closely behind Christian, carefully leading Evy out of the trees and into the water as Dexter angled the boat toward the shore.

"Good job, Dex," Christian said as he hauled himself up onto the swim platform at the stern of the pontoon boat.

Once aboard, he and Dexter reached down and pulled Evy and Laura aboard. Laura led Evy to one of the padded leather seats and wrapped a towel around her.

"What's the plan?" Dexter asked as he moved over, allowing Christian to take the helm.

"I'm not sure yet. For now, just head for the marina."

CHAPTER FIFTY-THREE

Lowery stood silently in the kitchen, waiting for Lincoln and Flannery to finish clearing the second floor. Keever positioned herself so that she could cover both the downstairs area as well as the staircase to the second floor. From where she kneeled, she could see Nate Boyle's broken body lying motionless on the first landing. Keever stole an occasional glance at Lowery, and she didn't like what she saw. She'd worked for Lowery for years, and they'd been involved in several serious encounters, but she'd never seen him lose his temper or make a bad decision. Tonight was different. They'd killed two coppers and at least three of the men protecting the Cota girl, but they still didn't have her, and they hadn't been able to kill the man who had murdered Callum. For the first time since she'd met the man, Lowery seemed to be on the verge of losing control.

Lowery's face was a mask of rage and hatred unlike anything

Keever had ever seen before, and it frightened her. They needed to leave. The police would be here anytime, and they'd be trapped on this damn peninsula with nowhere to run.

"Nessa, go get the priest." Lowery's voice shook with the barely- contained rage that was boiling inside of him. "We need to get to the boat and get out of here before the authorities arrive."

"Yes, Padraig."

"The second floor is clear," Flannery said as he and Lincoln came back down the stairs. "There's no sign of the girl or the man."

"They've escaped." Lowery fought to control his anger. He could not let his emotions run wild right now. He had to keep a clear head. He had to get away before it was too late.

Lowery's thoughts were interrupted by Keever when she came storming back through the front door.

"The fecking *priest* is gone, Padraig!"

Flannery was the first to respond, "What do you mean gone?"

"Gone, you fecking twat. He took the vehicle and ran away."

"Enough." Lowery's order was all the more terrifying due to his complete lack of emotion when he spoke. "The priest can wait. Right now, we need to get to the boat and head for the marina. The police will be swarming the entire area soon. I don't plan to be trapped here."

"But, Padraig, what about the *priest*?" Keever's hatred for the little man radiated from her.

"Another day, Nessa. We will find him and kill him, but not now. Right now, we need to get out of here."

Keever screamed in rage as she unloaded a full magazine from the AK-47 up the stairs and into the ceiling. When the bolt locked back on the empty magazine, Keever stood panting, trying to regain control.

Lowery took Flannery by the arm and pulled him close. "Let's go. Get us to the boat." When Flannery hesitated, Lowery shoved him toward the glass door Solomon had destroyed on the way in. "NOW!"

Flannery went out into the darkness first, with Lincoln following close behind.

Lowery grabbed Keever by both arms and shook the angry woman. "Get your head back in the game, Nessa. We have to run." He pushed her through the shattered door and onto the deck.

Flannery led the group through the trees lining the property and across the lawn to the dock on the far side of the boathouse. Once everyone was aboard, Lincoln untied the boat while Flannery started the engine and pushed the boat away from the dock. As soon as the boat cleared the dock, he turned south toward the marina.

They'd been traveling across the lake with their running lights off for about five minutes when Flannery thought he could make out the white-capped wake of a boat traveling about a half mile ahead of them.

"I think there's a boat ahead of us."

"Where?" asked Lowery.

Flannery pointed where he could just make out what he believed to be a boat's wake.

"Is it them?"

"I can't tell, but they're running lights are off, and they're going too fast to be trolling for fish."

"Can we catch them?"

"Not before they reach the marina, but we won't be far behind them by the time they dock."

Keever started to raise her rifle to her shoulder, but Lowery reached over and pushed the weapon back down.

"They're too far away, Nessa. All you'll do is warn them if you start shooting now."

Keever lowered the weapon and sank back into her seat, her eyes like laser beams locked on the barely visible wake of the boat in the distance.

Flannery pointed his bow at the stern rail of the fleeing boat and pushed the throttle wide open. Though they were slowly closing the distance on their prey, the lights of the marina were drawing closer every second, and it became apparent to everyone aboard that Flannery had been correct. They wouldn't overtake the boat before it reached the docks.

Five minutes later, Flannery looked at Nessa and shouted, "We may be close enough now for you to take a shot!"

The crazed look that crossed the woman's face as she moved

to the bow sent chills down Flannery's spine. He'd never encountered anyone as evil as Nessa Keever.

Keever sat in the open bow, struggling against the violent movement of the boat to aim at her target. She finally gave up obtaining the proper sight picture and simply started firing round after round at the fleeing boat ahead.

CHAPTER FIFTY-FOUR

"Shit."

When Dexter said that, Laura looked up from where she was seated next to Evy, trying to keep the girl calm, and asked, "What is it?"

"It looks like we've got company. There's a boat about a quarter of a mile back, and they're closing in on us."

"Is it them?" Evy asked.

"Hard to tell in the dark, but whoever it is, they don't have their running lights on."

Christian looked back from where he sat driving the boat and could just make out a boat trailing them across the night-shrouded lake. He did a quick calculation in his head and said, "We'll reach the marina ahead of them, but not by much."

Dexter kept calling out the distance between the boats as Christian concentrated on finding the best place to land their boat to give them the most time to reach the Jeep and exit the parking lot unseen.

Suddenly, muzzle flashes erupted from the boat.

"Laura, get Evy down! They're shooting at us!"

Dexter picked up the Daniel Defense MK18 rifle from where he'd stowed it when they came aboard and moved to the switchback lounge at the rear of the boat. He sat down and raised the rifle to his shoulder. The MK18 was not designed to be a sniper rifle. Its 10.3-inch barrel and 5.56mm ammunition made it an excellent weapon for mid- to close-range combat applications. Since the bouncing of the boat made for a horrible shooting platform, Dexter didn't even bother switching on the EOTECH holographic red dot sight mounted to the top of his weapon. He knew his best chance of hitting the vessel chasing them was if he used the good ole 'spray and pray' method.

"Here goes nothing," he said as he squeezed the trigger, sending a three-round burst of Hornady 68-grain BTHP ammunition traveling at 2960 feet per second flying across the dark lake at their pursuers.

The darkness surrounding them, coupled with the bouncing of the boat as it traveled at top speed across the lake, made it impossible to determine if he hit anything. Dexter just kept sending three-round bursts in the direction of the trailing boat and hoped for the best. He was further hampered by the fact that he needed to aim low to avoid any errant rounds traveling the relatively short distance to the far shoreline and accidentally striking someone in one of the lakefront homes.

They were quickly approaching the marina, and Christian had to make up his mind about where he was going to dock the boat. He knew their pursuers would only be minutes behind them, so he had to maximize the time they had to get to the Jeep. He remembered seeing a space of open water along the west side of the covered docks when they'd boarded the boat earlier. The open space led to a grassy slope between the parking lot and the Lake Placid boat tours building. Christian knew it would be tight, but he thought that would give them the best chance of reaching their vehicle in time to escape the parking lot.

They were approaching the docks at high speed, and Christian could just make out the small opening separating the westernmost dock from the building next to it. They were coming in too fast, and Christian struggled to keep the pontoon boat lined up with the small opening between the dock on the left and the building on the right. The slightest miscalculation in either direction would end in disaster. Christian waited until the bow of the boat had entered the narrow space before he threw the engine into reverse to try to slow down before they hit the grass-covered slope ahead.

When the boat made contact with solid land, it came to a complete stop, throwing everyone aboard violently forward. Christan's already-wounded hip slammed painfully into the control console, spinning him around and onto the deck. Though dazed and in pain, he didn't stay down for long. Once he'd pulled himself back to his feet, he rushed to help the others recover from the rough landing.

Laura had used her body to cushion Evy as much as possible. She was thrown into the seat back in front of her and now lay semi-conscious on the deck. Evy had escaped the radical maneuver unharmed and quickly moved to help Laura.

Dexter had been tossed over the side of the boat on impact, landing half in and half out of the water. Years of martial arts training had kicked in, and Dexter rolled as he landed, helping to bleed off the momentum of the collision and saving him from serious injury. He came to rest, sitting up, facing back toward the lake. He could see the collapsible stock of his rifle sticking out of the soft sediment of the lake bed, and he crawled over to recover the weapon.

Christian quickly checked Evy over for any possible injuries. When he was satisfied that she was unharmed, he turned to check on Laura.

"Hands off, big boy. You're not using this sad excuse to cop a feel." Laura pushed Christian's hands away and tried to stand on her own. When she stumbled, Evy and Christian each grabbed one of her arms and pulled her upright.

"Get her to shore, Evy." Christian looked around and finally spotted Dexter crawling back into the lake to retrieve his rifle. "You okay?" he called out.

Dexter looked up and, not having the energy to answer, just gave his friend a thumbs up.

Christian quickly gathered their weapons and leaped over the side of the boat. He helped Dexter get to the parking lot, where he found Evy looking scared but determined as she used her left arm to support Laura.

"Are you alright?" he asked Knight.

"I'm fine. Just got the wind knocked out of me. Maybe a few bruised ribs, but I'll live. Let's get moving before they get here."

The sound of their pursuer's boat caused them all to look back toward the water. The lake was still too dark to see the boat clearly, but the white caps formed by its wake were easily visible.

"Dex, get everyone to the Jeep. I'll slow them down."

Christian grabbed his MP7 from the ground next to him and climbed up onto the covered dock. As he ran along the dock, he used his tactical knife to cut the mooring lines of each docked boat as he passed by. He pushed several boats away from their slips on each side, causing a log jam of boats to drift out into the lake, slowing their attackers down.

When Christian reached the end, he sent thirty rounds of 4.6 mm x 30 ammunition screaming toward the rapidly approaching boat.

By the time his magazine ran dry, the boat had moved close enough to the shore for Christian to be able to make out its outline. He watched the boat veer off to his right to avoid taking any further fire as he stripped the spent magazine from his weapon and replaced it with a full one. He sprinted back along the dock, once again taking the time to shove several of the boats he'd previously cut free out into the lake.

Dexter was just pulling the Jeep up to the edge of the dock when Christian reached the parking lot. He quickly got in the passenger's side and said, "I bought us a little bit of time, but not much."

"Where are we going?"

"I'm working on that."

CHAPTER FIFTY-FIVE

"Get down!" Flannery yelled when he saw muzzle flashes coming from the boat up ahead.

He no sooner sounded the warning when a round shattered the windscreen in front of him, causing pieces of plexiglass to carve several bloody furrows into his face. Flannery began to turn the wheel, weaving the boat back and forth to throw off the shooter's aim.

"Easy, Brandon," Lincoln warned. "At this speed, you'll flip the boat and kill us all."

Flannery didn't waste time replying. He was too busy concentrating on not getting shot or dumped into the lake.

"If they don't slow down, they're going to do our job for us," Flannery said as he watched the boat they were chasing approach the marina at high speed. He stared in disbelief as the boat turned to the right of the docks and continued up onto the shore without slowing.

"What just happened?" Lowery asked, still crouched in his seat to avoid any further gunfire.

"The crazy bastard just grounded the boat next to the dock."

Flannery began to slow down as they got closer.

"What are you doing?" Lowery asked as he moved up next to the helm. "Speed up. I want to catch them before they have a chance to get to a vehicle."

"I'm trying not to wreck us the way they did."

Lowery pulled his handgun and aimed it at Flannery's head. "Follow them. Ram their boat if you need to."

Flannery began to push the throttle forward when he saw boats along the dock begin to float away from their slips. He again slowed the boat, this time to try to find a safe way to approach the grounded boat without hitting the boats moving slowly into his path. He was still thirty yards from the dock when gunfire rang out and bullets began to impact the boat around him. He spun the wheel to the left and pushed the throttle to its stop. The radical move threw Lowery to the deck as Flannery brought the boat hard to port, placing the second dock full of moored boats between his craft and the gunfire.

"There's a boat launch on the far side of the marina. I'm going to put us in there." Flannery sank down between his seat and the control console, keeping as low as possible while still being able to see where he was going.

Lowery turned to the others on the boat, his face twisted into a hideous mask of rage. "Grab your weapons," he ordered. "As soon as we touch land, I want everyone ashore to stop these bastards before they get out of the parking lot."

CHAPTER FIFTY-SIX

Christian turned in his seat to check on Laura as Dexter sped toward the marina exit.

"How is she?" he asked Evy.

"I'm fine. Stop worrying about me and get us out of here." Laura had a small cut above her hairline, and blood covered her face. Her eyes looked clear, though, and she was sitting up straight.

Christian laughed despite the seriousness of the situation. "I forgot how hardheaded you are." He turned to Evy next and said, "How about you? You okay?"

"I'm fine. Just a few bumps and bruises. I've had worse training for the show."

Christian was impressed. There was no longer any fear on the young woman's face. Now her eyes were bright with anger, and her jaw was set in dogged determination.

"We'll get you out of this, I promise."

"I know you will." There was no doubt in Evy's voice, just complete trust, and it brought another small smile to Christian's battered face.

"What?" she asked when she caught his smile.

"Two hardheads. I'm not sure I can handle that."

Dexter slowed as they reached the marina exit. "Where to?"

"Turn left and go around the lake. I don't want to drag this through downtown. He turned to Laura again and said, "Call Valentine and put him on speaker. I'll bring everyone up to speed at once."

Valentine answered on the first ring. "What the hell happened? Is everyone okay? I just got off the phone with Chief Nilsen. He says it's like a war zone out there, and he's lost contact with the two officers he sent out to keep an eye on the safe house."

Christian cut him off. "Listen to me, Arthur. We don't have time to play twenty questions."

Christian explained everything that had taken place from the time they reached the safe house after dinner. Laura had been upstairs trying to comfort Evy down when the attack began, so, like Valentine, the women were hearing much of it for the first time.

"Jesus Christ," he whispered as he tried to absorb what Christian had just told him. "Have you called Chief Nilsen since the attack?"

"No. We've been a little busy trying to stay alive. They used two people wearing police uniforms to breach our security, Arthur. I'm not taking any chances."

"I get it. I'll call him when we hang up. What's your plan?"

"There's no sense going to the police station. Every cop in the region is going to be responding to the house. Can you arrange a charter flight to meet us in Albany so we can get Evy out of here?"

"That won't be a problem. I'll send Abby and Simon in. They can get you to D.C., and we can figure out where to go from there." There was a brief pause, and Christian could hear Valentine giving orders to someone in the background. "Abby says she'll be in Albany in two hours."

"That works. It's going to take us around two and a half hours to get there from here."

"What about the ones that followed you in the boat? Do you want me to call the state police?"

"Yes. Give them information about the boat at the marina. Maybe they'll get lucky and nail them trying to steal a vehicle, but don't tell them about us. They're going to want to take everyone involved into custody while they figure out what happened at the house. I'd prefer to get Evy out of here just in case Lowery or Fabrizio slip through the cracks again."

"Done. I'll let you know as soon as Abby is wheeled up. Stay safe."

CHAPTER FIFTY-SEVEN

Flannery stayed low behind the controls as he maneuvered the boat around the docks and away from the gunfire.

Up ahead, a single streetlight bathed the boat launch in a weak yellow light. Aiming the bow for the center of the launch, Flannery slowed the boat just enough to avoid scattering his passengers when they made contact.

"Hang on," he warned, as the chin of the boat ground into the concrete ramp. Flannery cut the engine as the boat came to rest, listing to port.

"Grab your weapons and get moving," Lowery exhorted his people.

Keever was the first one over the side. She was checking her weapons when the sound of an engine drew her attention toward the roadway. She looked up just in time to see a green Jeep Grand Cherokee drive past, heading toward the exit.

"That's them!" She pointed at the Jeep as she yelled to

Lowery. "It's the same vehicle they were in on Main Street."

Lowery grabbed Flannery and spun him around by the arm. "Where's the damn vehicle?"

Flannery pulled his arm out of Lowery's grasp and pointed toward the marina offices, saying, "On the other side of the building, in the main lot."

"Quick, let's go!" Moving faster than a man his age had any right to, Lowery sprinted to keep up with Flannery as he raced for the vehicle.

They were halfway across the parking lot when the clouds opened up and heavy rain began to fall. When they reached the GMC, Flannery retrieved the keys from where he'd hidden them on the driver's side rear tire and got behind the wheel. He started the engine as Lowery settled into the passenger's seat. Once Lincoln and Keever jumped into the back seat, Flannery put the big SUV in gear and headed for the marina exit.

"Which way?" Flannery asked when he reached the exit.

"Left," Keever said.

"Are you sure?" Lowery knew if they went the wrong way, it was over. They wouldn't have time to turn around and try the other direction. By now, every cop within fifty miles would be flooding the area, and Lowery knew they'd be lucky to make it out of town without being stopped.

"I saw their taillights go left when we were running across the lot." Nessa looked Lowery in the eyes. "Trust me, Padraig. They went left."

Lowery nodded his head and said, "Go left, Flannery. Catch those bastards."

The heavy rain had begun to pool on the surface of the road, and the big SUV fishtailed as Flannery pressed hard on the accelerator, causing the rear tires to lose traction.

"Be careful, you shite!" Keever yelled from her place behind Flannery.

Flannery quickly regained control of the vehicle and took off after the fleeing Jeep.

Lowery tried to call Jimmy King as soon as they were in the vehicle, but the smuggler wasn't answering his cell phone.

"Where is that fecking idiot?" he muttered out loud.

"Who, Padraig?" Keever asked.

"King. He's not answering his phone. He was watching the house from this side of the damn lake. I want him here to help take the vehicle down."

They had just rounded a curve in the road and were passing Reservoir Road when Flannery interrupted Lowery.

"I think that's them."

Lowery forgot about King for the moment as he looked out the rain-covered windshield to see the taillights of a vehicle about a quarter mile ahead of them.

"Speed up and catch them!"

Flannery slowly accelerated, not wanting to lose control of the vehicle again. They had pulled to within seventy-five yards of the Jeep when the vehicle began to slow.

"What the hell are they doing?" He sped up and closed to within twenty-five yards when the Jeep turned left onto Northwood Road without braking.

Flannery had to brake hard to try to follow. The big vehicle went into a slide on the slippery road and drifted past Northwood Road. By the time Flannery regained control and made the turn, the Jeep had increased the distance between them to one hundred yards. He accelerated to over eighty miles per hour, rapidly cutting the distance between them in half.

Lowery again tried to reach King, this time using the tactical radio. After trying five times and receiving no answer, Lowery threw the microphone at the dashboard. "I'm going to kill that bastard!"

"This road T's out up ahead," Flannery said. "He can turn right and head back into town, or he can turn left and head out into the sticks."

"Get up on him and force him to go left! The police are going to concentrate on the town."

A brilliant bolt of lightning arched across the sky, followed immediately by an earth-shaking clap of thunder. The heavy rain swiftly became a monsoon, with high winds driving sheets of rain horizontally across the road in front of them. Even on high, the windshield wipers couldn't keep up with the deluge.

The Jeep was slowing down as it approached the Route 86 intersection, allowing Flannery to close the remaining distance between the vehicles. He took his foot off of the accelerator and edged the GMC onto the muddy right-hand shoulder of the road. Flannery brought the Denali alongside the Jeep just as the Jeep attempted to turn right. Flannery angled his vehicle into the front quarter panel of the smaller SUV, striking it just behind the front tire. He used his heavier, more powerful vehicle to force the driver of the Jeep to turn left and head away from town and any possible help from the police converging on the area.

CHAPTER FIFTY-EIGHT

High Falls Gorge
Wilmington, New York

The wind and rain that had begun just as they were exiting the marina were steadily intensifying, forcing Dexter to drive slower than he would've liked in order to maintain traction on the rain-swept road.

"Shit."

"What?" Christian looked over at his friend.

"We have company," Dexter said, looking in the rearview mirror.

Christian twisted in his seat to look out the back window. Rain obscured his view, but there was definitely a set of headlights moving toward them at a high rate of speed.

"Speed it up."

"I'm trying, but the roads are getting slick, and we won't get very far if I put us in a ditch."

"What's up?" Laura asked.

"It looks like they had a vehicle at the marina."

Evy looked over the back seat. "Are you sure?" Christian could hear the fear in her voice.

"Make sure your seatbelts are on tight."

Dexter was shifting his eyes from the road to the rearview mirror. "He's closing in fast."

"There's a left-hand turn up ahead. Take it. Maybe it's not them."

Dexter took his foot off the gas and allowed the Jeep to slow down without touching the brakes. The vehicle behind them continued to close in as Dexter waited until the last second before he swung the steering wheel to the left, causing the Jeep to rock hard to the right and lose traction on the road. Dexter expertly steered into the slide the radical move had caused and quickly regained control of the Jeep.

Laura had twisted around in her seat to watch the unknown vehicle. "They're definitely following us. The driver damn near wrecked just now, trying to make the turn."

"When we get to the end of this road, turn right and head back toward town. If we're lucky, we'll run into some cops heading to the shooting."

Laura was keeping watch out the back window as Dexter guided the Jeep over the slippery road as fast as he dared.

"They're right on our tail, Dex!"

"I know. I can see the stop sign up ahead."

Christian was looking in the sideview mirror when the big GMC moved onto the shoulder of the road and attempted to draw alongside them. "He's trying to come up on the right, Dex!"

Dexter was too busy concentrating on the fast-approaching intersection to respond. He began to ease the wheel right when the Denali swept up the passenger's side of the Jeep and slammed into the front quarter panel. The heavier vehicle began to push the Jeep straight into the intersection. Dexter knew that if he didn't turn left, away from the contact, they would be forced across the intersection and off the road.

In desperation, Dexter swung the wheel left. The Jeep shot across the road and into a small driveway that wrapped around a brown, clapboard-sided building. There were large chunks of Adirondack boulders bordering the driveway at three-foot intervals, and the Jeep's driver-side front tire slammed into one of the rocks. The vehicle was lifted into the air and turned ninety degrees to the left. When the Jeep landed, Dexter fought to regain control as they slid down a small, grassy slope, severing a street sign before entering the roadway. As the tires made contact with the blacktop of Route 86, the entire vehicle rocked up onto the passenger side tires, almost flipping over. Dexter steered to the right, bringing the wheels back down to the road with a bone-jarring crash.

"Shit!" Christian yelled as he looked up, seeing the headlights and emergency lights of an oncoming New York state police cruiser. He watched as the trooper driving the vehicle executed a perfect crash avoidance maneuver. She locked up her brakes, and as the vehicle went into a skid, she took her foot off the brake and rapidly spun the steering wheel to the right. The vehicle reacted by literally jumping a full car width to the right, narrowly avoiding striking the Jeep head-on. The trooper's vehicle left the roadway and smashed directly into the heavy log beam and granite stone sign for the Cobble Mountain Lodge. The force of the impact severed one log completely and collapsed the entire sign on top of the police car.

Dexter didn't have time to check and see if the trooper was okay. He pushed the accelerator to the floor and fled north on Route 86.

Laura was cradling Evy as much as their seatbelts allowed in the back seat. The side impact airbags had deployed when the Jeep had landed after striking the rock, and they now hung like deflated balloons covering the side windows.

Laura turned to look out the back window. "They're still behind us."

"I see them," Dexter replied as he watched their pursuers' headlights gain on them in the rearview mirror. The Jeep was shuddering violently as they sped down the highway. "Something broke in the front end when we hit that rock."

"Keep going for as long as you can, Dex." Christian turned to the women in the back seat. "Are you two okay?"

Laura checked Evy over for injuries before replying, "We're good."

"I hope so because it looks like we're going to have to ditch the vehicle pretty soon and take our chances in the woods."

"What do you mean?"

Christian could hear the terror in Evy's voice. He said, "Evy this vehicle is just about shot. If we can get ahead of them a little and get into the woods, we can hide and wait for help. When we stop, I'm going to need you to stick to Laura like glue. Can you do that?"

"Yes."

Christian saw a mixture of fear, anger, and determination in the young woman's face. Evy was doing her best to be brave, and Christian admired her for it.

"They're gaining on us, Christian."

Christian looked over the seats and out the back window. The collision at the intersection appeared to have damaged the other vehicle as well. A single headlight was quickly closing the distance with them.

"Keep pushing it, Dex. There's a place a few miles up ahead called High Falls Gorge. If we can get there, we can use their trail system to hide, and it'll give the cops an exact location where to respond."

"It better not be too much further. This baby is coming apart at the seams."

Christian was amazed at Dexter's calm demeanor, even in

their current life-or-death race. He couldn't have asked for a better person to be by his side.

The front end of the Jeep was jerking around so violently that Dexter was using every ounce of muscle he had to keep it on the road. The heavy rain continued to fall, and the winds sweeping down off the surrounding mountains drove the rain sideways across their path. Christian stole a quick glance at his watch. It was just past 5 a.m. Even with sunrise over an hour away, the skies to the east should've begun to lighten, but the heavy cloud cover and steady rain left their world shrouded in darkness.

Christian drew his tactical knife and was just starting to cut the deflated airbag away from his window when the rear window exploded inward, showering Laura and Evy with glass. Muzzle flashes lit up the dark night like fireflies when Christian looked out through the shattered back window. He turned back toward the front, and up ahead in the distance, he could see a spot-lit sign on the left.

"Give it everything it's got left, Dex. That's the gorge up ahead." He grabbed his MP7 from the floorboard and swung it around. "Get down as low as you can," he ordered Laura and Evy as he aimed the submachine gun out the back window.

Christian flipped the selector switch to single-shot and began to slowly fire rounds at the vehicle behind them. On the fourth shot, the lone working headlight dipped toward the roadway and swerved hard to the right as the big SUV braked hard and tried to avoid incoming rounds.

Christian turned back around and said, "I bought us a few more seconds."

Dexter began to slow as they neared the poorly lit parking lot. A spotlight lit the large sign welcoming them to the High Falls Gorge Waterfall Walk.

When Dexter started to pull into the parking lot just beyond the sign, Christian said, "Keep going!"

"Why?"

"Pull up in front of the building. We're going through the front doors. It's the quickest way onto the trails."

Dexter straightened the vehicle out and drove the final fifty yards to the front of the main building. As he turned the wheel left to ease into the small gravel parking area, the driver's side front tire broke free from the vehicle. The tire bounced along the gravel lot, hopping over the two-foot-high stone wall that bordered the parking lot before crashing through the white picket railing of the entranceway and demolishing the plate glass front door.

The driver's side axle dug a deep furrow in the narrow gravel parking area before the Jeep slammed into the low stone wall, coming to an instant stop. The Jeep had barely come to rest before Christian was out of the vehicle, urging the others to hurry.

"Come on, let's go. They're right behind us."

Dexter was already out of the vehicle and firing rounds at the GMC as it rapidly approached the building. Laura and Evy both climbed out of the passenger's side of the vehicle, using the body of the Jeep as cover.

Christian grabbed Evy's arm and led her to the front door, with Laura close behind. When they got to the entrance, Christian found the Jeep's front tire lodged in the doorway, partially blocking the way. Two quick kicks sent the tire rolling further into the building and provided them with a clear path inside.

Christian guided the women inside the building before looking back to where Dexter was hiding behind the Jeep, exchanging gunshots with their pursuers.

"Dex, let's go!"

As Christian called out to Dexter, the door frame around him exploded as rounds began to impact the demolished entryway. He ducked back inside and waited for a lull in the incoming rounds before he popped back up and began to fire at the big SUV that had stopped thirty feet behind the demolished Jeep. Christian's return fire provided Dexter the cover he needed to leave the questionable safety of the stricken vehicle and hobble past him into the building.

"You okay?"

"I took a round to the hip. I don't think it hit anything important, though," Dexter matter-of-factly informed his friend.

"Can you run?"

"Try to keep up," Dexter quipped as he moved deeper into the building.

Christian moved past Dexter and found Laura and Evy crouched behind the checkout counter on the far side of the gift shop they had entered. Subdued recessed lights in the ceiling provided enough illumination to take in their surroundings. The large space was filled with shelves and heavy wooden display tables holding all types of gift merchandise. Old-fashioned snowshoes, cross-country skis, and fly-fishing rods adorned the walls. Off to the right was the entrance to the River View Café. The door directly across from the shattered main doors led to the entrance to the gorge hiking trails.

"Come on. We need to be in the woods before they make it into the building."

Christian took Evy by the arm, and as gently as possible, while still trying to hurry, he pulled her from behind the sales counter and toward the exit doors. Laura followed, with her MP7 at the ready. Dex brought up the rear, limping backward and watching the entranceway they had just come through.

CHAPTER FIFTY-NINE

Flannery struggled to keep the big Denali from sliding off the rain-slickened roadway as he tried to close the distance with the Jeep up ahead. The SUV's wipers could barely keep pace with the wind-driven rain, and Flannery occasionally lost sight of the vehicle as even heavier gusts of wind and rain turned the windshield into a waterfall.

"Stay with them!" Lowery shouted above the combined noise of the heavy rainstorm and the roar of the engine.

"I'm doing the best I can," Flannery replied through gritted teeth.

For about the hundredth time since this whole ordeal had begun, Flannery found himself wishing he'd never met Padraig Lowery or his sadistic witch, Nessa Keever. The man was well into his seventies but had the strength and vitality of someone half that age. The old man's quiet intensity and barely-controlled anger were bad enough. Worse still was the woman. She seemed to believe threats and violence were the only way to motivate the men. Flannery had no doubt she'd just as soon kill him as work with him. *If I get out of this alive, I'll never do another favor for my grandfather or anyone else from back home,* he silently vowed to himself.

"If you let them escape, you're a dead man."

Flannery's eyes met Keever's in the rearview mirror as she spoke. He had no doubt the crazy bitch would jump at the opportunity to kill him if Lowery ordered her to.

Up ahead, beyond the fleeing Jeep, Flannery could just make out the lit Welcome sign at High Falls Gorge. Flannery had pulled the big Denali to within a hundred yards of the Jeep when the smaller vehicle began to slow down and angle toward the main building at the gorge. The smaller vehicle had just left the roadway when the front driver's side tire tore loose from the axle and bounced off into the darkness. The Jeep slammed into a low stone wall that surrounded the main entrance to the gorge and came to a dead stop.

"Hold on tight!" Flannery yelled to his passengers as he left the paved road and entered the narrow gravel parking area just behind the Jeep. He slammed on the brakes and brought the big vehicle to rest just thirty feet from the rear bumper of the Jeep.

The first person out of the crashed Jeep was the driver. He raced around the back of the vehicle, took cover behind the engine block, and began firing at the Denali. The big blond Lowery had shown them the photos of climbed out of the passenger's side door and appeared to be assisting two people out of the wreckage and into the main building of High Falls Gorge.

"Out! After them now!" Lowery's voice overpowered a crash of thunder as he shouted his commands.

Flannery opened his door and stepped out into the deluge just as three rounds penetrated the windshield and slammed into the seat he had just vacated. He dropped to his stomach and rolled under the SUV. The AK-47 he was carrying as he exited the vehicle was now trapped between his body and the gravel parking area. He had almost freed the rifle when he heard several weapons begin to fire back at the Jeep.

"Hurry up; they're going inside the building." Keever's voice pierced the stormy darkness like a demon's howl, causing Flannery to shiver from more than the icy rain.

Flannery crawled out from under the SUV and moved to a kneeling position near the front quarter panel. He made sure to keep the engine block between himself and the Jeep. Flannery sensed movement off to his right and looked over just as Lincoln sprinted across the road and dove over the guardrail. A few seconds later, he slowly rose up and began firing his rifle into the Jeep.

Flannery was so transfixed by watching Lincoln that he never heard Keever move up next to where he crouched. His first warning that she was there was when she grabbed his shoulder in a vice-like grip and turned him toward her.

"Get moving. We have to get inside that building before they get away."

"Get away *where?* Their vehicle is fucked, and there's nothing around for miles but mountains, the forest, and the river. The cops are going to be all over the area at any time. We need to get out of here."

"We'll not be going anywhere until the man is dead."

Flannery had been so fixated on Keever that he hadn't noticed Lowery kneeling behind her. He turned his angry gaze from the building to Flannery. "Do you understand me?"

Flannery was no coward, but Lowery's eyes were so filled with evil and hatred that the young Irishman's bladder failed him. The warm urine leaking into his cold, drenched jeans filled him with humiliation and dread. He was glad the darkness of the storm obscured his face. He had no doubt Keever would kill him if she thought he was about to give up and flee.

"I understand," he replied with more force than he'd intended.

The humiliation that Flannery felt was turning his fear into anger. Anger at the man and woman threatening him. Anger at his grandfather for getting him into this mess, and anger at the people fleeing them. Why couldn't they just accept their fate and die so that he could go back home to Montreal and forget he'd ever met any of these psychopaths?

"That's better," Lowery said, apparently mistaking the force of Flannery's reply for determination rather than the fatalistic resignation that it really was. "Now move out to the left and try to flank the Jeep."

When Flannery hesitated, Keever pushed the barrel of her rifle into his kidney and prodded him forward. Flannery had gone about ten feet when gunfire from the entrance caused him to flatten out in the dirt once again. He heard Keever and Lowery firing back at the building, and then Keever yelled for him to get moving. He had just started toward the Jeep again when he saw someone scurry away from the vehicle toward the building. He heard gunfire and watched as the subject flinched after being struck by a round fired by Lincoln from across the road. Flannery brought his rifle up and fired at the man as he dove through the doorway into the building. He couldn't tell if any of his rounds had found their mark or not.

Flannery was pushing himself to his feet when Keever grabbed his shoulder and pulled him up. "Let's go before they make it out of that building and into the forest."

They slowly approached the smashed doorway, all weapons trained on the open portal. Flannery stepped over the wooden railing the Jeep tire had partially destroyed, followed closely by Keever. Lowery hung back and motioned for Lincoln to cross the road and take up a position on the other side of the door frame. Everyone crouched low to avoid being seen through the large windows located on both sides of the entrance.

Flannery looked over his shoulder at Lowery and waited for the man to make a decision. Behind him, he could hear Keever drawing in deep breaths as she, too, waited for Lowery to come up with a plan.

After just a few seconds, Lowery said, "Nessa, move to the foot of the stairs and get a better angle on the doorway.

Keever slowly moved to the bottom of the entryway porch, using the wooden railing to both hide her movement and provide at least a little cover in the event someone inside started shooting. She aimed her rifle toward the interior of the building and activated the flashlight mounted under the barrel of her rifle. Flannery and Lincoln knelt on opposite sides of the doorway and aimed their rifles into the building. The light from Keever's rifle caused shifting shadows as the beam passed over display cases, clothing racks, and the rustic décor that filled the large gift shop.

"I don't see anything," Keever reported.

"What about you two?" Lowery looked from Flannery to Lincoln as he spoke.

"Nothing..."

"Me neither." Flannery struggled to keep his voice from shaking.

"We can't wait around out here all night. When I tell you to, I want all three of you to open up on the interior. When I tell you to stop, I want Flannery and Lincoln to hurry inside and find cover. Once you're in a position to cover us, Nessa and I will follow you in. Do you understand?"

Lincoln simply nodded his head, but Flannery didn't care for the plan at all. "What if they're waiting inside for us to come in? We'll be sitting ducks rushing through the door."

"Coward," Keever growled but fell silent when Lowery raised his hand.

"Once you've fired a few hundred rounds into the building, anyone inside will either be dead or trying to stay hidden." The shiver that ran through Flannery's body had nothing to do with the cold. Lowery had fixed his maniacal gaze on him, and Flannery knew without any doubt that the crazy terrorist would kill him where he knelt if he failed to comply. After a short pause that felt like about an hour to Flannery, Lowery spoke again. "Any questions, boy?"

A whispered "no" was all Flannery could manage.

"Good. Now get ready." Lowery let his gaze sweep over the three remaining members of his crew and prayed they'd be enough to allow him his vengeance for his grandson's murder.

"NOW!"

Three rifles began to pour hot rounds into the building. The noise from the three Ak-47s firing their 7.62 mm rounds into the building was deafening. Wooden display racks splintered and blew apart as glass and ceramic souvenirs shattered and crashed to the floor. Clothing and blankets bearing the High Falls Gorge logo were shredded, and bits and pieces of fabric filled the air.

After almost a minute of near-non-stop firing, Lowery's voice bellowed above the din of gunfire.

"NOW! Get inside. Quickly!"

Lincoln didn't hesitate. He kept his rifle raised as he swung around the smashed door frame and searched for a spot to take cover. Flannery was only seconds behind Lincoln as he also swept through the doorway and went in the opposite direction, looking for a place to hide from incoming bullets. Both men found heavy wooden display tables to take cover behind. The tables were riddled with bullet holes but somehow stayed upright during the onslaught of heavy rifle fire. Keever's weapon-mounted flashlight, coupled with the low lighting from the recessed ceiling lights, provided ample illumination on the inside of the shop. Flannery and Lincoln slowly panned their weapons around the interior for several minutes in search of any threats.

"Is it clear?" Lowery shouted from outside.

Flannery looked over at Lincoln where he crouched, partially hidden behind the display table, and shrugged. Lincoln returned the gesture before returning his attention to searching the destroyed gift shop for possible threats.

"Well, ya fecking wanker? Is it clear or not?" The sound of Keever's voice was like nails on a chalkboard.

"I think so. We don't see anyone."

"We're coming in!" Lowery shouted. "Don't shoot us."

A thought briefly flashed through Flannery's mind. *I could shoot them as they come in, and then Lincoln and I could get the fuck out of here.* As quickly as the thought entered his head, Flannery dismissed it. He was almost convinced Keever was some sort of demon who would undoubtedly search him out and eat his soul if he tried to betray them.

"We've got you covered."

CHAPTER SIXTY

Christian practically dragged Evy through the rear doors of the gift shop and back out into the stormy darkness. Laura came through the door next, followed closely by Dexter.

Christian let go of Evy's hand and faced the small group. Laura stood with her arm wrapped around Evy, hugging the scared woman to her side and alternating her gaze from Christian back to the gift shop. Evy leaned into Laura, but she held her head up as water streamed over her beautiful features. Dexter had positioned himself several feet behind the group and was keeping his eyes on the doorway back into the gift shop. He had his left hand pressed against his hip as he tried to stem the bleeding from the gunshot wound he'd suffered.

"Are you okay?" The concern in Christian's voice carried clearly even in the driving wind and rain.

"I'm fine. Just a graze."

Laura gently extricated herself from Evy's hug and moved to Dexter's side. She pulled a mini Streamlight flashlight from her pocket and tried to examine Dexter's injury.

"We don't have time for this," Dexter said as he pushed Laura away. "We've got to move."

No sooner had Dexter spoken when heavy gunfire erupted behind them.

"Everyone get down!" Christian dove and tackled Evy to the ground, using his body to shield her from injury as they fell. When the gunfire ended, Christian stood up, pulling Evy to her feet with him. "Let's move. We need to get across the bridge and into the woods."

"Then what?" asked Laura.

"I'll let you know once I've figured it out. No more questions. Just get moving."

The heavy wind and driving rain drowned out the sound of the river that ran beneath the bridge, and the thick cloud cover allowed for only brief glimpses of the rushing water below their feet.

They had just crossed the bridge and turned right onto the dirt and pine needle pathway when a shot rang out. Dexter shouted in pain and collapsed to one knee. Christian turned back toward the building but couldn't see anything in the darkness. He raised his MP7 and fired two rapid three-round bursts through the doorway, then moved to help his friend.

Laura and Evy had already reached Dexter and lifted him

back to his feet by the time Christian reached them.

"I'm fine," he growled through gritted teeth. "The round just grazed my shoulder."

Christian searched Dexter's face and found only stoic determination. No matter how badly he was wounded, Dexter was going to soldier on. "Fine. Then stop being a wimp and get moving."

Dexter chuckled, but Evy just shot Christian a withering look before moving to Dexter's side to help him get going.

"I'm fine, Evy. Just stay near Laura and keep moving."

Christian fired two more three-round bursts into the building before moving to join the rest of the group as they headed out onto the trail along the deep gorge. The trail was slick from the rain, making their progress slower than Christian would've liked. Dexter struggled to keep up as the wound to his hip was causing a lot more pain than he was willing to admit.

As they fled along the trail, Christian's mind worked to come up with a way out. He looked back toward the gift shop as a flash of light illuminated the entire area. In the brief millisecond that the lightning flash lit the world up, Christian saw four people exit the building. He also saw something that gave him an idea. It was a long shot, but if they could get a little distance ahead of their pursuers, it just might work.

They moved steadily along the trail until they came to a steep staircase. Christian stopped the group.

"Listen up. We're going to go down these stairs to the

elevated wooden walkway that runs along the wall of the gorge. With any luck, Lowery and his men will think we stayed on the main trail, which runs back up into the woods. There are two more bridges across the river. My plan is to cross one of them and work our way back to the main building."

"And then what?" Dexter's question came out in small gasps as he fought the pain in his hip and shoulder.

"And then we're getting out of here. There's a pickup truck parked on the side of the building. I saw it when the lightning flashed. If we're lucky, they left the keys in the cab since the vehicle is behind a gate and can't be seen from the road."

"And if we're not lucky?" Laura asked.

"Then we see how well I remember what I was taught in survival school about hotwiring a vehicle. Now let's get moving before they get across the bridge. This is going to get a lot harder if they are breathing down our necks the entire way."

They had almost reached the bottom of the long stairway when Christian's hope of escaping unseen was shattered. Several shots rang out, and sections of the wooden railing around them exploded as rounds struck it.

Christian turned back and could see muzzle flashes coming from back down the trail they had just left. He raised his MP7 and returned fire. He couldn't tell if he'd hit anyone in the darkness, but his suppression fire had done its job, at least temporarily, as the gunfire had stopped.

"Okay, keep going. We can still get back across the gorge

ahead of them." He moved aside and kept his rifle trained on the trail above them as the rest of the group slid past him.

Dexter leaned in as he came up beside Christian. "I'm slowing you down, brother." When Christian attempted to stop him from talking, Dexter grabbed the front of his best friend's shirt and continued. "No! Let me finish. I'm slowing you down. I'm going to hang back and slow them down so you can get Evy out of here. She's the mission."

Christian took Dexter by his injured shoulder and attempted to pull him along. "Come on, numb nuts. I'm not leaving you behind."

Despite his wounds, Dexter was still a powerful man. He rotated his shoulder and swept his arm up and over Christian's. The quick move took Christian by surprise, and before he could react, Dexter had him in a painful arm bar.

"Stop being an ass. Get the girl out of here. I'll slow them down. Once I'm sure you've gotten across the river, I'll move back into the trees and hide. Just remember to send some help. I don't want to bleed to death in these damn woods."

Christian looked Dexter in the eyes. Both men knew he was lying. Dexter wouldn't just fade into the woods. He'd keep fighting until he'd either killed everyone chasing them or until he was dead. When Dexter sensed Christian was relaxing his arm, he released the arm bar.

"Get moving. Evy needs to make it back home."

"Don't go trying to be some kind of fucking hero. Slow them

down for a few minutes, and then head up into the trees. They're after Evy, not you." Christian drew his closest friend into a quick hug and then turned to catch up with Laura and Evy.

"Where's Dexter?" Laura asked, trying to look past Christian. Christian didn't need to reply. The look on his face told Laura all she needed to know.

"Let's get moving," Christian said as he stepped past the women.

Evy looked from Christian to Laura, clearly confused. "Where's Dexter?"

"He's covering our trail. He'll join back up further along."

"We can't leave him!" The anguish in Evy's voice was clear above the sound of the storm and the raging river below. "This is my fault! We can't leave Dexter behind." As she spoke, she tried to push past Laura and go back to find Dexter.

Laura wrapped her arms around the girl and held her tight. "Dexter knows what he's doing, Evy. He wants you to be safe."

"Dexter can take care of himself." Christian's voice held none of the desperation or sorrow he felt. He couldn't let Dexter's sacrifice be for nothing. They absolutely had to get Evy out of there. "Now, stop acting like a child and let's move."

Evy glared daggers at Christian's back as she let Laura draw her along the trail. "I hate you," she said into the storm. If Christian heard her words, he gave no sign.

A short distance further along, the trail passed beneath another bridge. There was a set of stairs leading up to the span, but Christian kept going.

"I thought we were going to cross back over," Laura asked in confusion.

"We are. There's another bridge further down the trail. If we try to cross this one, we may be within sight of Lowery and his goons, and we'd be sitting ducks stuck out on the bridge."

Moments later, several gunshots rang out. The silence that followed was suddenly pierced by a terrified scream.

CHAPTER SIXTY-ONE

Dexter rested silently against the railing as he watched Christian rush down the trail to catch up with Laura and Evy. "Well, this sucks," he whispered softly into the storm.

He pushed himself upright and began moving as quickly down the dirt path as his wounded hip would allow, then passed under the bridge that Christian and the women had gone by just moments earlier. Several feet beyond the bridge, Dexter came to a viewing platform on his right. It jutted out over the raging river twenty feet below. Across the trail from the viewing platform was a wire mesh barrier. A brilliant flash of lightning allowed Dexter to see the sign next to the barrier just long enough to read the top two words. Master Pothole was all he'd been able to read before darkness reclaimed the world around him. Dex pulled a mini flashlight from his pocket and placed his hand above the bevel. He flashed the light quickly, hoping to make out details of the trail ahead of him. On the other side of the barrier guarding the pothole, there was a small cutout next to a short staircase running deeper into the gorge. A hasty plan began to form in Dexter's head as he moved to crouch in the small, hidden spot.

Dexter took one step toward the cutout before several shots fired from behind him struck the railing and hill off to his left. Dexter dove for the questionable cover provided by the small alcove. As he struck the wooden deck that led to the short staircase, Dexter lost his grip on his rifle. Before he could react, the rifle skidded along the wet decking and disappeared under the railing.

"Shit!" Dexter scrambled to get into a tight crouch, trying to hide as much of his body in the small space as possible.

When Dexter fled the house during the initial assault, he didn't have time to grab his backpack, which was where he had stowed his Glock handgun. He'd fled through the window with just the DD MK18 rifle he'd just let slip into the raging river below him. The only other weapon Dex had was the Dynamis Razerback knife Christian had given him for Christmas last year. He drew the knife from the sheath tucked inside his waistband and waited.

The storm continued to intensify as Dexter remained motionless, trying desperately to hear anyone approaching above the noise of the storm. The pain from Dexter's wounds had settled into a constant agony that throbbed with each heartbeat. He employed the box-breathing technique Christian had taught him to bring his adrenaline-fueled heart rate back under control.

Dexter had just begun to think that perhaps their pursuers had given up and fled before help could arrive when a figure suddenly appeared on the path directly across from him.

The man was around Dexter's size and carried an AK-47 rifle held up in front of him as he peered intently down the trail ahead. Dexter reacted without thinking. He'd been sitting in the cold rain for so long that his injured and weary legs protested in pain as he thrust himself diagonally up and into the man before him. He drove the 3.75-inch razor-sharp steel blade of his knife into the man's chest as he slammed his right shoulder into the man's midsection and strained to lift him off his feet.

Dexter released the buried knife, wrapped his arms around the man's upper body, and continued to lift as he drove the man back with his legs. His wounded hip threatened to give way as he performed a tackle worthy of an all-pro NFL linebacker. Dexter continued to drive the man backward across the path until they crashed into the railing on the observation platform. When they slammed into the railing, the wooden and mesh cross section gave way, and they plummeted into the raging waters below. The man's terrified scream was the last thing Dexter heard before he struck the surface of the river and the rapidly moving water began to drag him downstream.

CHAPTER SIXTY-TWO

Ben Lincoln was just fifteen feet behind Brandon Flannery as they slowly moved along the trail above the gorge. Both men had flashlights mounted under the barrels of their rifles, but neither man wanted to use them and take the chance of giving the people they were tracking something to aim at in the darkness.

Suddenly, without any warning, a dark figure charged out of the darkness and carried Flannery through the railing and into the river far below.

"Brandon!" he yelled, knowing he was too late to help his friend even as he rushed forward to try.

When he reached the viewing platform, Lincoln stopped and peered into the darkness, his friend's final horrifying scream echoing inside his head as he tried in vain to catch a glimpse of him in the rushing water below.

"Keep moving," Nessa Keever hissed as she suddenly

appeared on the platform next to him.

He had been so focused on trying to locate his friend that he hadn't noticed the crazed bitch coming up behind him, and he nearly lost his balance and joined Flannery in the angry waters when she spoke.

"Brandon fell into the river. We've got to help him."

Keever ignored the anguish in the man's voice as she stepped closer and grabbed him by the front of his shirt. She turned him toward her and pushed her face to within inches of his. "He's gone. You'll be next if you don't get moving."

"We can't just leave him." Lincoln had worked with some dangerous people over the years, but no one he'd ever met rivaled the absolute evilness of the crazy Irishman and the ungodly woman who served him.

"We can and we will, boy," Keever growled. She shoved him away from the edge and back onto the trail. "Now get moving before I slit your throat and you can join your dead friend."

"What's the holdup?" Lowery asked when he reached the pair. His seventy-four years were beginning to catch up to him. His breath was labored as he looked from Keever to Lincoln.

"One of them stayed behind and took Flannery out."

The matter-of-fact way she spoke about Brandon made Lincoln want to shoot the bitch in the face.

"Damn it." Lowery almost spit the words out. The thought of how angry the boy's grandfather would be entered his mind and just as quickly faded away. That didn't matter. All that mattered was avenging Callum's murder. He'd deal with Sean Flannery if he managed to make it back to Ireland.

He grabbed Lincoln by the shirt. "There's nothing we can do for Flannery now. The best you can do is to kill the people responsible for his death." When he finished speaking, he turned Lincoln back toward the path and shoved him hard. "Now get moving, you worthless sod, before we lose them in the woods."

CHAPTER SIXTY-THREE

"We have to go back," Evy sobbed when she heard the heartbreaking scream. "Dexter's in trouble."

"That wasn't Dex," Christian said with absolute certainty.

"You don't know that!" Evy struggled to free herself from Laura's grasp.

"Yes, I do. Dex would die before he'd let out a scream like that."

"How can you be so sure?" Laura asked.

"Believe me, Dexter wasn't the one screaming. He was the one who caused the scream."

Christian looked back down the path they had just covered and nodded his head in silent tribute toward his unseen friend. He turned back around and guided Laura back toward the path, giving her a gentle push to get her and Evy moving.

Though the storm continued to rage around them, the sky

began to brighten ever so slightly. Up ahead, in the gloom, Christian saw the final bridge.

"The next bridge is just ahead. We're going to cross back over the gorge and work our way back toward the building."

Evy peered through the darkness, where she could just make out the span over the gorge. "What good will that do? What's to stop them from following us across?"

"Nothing, Evy. The goal is to get back to the building far enough ahead of them to get out of here before they make it back."

"This is pointless. They'll just follow us and kill us." The stress caused by her constant fear was finally starting to undermine Evora's determination to survive.

"Enough, Evy. Just do what we ask. Christian knows what he's doing." As Laura spoke, she looked closely at Christian, hoping for some sign of what he had planned. She struggled to hide her concern when he only shook his head then nodded for her to proceed across the bridge.

Laura and Evy reached the far side of the bridge first, with Christian bringing up the rear, stopping every couple of seconds to look back down the trail, trying to spot their pursuers.

When he finally joined the women, he stopped and drew them both close so they could hear him over the wind and rain. "They're still behind us, but Dex did his job. They're not sure where we are, and they're moving more slowly now so they don't fall into another trap."

Christian wiped the rain from his face with one hand while setting the stock of the rifle on the ground at his feet. His left eye was swollen almost to the point of closure thanks to Nate Boyle's headbutt, and the bullet wound in his hip throbbed. The pressure bandage Laura had applied to the knife wound in his arm had torn free. Blood from the deep cut flowed freely down his arm, mixing with the rain and running off his fingertips.

"We're going to move away from the path and go as far back up into the trees as the terrain will allow and work our way back to the building. If we get really lucky, the people chasing us will think we crossed over and continued downstream."

"What are the chances that will happen?"

"Evy, please…" Laura began before Christian cut her off by gently touching her shoulder.

Christian was tired, and he hurt all over. He just wanted to lay down in the wet pine needles and let the storm absorb him. He didn't have the energy to deal with a petulant, spoiled girl. He looked up into the storm and let the rain wash the mud and sweat from his face. He caught some of the cold rain in his open mouth and swallowed it to soothe his parched throat.

"Honestly, Evy, I don't know. The man chasing us is a terrorist who helped fight the best the British army had in Ireland for decades. The woman with him was trained by the British Army. I have no idea how many men he has with him or where they came from. I just left the best friend I've ever had back there to cover us and give us a fighting chance to escape." He paused for a second to stare back across the bridge before he continued. He turned back to Evy and looked her directly in the eyes. "What I do know is that I'm well-trained, and so is Laura. We've both been in tough spots in the past. We swore we'd protect you, and that's what I plan to do as long as I'm breathing. So please do me a favor and stop with the questions. Just do what I ask, and maybe, just *maybe*"— He emphasized the last two words—"we'll all get out of this, and Dexter and the men who died back at the house trying to protect you won't have done so in vain."

When he finished speaking, he didn't wait for Evy to respond. There was nothing she could say that mattered at that point. He took her arm, gently turned her toward the woods on the far side of the trail, and gave her a push.

"Let's get moving while we still have time."

As they climbed the steep slope into the trees, Christian slipped and fell. Laura came up from behind, hooked him under the right arm, and helped him right himself as he struggled to stand.

"I'm losing a lot of blood." He held his left arm up, and Laura could see the blood flowing freely from the deep cut Boyle had inflicted during their fight.

"We need to get that wound closed up again."

"Not yet. We don't have time." Christian took a couple of stumbling steps up the hill before steadying himself.

"You won't make it much farther if we don't stop the bleeding," she insisted.

Christian slowed down and looked around. Twenty feet further up the slope was a giant Adirondack boulder.

"Come on. We need to get behind that rock, and then we can take care of my arm."

Laura looked over her shoulder and said, "Evy, help me here."

Evora half walked and half slipped back down the wet trail until she reached them. She put Christian's right arm over her shoulder, just as Laura did the same with his left. The trio moved awkwardly up the hill until they reached the relative safety of the massive boulder.

Once they were hidden from the trail below, Christian handed his Glock 43 to Evy. "I know you've had weapons training for the show. Keep an eye back down the hill. If they realize where we are and try coming up the hill, I want you to start shooting." Christian was surprised by the expression on Evy's dirt-smeared face. The fear and panic he had observed on the young woman's face just moments earlier were quickly replaced with a look of anger and determination. "Can you do that?"

"They killed Dexter." A single tear escaped her left eye and mixed with rainwater as it rolled down her face. "I'll kill them all if I have to."

"I bet you will." Evy's savage response brought a small smile to Christian's face, despite the pain and exhaustion he felt.

Laura kneeled next to Christian and gently turned his left arm so she could see the deep knife wound. Blood oozed from the cut and dripped from his elbow and finger. There was dirt caked in the wound, so she unbuttoned her jacket then quickly pulled the hem of her shirt out of her pants and used it to wipe as much of the dirt away as she could while trying not to cause too much pain. She used the fingers of both her hands to open the wound slightly and let the driving rain wash as much debris from the deep cut as possible. Christian grimaced but held as still as he could.

"Christ, that cut went deep. You're lucky you can even use your arm."

"Yeah, I feel very lucky." Christian grimaced again as Laura cleaned the wound as much as possible.

Laura let go of Christian's arm and removed her jacket. Next, she pulled the long-sleeved shirt she was wearing over her head, leaving only her bra to combat the cold. She took the folding knife she had clipped inside her front pocket and cut both sleeves off the shirt. Laura folded one rain-soaked sleeve into a rectangle and placed it over the wound. She took the second sleeve and cut it in half, then slit each half open the long way, creating two strips of cloth to secure the bandage she'd placed on the wound. She looked up at Christian to see how he was holding up.

"Christ. We're sitting in the woods in a rainstorm being pursued by homicidal maniacs with you bleeding to death, and here you sit staring at my chest."

Christian chuckled as he looked Laura in the eyes. "Just trying to take my mind off what you're doing."

"Men," she muttered as she finished binding the wound. She

gave the last strip of cloth an extra-hard pull, causing Christian to gasp as she released his arm. "The shows over," she said as she pulled the now-sleeveless shirt back over her head and slipped her jacket back on.

"I think they're across the bridge," Evy whispered from where she knelt, peering around the boulder.

"Stay still. The human eye is drawn to movement." Christian flexed his arm several times, checking the tightness of the field dressing Laura had applied. "Nice job," he whispered before he moved up behind Evy so he could take a look.

Christian slowly pulled Evy back away from the edge of the boulder and took her place. The woods had brightened perceptibly in the past twenty minutes as the rising sun fought to penetrate the storm clouds. Christian could see movement down below, and he could hear voices but couldn't tell what they were saying.

"Okay. Here's what we are going to do. We are going to move further up the slope, keeping the boulder between us and them. Once we're far enough away from the trail so they can't see us, we'll head for the building." He checked to make sure both women understood. "Take it slow. The noise from the storm should cover our movement, but I'd rather not take a chance."

Christian nodded toward Laura, and then, with his chin, indicated he wanted her to go first. He reached out, grabbed Evy's arm, and held her back.

"Let Laura get about ten feet ahead of you before you move.

We don't want to bunch up and give them an easy target."

Evy nodded in understanding, then knelt back down and watched Laura as she slowly picked her way up the slope. When she estimated Laura was far enough ahead, she slowly moved to follow. Before she started up the hill, she turned to Christian and said, "Here." She held out the gun he had given her.

Christian shook his head. "You keep it. I may need you to help deal with our friends down there," he said, nodding his head down the hill.

"Thank you." Evy tucked the weapon into her jacket pocket and carefully began to climb the hill behind Laura.

Christian kept his MP7 trained on the trail below as he alternated between watching for their pursuers and seeing how Evy was doing. Once she was about fifty feet up the hill, he slung the submachine gun so that it hung down the middle of his back and set off up the hill. The heavy rain was a double-edged sword. While the rain made the forest floor quiet to walk on, it also made it slippery with mud under the fallen pine needles and leaves. Twice as they climbed, one of Evy's feet slipped on the slick surface, and she almost fell. Each time, they all stopped and held their breath, praying their pursuers hadn't heard the noise.

"They're sticking to the trail, but that crosses back over the middle bridge about halfway back to the building. If they want to stay on this side of the gorge, they're going to have to leave the trail and do the same thing we're doing."

"Where are they?" Laura was busy dividing her time between

negotiating the slippery terrain and making sure Evy was okay. She left the task of keeping track of Lowery and his people for Christian.

"They're about twenty yards behind and fifty feet below us, moving slowly. They know we came across the bridge, but I don't think they're positive we came this way."

They moved quietly for another ten minutes before Christian held up his hand, stopping the women. "The hill narrows up ahead. There's a sheer wall up to the roadway and a narrow strip of open terrain before we make the final climb to the building."

"Why not just climb up to the road? Wouldn't it be easier than this?" Evy held her arms out, taking in the drenched woodland around them.

"It's open rock with no cover. If we are spotted, we can't hide. Plus, in this rain, it would take an experienced climber with the right gear to make it up the cliff face."

"How much further?" Laura asked as she wrapped her arm around Evy and pulled her close. The determination and physical abilities Evy had displayed so far had impressed both Laura and Christian. She was a young actress completely out of her element, yet she fought the fear she was obviously feeling and kept moving forward.

"We'll reach the open section in about fifty feet. Once we cross that, it's a short climb to the back side of the building."

Christian took over leading the way when they reached the open area. "Be very careful on the rocks. Make sure of every foot placement and handhold. This rainstorm has probably saved our lives, but it could just as easily kill one of us if we slip and fall back into the gorge."

Christian moved out onto the open rocks first. He motioned for Evy to follow closely so he could help her if she had difficulty. Laura let Evy get about ten feet out onto the open rocks before she followed.

The main waterfalls of the gorge thundered below them. The distinctive wedge of rock that divided the flow of the water was barely visible in the low light. Evy was about halfway across the span when she stopped to rest. Her fingers ached from finding crevices and small outcroppings to hang onto, and her thighs shook from the strain of crabbing along the cliff face. She allowed her mind to wander as she stared, transfixed at the torrent of water rushing by below them.

"Don't look down, Evy." The urgency in Christian's voice cut through the haze that had threatened to overwhelm Evy's fatigued brain. She shook her head and turned away from the waterfall below to see Christian's concerned face just a few feet away from her. "We're almost there," he said reassuringly.

"I'm okay. Just tired."

"We're all tired, Evy. Just a little further." Evy turned toward the sound of Laura's voice and found her clinging to the rock face just a few feet behind her. "We can rest once we're across. I promise."

"Let's go, ladies. We can chat later."

Christian began to climb across the last few feet of the cliff. Once he reached the wood-covered slope again, he turned and reached out to pull Evy to him. When he held out his hand to Laura, she waved him off.

"I've got it. Thanks." Laura finished crossing the cliff face under her own power. She turned her face to the sky and let the rainwater wash away a little of her exhaustion.

Christian didn't give them long to rest. "Ten more feet and we're there. We can rest once we reach the top."

Evy groaned and pushed herself back to her feet. Laura held out her hand, and Christian grabbed it and pulled her up.

"Laura, go first. I'll follow Evy up."

Laura chose a foothold and began her ascent. When she reached the top, she scrambled over the edge and then turned and got down on her stomach so she could reach out and help pull Evy up the last few feet.

Christian stayed close behind Evy, catching her foot twice when she slipped on the wet foliage. As she neared the top, Christian placed his hand on her backside and gave her a push as Laura pulled her up the last few feet.

Christian climbed up onto the ledge next to where the two women lay, gulping lungs full of air. In front of him sat a red Ram 2500 bearing the High Falls Gorge logo on the doors. The truck looked to be about ten years old but was well-maintained.

"Your chariot, ladies," he said as he pointed at the truck.

Just as he spoke, a gunshot rang out from below. Christian

looked back down the rock face and saw three people standing at the very edge of the trees. Rounds began to slam into the ground around them as well as the building at their back. Wet dirt and leaves kicked up into the air, joining pieces of wood that rained down as bullets continued to fly toward them.

"Quick. Get in the truck!" Christian yelled.

He moved to let the women get past him before he began to return fire. The bolt on his MP7 locked open as the weapon ran empty. He pulled the spent magazine from the submachine gun and replaced it with his last thirty-round magazine. As much as he wanted to continue to shoot at the people trailing them, he knew he had to conserve the last of his ammunition, so he turned and ran for the truck.

When he reached the truck, he found Evy and Laura crouched on the far side of the vehicle, using the engine block for cover. He prayed one of the incoming rounds didn't hit either of the two one-hundred-pound propane tanks sitting next to the building behind them. He tried the driver's side door and silently thanked fate when he found it unlocked. He reached across, opened the passenger side door, and yelled, "Get your asses in here!"

Laura pushed Evy in first and then climbed in behind her. Evy quickly slipped over the armrest and into the back seat, where she sat down on the floorboard and covered her head.

"Keys?" asked Laura.

"Check the glove box." Christian turned down both sun

visors, praying the last worker in the truck had left the keys inside.

"Nothing here," Laura said as she frantically pulled everything from the glove box.

"Check the armrest," Christian ordered as he reached under the driver's seat and swept his arm back and forth. He felt his finger strike something metal and knock it deeper under the seat. "Damn it," he muttered. He bent over in the seat and reached as far back as he could but didn't feel anything. He sat back up and looked in the back seat, where Evy sat on the floor.

"Evy, reach under my seat. I think the keys are there."

Evy slid her left hand under the seat and quickly found it. "I've got it," she said as she pulled a key ring with a single key attached from under the seat. She handed it to Christian, who slipped the key into the ignition and hoped the battery was charged. When he turned the key, there was a short electrical clicking sound followed by nothing.

"Shit!" Christian turned the key again, knowing it was futile. "Sit tight. Let me check and see if they have a jumper pack in the back."

He opened the driver's door and slid to the ground. Once out of the truck, he moved around the front of the vehicle, keeping the engine block between himself and the gunfire as much as possible. When he reached the back of the truck, he climbed over the bedrail. A black aluminum toolbox was mounted to the bedrail against the cab of the truck. Two Master Lock padlocks held the heavy-duty toolbox closed.

"Shit!"

Christian searched the truck bed and found a three-foot length of rusted and bent chain link fence post. He grabbed the post and tried to wedge it into the hasp of the padlock, but it was too wide. He rose up on his knees and started to hammer at the first lock. After a half dozen strikes, the lock snapped open. He turned his attention to the second padlock and went to work. Unlike the first lock, the second refused to break. He knew Lowery and his goons would be across the rock face and up the slope soon. They were running out of time. He stopped hammering on the lock and began to box breathe to calm himself. Christian only spared enough time to complete one cycle of breaths, but it was enough to bring his heart rate and breathing back under control. He turned his attention back to the fence post.

Christian placed the top edge against the truck bed, and then, using his foot, he slowly bent the post to a 90-degree angle. He took hold of the bottom half of the post and, using the bent end like a hammer, began to pound on the lock again. It took another half dozen strikes before the lock surrendered. He threw the fence post down and tried to open the toolbox. The lid wouldn't budge. The box had another lock set in the latch. Christian retrieved the fence post again and wedged it under the latch. Using his rapidly waning strength, he shoved the post upward, snapping the cheap internal locking mechanism. Christian set the fence post aside and opened the box. He knew that if there was no jumper pack, they would be in serious trouble. He lifted the lid, and there, nestled among greasy rags, a tire iron, and a portable tool kit, sat a large black battery pack jump starter. He whispered a quick prayer of gratitude and grabbed the pack. As he slid over the bedrail, the rear window of the truck shattered, and rounds began to impact the tailgate. Christian stole a quick glance back toward the cliff and saw a head behind the sights of a rifle. He raised his MP7 and fired two three-round bursts, and the head disappeared. There was no way to tell if he'd struck the target.

"Laura, pop the hood!" he yelled as he moved to the front of the truck.

When he heard the lock pop, he reached under the hood and pulled the release lever then pushed the hood up and set the retention bar in place. He attached the alligator clips on the jumper pack to the battery posts and waited for almost a full minute to allow a small charge to be transferred to the dead battery.

"Try it!" he yelled to Laura.

The 6.7-liter Cummins turbodiesel engine coughed and growled before finally roaring to life. Christian disconnected the jumper pack and slammed the hood down. He raced around the truck, flinging the jumper pack out of the way as he ran. He pulled the driver's door open just as two rounds struck the door jam. Christian looked over his shoulder and saw muzzle flashes from a rifle poking over the lip of the cliff.

"Get down!"

Christian bent low over the steering wheel as he slammed the vehicle into drive and stomped on the gas pedal. A six-foot chain link fence stood in front of the truck with a set of double doors secured with a padlock and chain. The 400-horsepower engine propelled the big vehicle through the locked chain link gate with ease, completely destroying the gate and metal posts as it passed. On the far side of the chain link gate was a narrow opening in a post-and-rail fence. The opening was bordered by large rocks. The big truck collapsed the wooden post on the driver's side, creating a makeshift ramp up and over the rock. Unfortunately, the post snapped in half as the front tire passed over it, and the frame of the truck came crashing down on the rock. The vehicle bounced into the air before settling back on top of the rock, with the driver's side rear tire hanging inches off the ground. Luckily, the passenger's side rear tire remained in contact with the gravel driveway and was able to push the truck over the rock and clear of the fence line.

CHAPTER SIXTY-FOUR

Christian knew they were in trouble as soon as they cleared the rocks. He stepped on the accelerator, and the big truck kicked up dirt and cinders as it thundered over the short driveway, but Christian had no steering. Something had broken loose as the truck had passed over the rocks, and though Christian was trying to turn left to head east on Route 86, the Ram proceeded directly across the road, smashing through the guardrail and coming to an immediate stop when the front bumper made contact with the bottom of the ditch on the far side.

When the front bumper of the truck slammed into the bottom of the ditch, the airbags deployed, stunning both Christian and Laura as they did their job of arresting the occupants' forward momentum. Evy, who had been sitting on the floor in the back seat, was slammed forward into the back of the front seats. She struck her head, causing a nasty cut above her right eye and dazing her.

The big diesel engine continued to roar, and the rear tires kicked up dirt and debris as the truck sat wedged against the bottom of the ditch and the steep slope leading up into the forest.

Christian quickly recovered from the impact. The combination of the airbag impact and the loss of blood was making it hard for him to concentrate. He shook his head to try to clear the cobwebs as he turned to Laura and saw that, though dazed, she was working to get her door open. He opened his door and slid into the muddy ditch, taking his weapon with him. He quickly crawled to the back door and opened it. Evy was still seated on the floor. Her face was a mask of blood, and her eyes were staring straight ahead, unfocused and confused.

Laura opened the back door on the far side of the truck, crawled inside, and began assessing Evy for injuries. While Laura checked on Evy, Christian crawled to the guardrail and looked back toward the building across the road. As he watched, he saw three subjects appear at the edge of the cliff and slowly move toward their stricken vehicle. Christian couldn't identify any of the subjects through the heavy rain and gloom. He took careful aim at the lead person and squeezed off a quick three-round burst. The subject yelled out in pain and collapsed to the ground, while the other two subjects split up and took cover.

Between the roar of the engine and the rear tire digging deeper into the ditch, Christian had no way to yell to Laura, so he quickly backed away from the cover of the guardrail and crawled back to the truck.

"She's okay," Laura said. "Just a little dazed from the crash."

"How's her head?" Christian knew head wounds bled excessively, and Evy's face was covered in blood and her eyes were wide open.

"She's got a deep cut over her right eyebrow and most likely a concussion, but she's alert, and she says she can move on her own."

"Good, because we're going to have company in a few seconds. I hit one, but there are at least two more out there."

As if to emphasize Christian's warning, rounds began to impact the guardrail where Christian had been taking cover. Several seconds later, rounds began to strike the back of the truck.

"Okay, help me get Evy out of the truck."

When Christian reached for Evy, the girl shoved his hand away. "I don't need any help."

Rounds continued to impact the truck as Evy scooted forward on the floor and lowered herself into the mud. Laura crawled out of the truck right behind her.

"We need to get up into the trees before they work up the nerve to cross the road." He took Evy by the arm and guided her into a small creek bed that was normally dry but now held about six inches of rapidly moving water as a result of the storm. "Try to stay close to the streambed as you climb. The sides will give you a little bit of cover."

Evy nodded her understanding and began to move up the hill.

Rounds continued to rip through the woods around them as their pursuers fired sporadically from cover across the road.

Laura moved up next to Christian and leaned in close so he could hear her over the noise of the truck and gunfire. "They won't wait much longer before they try to cross the road."

"I know," he said. "We need to try to get up the slope and find some decent cover. We can try to call in the cavalry and hope they get here before we run out of ammunition."

Laura was about to reply when she screamed and collapsed into Christian's arms. "I'm hit," she gasped.

Christian laid her down and unzipped her coat. A dark crimson stain was spreading from her lower abdomen, and she was struggling to breathe. He lifted the hem of her shirt and saw blood welling up from a quarter-sized hole on Laura's lower left side. He gently rolled her on her side and saw a smaller entry wound in her back.

"It went straight through." He tore a large chunk of material from what was left of her tattered shirt. He gripped the edges of the material and tore it in half and then in half again.

As he was working on Laura, Evy slid back down the creek bed to see what was happening. When she saw Laura lying in the mud, she hurried to her side and tried to wrap her arms around the woman.

"Evy, we don't have time for that," Christian said as he peeled the young girl off Laura. He handed her pieces of the torn shirt that he had folded into squares. "I need you to hold those bandages here and here." He indicated the entry and exit wounds in Laura's torso. With Evy holding the two makeshift pressure bandages in place, Christin used the remaining two strips of cloth to bind the dressing in place as tightly as he could. Laura gasped in pain as Christian pulled the strips of cloth tight. Once the wounds were covered, he helped Laura sit up.

"Can you walk?"

Laura pushed herself into a crouch, inhaling sharply as the pain flooded her body. "I can if Evy helps me."

"Evy." When the girl didn't look at him, Christian took her by the arm and turned her toward him. Just as he pulled her close, the truck engine finally had enough, and with a loud bang, it ground to a halt. Dark black smoke began to billow from under the hood, obscuring the already gloomy woodland even further. The silence was deafening. Also gone was the sporadic gunfire from across the road. Christian quickly stole a glance back and saw three people fanning out and crossing the ribbon of blacktop. One of them held their hand tightly to their side as they moved. *So I did hit the son-of-a-bitch,* he thought with grim satisfaction.

Turning back to Evy, Christian said, "Do you see those boulders just above us?" He pointed up the hill where four giant Adirondack boulders formed a semi-circle.

"Yes."

"Can you help Laura get up there?"

Evy wiped a mixture of blood, mud, and tears from her face before she replied. "I think so."

"You have to, Evy. She can't make it on her own."

"What about you?" She was clearly confused, and her head injury wasn't helping.

"I'm going to slow our guests down." Christian nodded back toward the road as he spoke.

"No! You have to stay with us." Evy's terror was clearly written on her blood-covered face.

"Evy, listen to me. We're low on ammunition, and both Laura and I are wounded. If we get pinned down in the woods, we're as good as dead. Now, get Laura up to those rocks and get your gun out. I don't want either of you to start shooting unless they get up to you. I'll be moving around down here, and I don't want to get shot by accident."

Evy threw her arms around Christian and hugged him tight. "Don't get killed." She kissed his cheek and quickly moved to where Laura knelt and helped her friend climb as quickly as her wound would allow toward the questionable cover of the boulders above them.

Christian turned back down the hill and quietly began to work his way toward the enemy.

CHAPTER SIXTY-FIVE

Lowery was tired. He'd been a warrior his entire life. He'd been wounded more times than he could remember during his years of war with the British invaders and their Irish coconspirators. Along the way, he'd lost more friends and loved ones than he cared to remember. Callum had been the last of his family. The boy's father, Lowery's only son, had been murdered by the godless members of the SAS, and his mother, a good Irish lass, had died of cancer when he was a wee lad. Now, as he moved as quietly as possible through the heavy woods of this foreign land, Lowery knew his time was near. He realized there was going to be no escape from the United States. They had killed two police officers, along with most of the men hired to protect the girl. The worthless priest had run off, and King, their guide back across the border, wasn't answering his phone. There were only two other members of his team left. The Canadian, Ben Lincoln, had been one of Brandon Flannery's men. He held no loyalty to Lowery, and he had no stomach for the fight they now found themselves in. He was a petty smuggler with no courage or commitment. He would've cut and run already if he wasn't so terrified of Nessa Keever.

Nessa was a different story. Her loyalty to Lowery was unshakable. She'd stay by his side until the job was done or she was dead. Lowery had no doubt about that.

Lowery had struggled to make it over the guardrail, and now he stood silent in the woods, listening for any sound that might give his prey away. His body was worn out from years of war, and he knew in his bones that this was his last battle. The man who murdered Callum had to die. Nothing else mattered. He no longer cared about the girl they had been contracted to kidnap. She had been the worthless priest's goal. If he found her, he would kill her, but the only thing that mattered was the big blond. *The Viking*. He had to die.

Off to his left, Lowery saw movement. It was Lincoln. The man had no skill whatsoever when it came to stealth. He wouldn't have lasted a week during 'the troubles'. As Lowery watched, the pathetic shite slipped between two pine trees before tripping and falling down.

On Lowery's right, further up the hill, he caught a quick glimpse of Keever before she disappeared among the gloom. She was his best hope of killing the man who had ended Callum's life in Rome.

"Why won't this infernal rain stop?" Lowery muttered to himself as he reached out and grabbed onto a small aspen tree to help pull himself further up the hill.

CHAPTER SIXTY-SIX

Christian had worked his way halfway back to the road when he saw the man he'd shot entering the woods thirty yards west of the wrecked truck. The guy stumbled from tree to tree, falling down twice. He clearly had no skill in the woods. The man kept one hand pressed to his left side as he moved. The AK-47 he had slung on his back kept swinging around, hitting trees as he stumbled between them.

Christian moved quietly toward the wounded man. He stopped in a small opening between three white spruce trees that had grown close together and watched as the man awkwardly continued to move toward him, completely oblivious to his surroundings. Christian leaned his submachine gun against the base of one of the trees, drew his tactical knife, and waited. It took the wounded man another three minutes to reach Christian's hiding spot. He let the man walk past him before stepping up behind him and wrapping his left arm around his neck. He placed the tip of his blade at the base of the man's neck and whispered in his ear, "Don't do anything stupid, and maybe you'll live through this."

The man froze. It was obvious that he hadn't suspected anyone was near him when Christian grabbed him.

"Please, man. Don't kill me."

"That depends on you."

As Christian spoke to the terrified man, he pulled him into his hiding space between the spruce trees. Christian unslung the tactical rifle from where it hung down the man's back and sat it down behind him before he took his arm from around the guy's neck and turned him around, quickly using his left forearm to pin him to the tree by his throat. He placed the tip of the knife blade just millimeters from his captive's right eye.

"Name."

Christian could tell that the man was tired and scared. He didn't appear to understand what Christian had said to him.

"What…?"

"What's your fucking name, asshole?"

"Lincoln," he croaked out. "Ben Lincoln."

"How many guys do you have with you?"

"Three. There are three of us left. There were four, but Brandon fell into the river."

"Who are the other two?" Christian already knew who they were, but he wanted to see how truthful this guy was going to be.

His answers would decide his fate.

"Two crazy Irish assholes."

"Names."

"The old guy is Lowery. He's in charge. The other one is a woman. Nessa something. She's worse than the guy. She's a really sick bitch, man."

"No one else?"

"We had a few more guys, but you took them out."

Christian was about to ask another question when Lincoln started talking again.

"There was one other guy. A little Italian guy Lowery calls 'the priest'."

"Where is he?"

"No idea, man. He took off when things went bad at the house. He and Jimmy King disappeared. Lowery's going to kill them both if he catches them."

Christian knew he didn't have time to continue interrogating Lincoln. He had to find the other two before they found Laura and Evy. He couldn't just kill the guy. He posed no threat. It wouldn't be self-defense at this point. It would be murder.

"Do you want to live, Ben Lincoln?"

"Yes! Please don't kill me. I had no idea what those crazy fuckers were going to do. Brandon said the Lowery dude was friends with his grandfather, and we'd make a lot of money smuggling him and his crazy bitch into the States and then helping them grab some girl. They never said anything about killing anyone."

"Turn around."

"Please, man, don't kill me!" There were tears running down the terrified man's face.

"I'm not going to kill you, asshole. Just turn around."

As he gave the man orders, Christian grabbed him by the arm and forced him to turn away. He quickly wrapped his left arm around the man's neck once again. He had his forearm on the right side of the guy's neck and his bicep pressing into the left side. He locked his left hand into the crook of his right arm and placed his right hand on the back of his head. Once he had the rear restraining hold locked in, he began to squeeze. The blood to Lincoln's brain was closed off, and the man passed out in seconds.

Christian lowered the unconscious man to the wet leaves and quickly used the laces from the man's hiking boots to tie his hands and feet together. Once he had the guy's hands and feet secured, he cut a strip of cloth from the man's shirt and stuffed it in his mouth to keep him quiet if he regained consciousness before Christian had dealt with his friends. He searched the guy and found his handgun, performing a press check to make sure it was loaded before he secured it in his waistband. He also took the man's cell phone. He sat quietly for several minutes to make sure he hadn't attracted any attention while dealing with Lincoln. When he was sure no one had heard the commotion, Christian set out to find the remaining two threats.

CHAPTER SXITY-SEVEN

Christian worked his way quietly through the heavy woods, taking care where he stepped to avoid snapping a twig or slipping on a rock and warning his prey. He'd only gone about twenty yards before he had to stop and rest. The blood loss was taking its toll on him. He raised his left arm and saw that the makeshift bandage Laura had applied was soaked through with blood. Christian used his tactical knife to cut two long strips of cloth from his shirt and then used them to apply another layer to the wound. He pulled the strips as tight as he was able to, using his teeth and right hand. He allowed himself a few seconds longer to perform a couple of cycles of box-breathing to bring his racing heart rate and labored breathing back under control.

As he leaned quietly against a tree, Christian saw a flash of movement a short distance away. Rather than look directly at the spot where he saw the movement, he trained his eyes several feet ahead, knowing his peripheral vision would be better able to pick up any movement. Christian had hunted the forests of the Adirondacks his entire life. He knew how easily an animal or a person could disappear among the trees, even when they were very close. He remained still and cleared his head of all other thoughts. His patience was rewarded when he once again saw movement. He moved a few feet to gain a better field of view, and there, slightly higher up the slope from him, was Padraig Lowery. The old man was clearly struggling to move from one tree to the next. He moved slowly, stopping often to lean against a tree to try and catch his breath and gather enough strength to move again. As Christian watched, Lowery raised a handheld radio to his mouth and spoke. Christian wasn't close enough to hear what the man said, but he heard the radio crackle as someone responded. *It has to be Nessa Keever,* he thought.

Lowery was using his current roost for far longer than his last few stops. Christian knew from their briefings that the man was in his mid-seventies, and the physical exertion of the chase and now climbing up the mountainside were obviously taxing the man to his limits.

Carefully moving from his concealed spot, Christian edged slowly closer to the struggling man. When he was directly behind him, Christian snapped a front kick to his right leg. As Lowery began to collapse, Christian grabbed the man's head, wrapping his left hand around to grasp his forehead and grabbing his jaw with his right hand. He twisted Lowery's head back and to the right. Lowery put up no resistance, and Christian slammed the big man to the ground, keeping his head pinned to the rocky earth as he placed his knee in the man's back and pulled his head up as far as he could.

Once he had the man immobilized, Christian leaned down and placed his lips next to Lowery's ear. "Don't make a sound, old man." When Lowery attempted to reply, Christian yanked the man's head back sharply, causing him to gasp in pain. "I said don't make a sound."

Christian forced Lowery's face into the dirt and knelt quietly on his back, listening for any sign their struggle had attracted Keever's attention. After several seconds of silence, he felt safe enough to continue. He searched Lowery, relieving him of his handgun and a folding knife. The AK-47 Lowery had been carrying still rested at the base of the tree where he had stopped to rest. *Where the hell did these guys get all the hardware?* the cop part of his brain wondered. He pushed the thought aside and got down to business. He grabbed Lowery by the shoulder and started to roll him over.

The wounds he'd suffered during his fight with Boyle back at the house were steadily sapping Christian's strength. His left eye was swollen, almost closed, from the viscous headbutt Boyle had landed, and Christian was fairly certain he had a concussion. The blood loss from the gunshot wound to his right hip and the deep cut to his left arm was making it difficult for Christian to concentrate. The result of his injuries had caused him to miss a knife Lowery had hidden in the front of his waistband. As Christian rolled the devious man over, Lowery drew the knife and drove it straight at his torso. Only fate and blind luck saved Christian from being skewered by the six-inch blade. Lowery's aim was slightly off target, and as the blade passed through Christian's billowing shirt, it became entangled in the material gouging a shallow wound along Christian's rib cage.

Christian's reaction was instinctive. He grabbed Lowery's right wrist and trapped the knife against his own side. He reached across his body and slammed his right forearm into the crook of Lowery's arm, causing the knife to rise up and allowing Christian to apply leverage with his left hand and drive the blade away from his body. Lowery used both hands to try to regain control of the knife, but it was too late. Christian was able to trap the blade in Lowery's hands and slowly begin to turn the tip back toward his opponent. Christian sat up and used his body weight to slowly sink the titanium blade into Lowery's chest. The razor-sharp blade entered Lowery's chest just to the left of his breastbone, allowing the blade to slide between his ribs and pierce the man's rapidly beating heart. Christian could feel the beating of Lowery's heart through the blade as he stared into the stricken man's eyes.

"You…murdered…my…grandson…" Lowery gasped out the words before using the last of his strength to spit a gob of blood into Christian's face.

"This is for Dex, you piece of shit," Christian snapped as he slowly twisted the blade and watched the life drain from the old terrorist's eyes.

Christian collapsed across Lowery's lifeless body and drew in deep, shuttering breaths. The exertion of the fight had taken almost more than he had left. Almost.

As he lay still, trying to summon the strength to move, Christian heard a scream, followed by a rapid string of gunshots ringing out further up the hill.

CHAPTER SIXTY-EIGHT

It had taken all of Evy's strength to help get Laura up the hill and into the protected space among a cluster of giant boulders. The young actress had never been so terrified in her life, but she was determined not to let her protectors—her friends—down. They'd all sacrificed so much to protect her, and now they were all either dead or badly wounded because of her. She would not fail them again.

Once they reached the rocks, Evy made Laura as comfortable as she could. The woman's face was a mask of blood from a shallow cut near her hairline, and the bandage Christian had fashioned around her abdomen was saturated dark with blood.

"Evy, listen to me."

"Shh. Don't speak. Just rest." Evy tried to keep Laura seated.

Laura grabbed Evy's wrists and pulled her down beside her. "Listen to me." She held the younger woman's wrists and waited to make sure she was listening. "Christian may not be able to stop them all. He's wounded and up against at least three people. We have to be ready to defend this spot." When she was sure Evy was paying attention, she released the girl's arms. "This is a good position. We have the high ground. That's always a plus. The boulders will shield us and stop anything they may have. The downside is that this is the best cover in the area and an obvious spot for them to check."

Laura moved to a kneeling position and used her hand to grab ahold of the rocks she'd been leaning against to steady herself when a wave of dizziness and nausea threatened to overwhelm her.

"Are you okay?" Evy moved to steady her friend.

"I'm fine, but I think I have a concussion. There's nothing we can do about that right now. Once we get out of here, we can get medical attention."

"You're bleeding pretty bad from your head." Evy used her hand to wipe some of the blood from Laura's face.

"Head wounds bleed a lot. It's nothing to worry about. Just pay attention." Laura waited for the dizziness to pass before she continued. "I need you to cover your side of the space and our rear. I'll cover my side and the front. That gives us 360-degree coverage. If you see movement, you need to quietly let me know. Don't shout. Just because you see them doesn't mean they've seen us. This next part is very important." Laura paused to make sure Evy was paying close attention. "Do not shoot at anything unless you're sure of your target. Christian is out there. If he can't locate and eliminate the threat, he may try to join us here to help hold them off until help arrives. I don't want you to shoot him by accident."

Evy nodded in understanding. She wouldn't let Laura down again. She'd abused the woman's trust when she sent the message that had drawn their attackers right to them. Evy was determined to make up for it.

"Where should I be?"

Laura positioned Evy so she could cover her assigned areas before moving to the opposite side of the opening among the boulders and positioning herself to cover the hillside down to the road.

The two women settled in and watched and listened for any sign of Christian or their pursuers. Several times, Evy was positive she'd seen movement. "How can you stand this?" she whispered. "I keep thinking I see something, but then there's nothing there."

"The woods can be tricky. There are squirrels, raccoons, and all sorts of small wildlife surrounding us. Our peripheral vision locates movement better than our central vision. If you think you see something, don't stare directly at that spot. Look off to one side and let your peripheral vision work for you."

Evy was staring intently down the hill when she heard rocks clattering down from above their hiding space. She turned just in time to see a woman dressed in a police uniform climb atop the boulders guarding their backs. At first, Evy thought they'd been rescued, but her elation was short-lived as she saw the woman raise the rifle she was carrying and aim directly at Laura's unprotected back.

"Laura, look out!" Evy's terrified scream echoed off the surrounding hills as she raised her Glock to stop the new threat.

Evy's scream saved Laura's life. Even wounded and tired, Laura reacted immediately. As she rolled to her left and spun to see what had spooked the girl, three rounds fired from Nessa Keever's AK-47 slammed into the ground where she had just been lying.

Before Laura could bring her submachine gun up to engage the threat, Evy was already firing round after round at Keever. Several rounds found their mark, and Keever shouted in pain as she collapsed over the back side of the boulder, falling out of view.

Evy pulled the trigger several more times before she realized she had run out of ammunition and the slide was locked back. Using the thumb of her shooting hand, she depressed the magazine release button and, flicking her wrist as she had been taught by the firearms trainers she'd worked with on the show, sending the empty magazine flying from the weapon. Once the spent magazine had been ejected, Evy slammed her last full magazine into the magazine well. She used her left hand to pull back on the slide, releasing it from the locked position and allowing it to chamber a round as it slid back into the battery.

Evy kept her weapon trained on the spot where Keever had

disappeared while using her eyes to sweep the area around her for further threats. She stole a quick glance at Laura and asked, "Are you okay?"

"I'm good, Evy." Laura winced in pain as she shifted her body weight to a more comfortable position. She, too, kept her weapon aimed at the spot where Keever had gone over the boulder.

"Wait here. I'm going to take a look." Evy moved to a crouch and began to edge toward the side of the boulder, keeping her weapon trained straight ahead as she moved.

"Just be careful, Evy. She could be playing possum."

Evy had never heard the term 'playing possum' before, but she understood Laura's meaning. She slowly worked her way around the boulder, using the technique known as slicing the pie. She moved in small increments as a larger and larger area came into view. After a few more steps, she spotted Keever lying on the ground, struggling to sit up. The woman's rifle lay on the far side of her just out of reach. Evy put the front sight of her handgun on Keever and slowly moved forward. When Keever finally spotted Evy, she made a halfhearted effort to reach for the rifle that was just out of the reach of her outstretched hand. Evy pulled the trigger one time, sending a 9-mm round sizzling into the fallen woman's exposed side. Keever fell back with a pain-filled yelp.

"Don't move again, you bitch," Evy spat through clenched teeth. She closed the remaining distance and stood over the woman, staring at her hate-filled face. "Where is he? Where is Fabrizio?"

Keever began to laugh but ended up coughing up a mouthful of dark red blood. "Feck you, girl."

"Where is he?" Evy's shrieked in anger.

"Gone...for...now." Keever struggled to speak as blood continued to fill her stomach and lungs. She spit out a great glob of dark blood and tissue before continuing. "He...has plans...for...you."

Evy was so engrossed in what the wounded woman was saying, she almost lost her life. The entire time she had been speaking, Keever had been slowly drawing the weapon she had holstered at her waist. The barrel of the handgun had just cleared the holster when Evy realized what was happening. She shifted her weight and stomped down hard on Keever's right hand with her left foot, trapping the hand and the weapon it clutched in the soft earth.

"You miserable bitch!" Evy hissed. She aimed her Glock at Keever's upturned face and pulled the trigger three times. All three rounds smashed into Keever's face, with the final round entering her left eye and blowing out the back of her head.

Evy had no idea how long she stood there, looking at what was left of Nessa Keever's ruined face. It could've been seconds or hours. Time just seemed to stand still.

A noise behind her drew Evy out of her trance-like state and caused her to turn and raise her weapon toward the sound.

"Easy, Evy. It's me, Christian."

It took Evy a few seconds, but her eyes finally focused, and she saw Christian covered in blood and limping as he struggled to reach her. To protect her.

She lowered her weapon, ran to him, and threw her arms around his neck. As Christian returned her hug with his injured left arm, he used his right hand to aim his weapon up the hill behind Evy as he searched for the threat.

Evy pulled back slightly so she could see Christian's face. "She's dead," she said quietly. "I killed her." Tears flowed freely down her face.

"It's okay, Evy. It was her or you. You did the right thing."

Evy buried her face in Christian's shoulder and wept harder. Christian let her cry for a few seconds and then gently pulled her arms from his neck.

"Where's Laura?"

"I'm over here."

Laura limped from behind the screen of boulders, holding her hand to her wounded abdomen. She leaned heavily against the nearest boulder and raised her face into the rain that continued to inundate the forest.

"Evy, go give Laura a hand."

"Where are you going?" she asked as Christian started to walk up the hill.

"I'll be right back," was all he said.

Evy and Lara had just finished collecting their things from

their hiding spot when Christian reappeared. In addition to the MP7 he'd been carrying, he now had the AK-47 Keever had tried to kill Laura with slung over his left shoulder.

"Let's get moving. I have no idea if there are any more of them out there."

They worked their way back down the mountain to where the truck had crashed through the guardrail. When they reached the truck, they sat down to rest and regroup.

"Now what?" Evy asked.

"Now I commandeer a vehicle and get us out of here." Evy didn't like the sound of the word 'commandeer', but she didn't interrupt. "I'm going to call Valentine and have him call Chief Nilsen. Hopefully, they get so tied up in the crime scene at the house and the one here that they forget about us for a bit, and we can make it to the airport."

"Laura needs medical attention, and frankly, so do you."

"I realize that. I'll have Valentine arrange it. If we show up at a hospital right now, the police will be called, and we won't be able to get you out of here."

"I don't care about that," Evy said.

"I do."

"So do I," Laura added.

CHAPTER SIXTY-NINE

The phone call to Valentine lasted a half hour as they worked out the details of a new plan. Once Christian had hung up, they sat back in the shelter of the trees along the side of the road, waiting for a good opportunity. Christian was amazed at the lack of traffic on the normally heavily traveled road. Laura suggested that the combination of the weather and the violence in Lake Placid was keeping people inside.

While they waited, Christian directed Evy in cleaning and redressing his and Laura's wounds with what little they had to work with. Once again, he was impressed with the girl's intelligence and ability to stay calm as he worked with her.

Evy had just finished redressing Laura's gunshot wound when Christian heard a vehicle approaching. He prayed it wasn't the police. Evy had suggested calling the police, but both Laura and Christian had convinced her that was a bad idea. First of all, they had no idea where Fabrizio was or how many more people he may have looking for them. The guy Christian had interrogated said they were the last, but he didn't trust the guy and had no way to verify his claim. Next, their goal was to get Evy out of the country as soon as possible. If the police found them, the best they could hope for was to be detained. It was a very real possibility that they'd be arrested. That would mean Evy would be stuck here with no way of knowing where Fabrizio was or what threat he may still pose.

"Wait here. I'm going to check it out."

Christian slid over the guardrail before either woman could object. He crept to the back end of the wrecked pickup truck and waited for the approaching vehicle to appear but didn't have to wait very long. As Christian watched, a white GMC Sierra crew cab pickup truck came into view, traveling west along the highway. When the driver spotted the wrecked truck, he began to slow down and pull to the shoulder. As the big heavy-duty truck came to a stop, Christian saw the driver's side door had the words Adirondack Aerial Adventures written on it. Below the lettering was a picture of a single-engine prop plane.

Christian sat the MP7 against the rear tire of the truck and slowly stood up and raised his hands.

"Hey there," he called out.

The driver never flinched. He raised his eyes from the wreckage and stared at Christian for a couple of seconds before he replied.

"Looks like you're having a bad day," he said in a deep voice. He looked from Christian to the two vehicles across the street and the caved-in door of the High Falls Gorge building and turned back to Christian. "That you?" The man's face never changed expression. If finding a wrecked truck, a blood-covered stranger, and obvious signs of a break-in surprised the man, Christian couldn't tell.

"Long story," Christian replied.

"I'd imagine." The dark eyes staring at Christian gave no hint of what the man was thinking.

I wouldn't want to play poker with this guy, Christian thought. "We could use some help."

"We?" Now the man's penetrating gaze swung to the wooded mountainside behind Christian.

"I have two friends back up the hill. We're all in rough shape. We could use a ride."

The man didn't respond right away. He appeared to be trying to decide what to do. After almost a full minute, he said, "Lots of state troopers are heading toward Placid with their lights going. A couple of helicopters buzzing around too. That you as well?"

"Like I said, it's a long story."

"Have your friends come out." Christian started to turn to call out to the women, but before he could speak, the dark-eyed man added, "And hey, leave the H&K right where it is."

Christian turned back to the man and saw that he now held what looked like a 1911 handgun in his right hand. The tan-colored weapon was resting on the open windowsill of the truck with the barrel pointed at the ground a few feet short of Christian, but he had no doubt the man could raise and fire the weapon before Christian could take two steps in any direction.

Christian slowly raised his hands again. "Hold on, buddy. We don't want any trouble."

"No trouble. Just leave the weapon where it is and make sure your friend's hands are empty when they come out."

Christian never took his eyes off the driver and his weapon when he yelled, "Laura, Evy, come on down!"

"Slowly and no weapons," the driver emphasized.

"Keep your weapons secured. We don't want any misunderstandings," Christian instructed the women.

It took almost five minutes before the women appeared from the woods. Laura was leaning heavily on Evy and holding her hand pressed to her wounded stomach. They stepped up beside Christian and stopped.

"Like I said, we're all in rough shape and could use a ride."

"Mind telling me why I'd give you a ride instead of calling the cops and holding you for them?"

"Listen, if you don't want to give us a ride, I get it. Just leave. We'll figure something out. I can't let you call the cops, though."

"*Let* me?" For the first time, there was just a hint of a sarcastic smile on the man's face.

Christian threw his arms up into the air, drawing the man's attention.

"Drop the gun," Laura said.

The man's gaze shifted from Christian to the woman. A brief look of surprise flashed across his face when he saw both Laura and Evy were aiming handguns at him. The look was gone as quickly as it appeared.

"Looks like we have a standoff, doesn't it?"

"No standoff. If you raise the barrel of your weapon, they'll shoot you," Christian said. "No one wants that. We need a ride. You can drive us, and I'll pay you a thousand dollars, or you can give us your truck, and I'll still pay you a thousand dollars. Either way, we get a ride, and you get the money."

"No one's taking my truck." There was no fear in the man's voice.

"I said drop the weapon." Laura tried to sound threatening, but the pain of her wounds robbed her of any menace.

"Not gonna happen, lady. This is a custom Kimber Warrior. Between the price of the gun and the customization, I've got almost twenty-five hundred dollars invested. There's no way I'm going to drop it out the window."

"At least put it away," Christian said. "We'll put our weapons away as well, so we can talk."

When no one moved, Christian turned to Evy and Laura and said, "Put the weapons away, ladies. We aren't going to shoot an innocent man. I don't care how badly we need a ride."

Laura lowered her weapon and slid it back into the holster tucked in the front of her pants. She drew a sharp breath, as even that simple move caused her wound to flare up in pain.

"I don't have a holster," Evy said as she lowered her Glock.

The driver slowly pulled his handgun back inside the cab of his truck. "You still haven't told me why I would give people that the police obviously want a ride anywhere."

Christian hesitated as he considered how much to tell the man. Finally, he looked to Laura, who nodded and said, "You may as well tell him. We need to get out of here." The look of pain on Laura's pale face helped make up Christian's mind.

"We were hired to protect the girl." Christian pointed to Evy. "The man after her is a psychopath. He's very rich, and he hired a band of criminals to try to kidnap her. We were hiding her in Lake Placid, but the guy somehow figured out where we were."

A look of regret and shame spread over Evy's beautiful face, and she lowered her head. "My fault," she whispered too quietly for the driver to hear, but Christian and Laura both heard her. Laura pulled the girl close.

"They found us tonight and attacked the house we were hiding in. We managed to escape, but they chased us. We wrecked our vehicle, and now we really need a ride."

"That wasn't really a long story." The man shook his head. "I'm probably going to regret this, but get in. Keep your weapons out of sight."

"Thank you."

"A thousand, correct?"

CHAPTER SEVENTY

Christian helped Evy and Laura get into the back seat of the truck before he climbed in next to the driver.

"Christian," he said to the man as he offered his hand.

"Nick." The man had large, callused hands and a firm handshake.

Nick looked to be around forty-five. He had long, dark hair that was just starting to gray at the temples. He kept his hair in a loose braid that hung down his back. Nick had the high cheekbones, dark eyes, and coppery skin tone that denoted his Native American ancestry. He was tall with a wiry, athletic build. Nick wore a red and gray flannel shirt with the sleeves rolled up, displaying tightly muscled forearms.

"Where are we heading?"

"To the airport in Plattsburgh. Do you know where that is?"

"I do. I was just coming back from there. I had to pick up

some parts for one of my planes."

Christian turned to the back seat. "How are you two doing?"

"We're good for now," Evy replied. She sat behind Christian with Laura's head in her lap. She gently stroked Laura's hair as they spoke quietly.

"Laura?"

"I'm okay, Christian. Just really tired."

"We all are. You have to stay awake, though. We'll be at the airport soon."

"Stop worrying about me. Concentrate on what you have to do."

Christian chuckled. His admiration for Laura rose more and more each and every day. "Okay, hard ass. I'm going to call Arthur and give him a sit-rep and see how long before the plane arrives."

Valentine answered on the first ring. The two men spoke for several minutes as Christian updated him on what had happened at High Falls Gorge. He hated giving out so many details with Nick sitting right next to him, but he had no choice. Valentine had to have the facts if he was going to cover for them. He pulled the phone from his ear and turned to Nick.

"How long before we reach the airport?"

"The rain is letting up, but I don't want to attract any attention, so I'm going to stay off the main roads as much as possible. Normally, it'd take about forty-five minutes to an hour from here. We're looking at probably an hour and a half, maybe an hour and forty-five minutes."

"Our driver says we should be there in less than two hours," Christian said. He waited for a reply and said, "I'll keep you posted. Call Nilsen and tell him we're in a black Toyota pickup truck and we're heading for the airport in Albany. He'll relay that to the troops, and they'll concentrate on the wrong vehicle in the wrong direction." He listened as Valentine responded and then said, "I get that, Arthur, but we don't have a choice. We don't know where Fabrizio is, and we have no idea how many more people he may have working for him. I want her out of here." He and Valentine spoke for several more minutes before Christian disconnected the call.

"Well?" Laura had kept quiet during the call, but she wanted to know what was going on.

"The plane should be in Plattsburgh by the time we get there. From there, we'll decide what to do next."

Christian and Valentine already had a plan in place, but Christian wasn't going to discuss the details in front of their new friend.

Nick kept his speed just over the posted speed limit, made sure to come to a complete stop at any traffic light or stop sign, and signaled each turn. From the way Nick kept a constant eye on his mirrors and obeyed the traffic law, Christian figured this wasn't the man's first rodeo.

"I've spent a lot of time in the Adirondacks, but I haven't been on many of the roads you are taking."

Nick's eyes never stopped surveying the area around them when he replied. "That's the point. Anyone who sees me isn't going to think I'm in a hurry to get anywhere using the roads we're on. Plus, it's real easy to spot a tail on these back roads."

"Sounds like you're speaking from experience." Christian watched Nick for a reaction, but the big man just kept his eyes moving.

"Back in my younger days, I did some stupid things to make money. I moved stuff across the border a lot. Untaxed cigarettes, stolen auto parts, stuff like that."

"Not anymore?"

"Nope. It's not worth the risk. I didn't want to end up in a cage. I'd rather be dead than locked up."

Again, it seemed like the man was talking from experience, but Christian didn't pursue it. The man was helping them escape the area. That was all that mattered.

"So now what do you do?"

"After I got out of the army, I bounced around a bit. Got tired of working to make other people rich. Now I own three planes and a helicopter and make my money taking tourists on aerial tours of the Adirondacks and ferrying hunters into the backcountry to try to bag the mythical monster whitetail or giant black bear."

They traveled another twenty minutes without speaking, and it appeared to Christian that that was the way Nick liked it. He had no problem with not talking. He'd always hated it when he was with someone who thought all the quiet space had to be filled with conversation. One of the many things he loved about Summer was that she could ride along listening to music and singing along to the songs she liked without the need for constant chatter. He did, however, think Nick deserved at least a little bit of an explanation for what was happening.

"So I guess you're probably wondering exactly what's going on?"

"Nope. The less I know, the less I can tell any cop that questions me."

"Very true."

Nick turned in his seat to check on his two female passengers. "Not sure what your plan is, but it had better include some serious medical help, or your one friend may not make it."

"It's being taken care of."

Nick just nodded and kept driving.

CHAPTER SEVENTY-ONE

Plattsburgh, New York

They drove the remainder of the way to Plattsburgh in silence. Nick was busy watching for possible problems, while Christian split his time between checking on Laura and running their hastily formulated plan through his head, looking for mistakes.

"We're here," Nick said.

Christian turned from checking on Laura and saw a large white sign sitting atop a granite stone base welcoming them to the Plattsburgh International Airport. Below the twelve-inch letters was the French translation in much smaller print. The sign featured a silhouette of an airplane shooting skyward with a looping contrail flowing behind. Floodlights surrounding the base of the sign easily cut through the rain and gloom, making it easy to read. The red terminal building with gray field stone pillars holding up a canopy to cover the drop-off and pickup area sat just beyond a large parking lot. The parking lot was well-lit by ornate light poles and appeared to be almost full.

Nick turned right off of Route 22 and asked, "Where to?"

"Pull into the lot and wait. I'll find out."

Nick found a parking spot as far from the terminal building as he could and backed in. They sat quietly as Christian made a phone call.

When Valentine answered, Christian said, "We're here."

"Stand by." Christian could hear the man speaking with someone else. "Okay. There's a gate to the right of the main terminal building. Security will let you through. The plane just finished taxiing up. They'll have the stairs down by the time you get there."

"Copy that. I'll reach out once we're airborne."

He disconnected his call and pointed toward the terminal building. "Apparently, security is going to let us pull out onto the tarmac behind the building. The plane's here already."

Nick pulled out without saying a word. He drove around the parking lot and onto the perimeter road. As he approached the terminal, a security guard wearing a bright orange hooded rain jacket that hung almost to the ground directed him to turn right and proceed through the opened chain link fence. Up ahead, just beyond the building, sat a Cessna Citation Longitude business-class jet. Nick pulled up about fifteen feet from the wing tip and stopped the truck.

"Nice plane. Maybe I should've asked for more money."

"About that…" Christian began.

"Let me guess. The check is in the mail?"

"Sort of. I don't have that kind of cash on me." He pulled out his wallet, took all the cash he had out, and counted it out. "I've got three hundred and sixty-five dollars on me. I'll give you that, and once we get where we're going, I'll arrange to send the rest to your office."

Nick held up his right hand to stop Christian. "No need. Give me a hundred bucks for gas. I would've just sat around all day bitching about the weather if I'd gone home. This was much more interesting."

"A hundred bucks won't get this gas guzzler back home. Just take what I've got. We'll work out the rest some other time."

Nick took the cash and stuffed it in his pocket. He looked out the windshield and said, "We've got company."

Christian looked and saw two men exit the plane. Both had the look of former military personnel. Obviously, Valentine wasn't taking any chances. Christian watched as a two-man security detail took up positions on either side of the staircase. Neither man displayed any weapons, but Christian was sure they were each armed with at least a handgun. The security team was followed by two men and a woman who hurried toward the truck.

"Don't get out, Nick. There's no sense letting anyone see you."

Christian climbed out of the big truck just in time to step in front of the three people.

"I'm Dr. Phillips," said the first man to reach him. "These two are my trauma team." He nodded toward the man and the woman with him. "Let's get you all on the plane and get out of here."

Christian helped Evy get Laura out of the truck, and the two trauma medics stepped up and took her aboard the plane. Evy followed them up the stairs. One member of the security team followed the group aboard while the other approached Christian.

"We have to go, sir."

Christian waited until Nick had driven back out of the gate and was on his way before he turned to the security guard and said, "After you."

CHAPTER SEVENTY-TWO

The Cessna Citation Longitude was designed as a luxury business jet. The plane was capable of carrying twelve passengers and their luggage comfortably. The aircraft Christian boarded had been reconfigured. The four rearmost seats had been removed and replaced with low-slung hospital beds complete with vitals monitors and IV drip racks.

Laura was already on one of the beds and being assessed by one of the medics by the time Christian boarded. As soon as he set foot inside, Doctor Phillips directed the second medic to get him on a bed and start doing her assessment. The medic took Christian's arm and attempted to guide him to the empty bed, but he shrugged the woman's hand off.

"Slow down. I need to talk with the pilots and make sure we're all set before you start poking and prodding."

"Stop being a pain in the ass, Christian."

Christian looked beyond Doctor Phillips and saw Abby Fuller coming through the cockpit door.

"Abby," he said in surprise.

"Abby my ass. Get your ass in bed and let them get to work. We don't have all day, and I can't get this bird in the sky until you're strapped in."

She pushed past the doctor and his medics and gave Christian a brief hug. "Thank you," she whispered in his ear before pulling away and moving to the bed that held her wife. She bent down, hugged her wounded wife, and gave her a soft kiss on the lips. They put their heads together for a few seconds and had a whispered conversation before Abby straightened up and turned back toward the cockpit.

"Are you still standing there?" She grabbed Christian by the shoulder and guided him to the empty medical bed. "Lay down and let them get to work. We'll be in D.C. in an hour and a half."

"Strip," said one of the medics. She stood around five feet four and had her light brown hair pulled back into a ponytail. She had a thin build, which was common among flight medics, as medicav aircraft didn't have much room. The name tag on her olive-green flight suit read LAWSON.

"What, no foreplay?" Christian couldn't help himself.

"Maybe later. Right now, let's see if it would be worth it." The woman never even cracked a smile.

Christian laughed out loud. It felt good after the tension of the last several hours.

He stripped out of his filthy, blood-covered clothes and laid down on the bed. The medic assessed his wounds and went to work. Dr. Phillips checked in periodically, but Lawson did all the work. When she was done stitching up Christian's forearm and the deep gouge Boyle's bullet had carved in his hip, she gave him a liter of blood as well as several injections to help with the pain and to prevent infections. She put an ice pack on his swollen eye and told him to hold it in place. When she was done, she helped Christian to the bathroom, where he used a small shower to get cleaned up. When he stepped from the shower, he found a neatly folded green flight suit, underwear, socks, and a pair of tactical boots all in his size sitting on the counter.

It took Christian ten minutes to finish getting cleaned up and dressed. When he walked back into the main cabin, he found Laura asleep. A blanket was tucked up under her chin, leaving just her left arm exposed. An IV was taped in place on her exposed arm, with the tube running up to a bag of clear fluid hanging from the IV tower mounted to the head of the bed. Someone had taken the time to wash her face. A heart rate monitor beeped softly above the bed.

Evy had fallen asleep in a chair next to Laura's bed. Even in sleep, she kept a tight grip on Laura's pale hand.

"How is she?" Christian asked the doctor.

"She lost a lot of blood, but we already took care of that. The bullet went straight through, but it missed anything major. It's hard to tell how much damage she has yet, but I think she got lucky. She's dehydrated and most likely has a concussion. The bullet wound and the cut on her scalp will leave scars, but she'll make a full recovery, and that's all that really matters."

"Thanks, Doc. That's great news." He tried to move past Phillips, but the man blocked him.

"As for you. . ."

"I'm fine, Doc."

"No, you're not. You also lost a lot of blood, but we topped you off. Phyliss—excuse me, Flight Medic Lawson—stitched up your arm and the GSW to your hip. She gave you antibiotics to help fight off any infections and pain meds. There are no broken bones in your face, and the ice will take care of the swelling. All in all, you also got pretty lucky. You need to take it easy for a few days and heal up."

"I'll try, Doc, but I still have a lot to do. For now, I need to call Valentine and give him a sit-rep, and then I want to check on Laura."

Christian soon learned there was no need to call Valentine because Abby had already given him an update. After grabbing a bottle of cold water out of the galley refrigerator, he sat down next to Evy and Laura and closed his eyes. Sleep eluded him, as each time he started to drift off, the face of his best friend filled his mind. He tried to box breathe, but even that didn't calm his mind. Dexter was gone, and it was his fault. He'd dragged Dex along on this crazy mission, and his always faithful friend had paid the ultimate price.

Tears welled up in his closed eyes as he struggled to accept the loss and the guilt. As the tears escaped his eyelids and rolled silently down his cheeks, Christian felt two small, warm hands wrap themselves around his left hand. He opened his eyes to find Evy staring at him.

"It's going to be okay." Tears flowed openly down her face as well, and Christian wasn't sure if she was trying to reassure him or herself.

CHAPTER SEVENTY-THREE

Ronald Reagan Washington National Airport

Arlington, Virginia

Christian was exhausted in mind, body, and soul. He finally dozed off with Evy holding his hand and her head resting on his shoulder. Though memories of Dexter filled his dreams, he slept until they landed at Ronald Reagan Washington National Airport. The thud of the aircraft's tires touching down on the runway roused him from his slumber. He blinked his eyes several times to clear the sleep from them and then gently moved Evy's head off his shoulder. He sat up straight and looked out the small window next to his bed and watched the landscape fly by. As the plane turned to taxi off the runway, Christian could see the dome of the capitol building gleaming in the bright sunlight off in the distance.

Fuller guided the plane past the main terminal, and Christian saw the airport fire station flash by as they continued on to the charter flight area. The plane finally came to a stop, and the security guards moved to the exit door. Before they could open it, Abby came out of the cockpit.

"I just got off the phone with the boss." She pointed at the two security guards. "You two are to assist in moving Ms. Cota to the jet inside the hanger bay. There is a full crew already aboard, as well as a security detail."

"I'm not going anywhere without Christian and Laura."

Christian took Evy's hand. "Evy, please, for once, just listen and do what you are asked without being a pain in the ass."

Tears welled up in her eyes. "I don't want to leave you guys."

"We'll see you again, I promise. For now, just get on the other plane. Valentine has a plan in place to keep you safe until they figure out where Fabrizio ran off to."

"I'm safe with you," she argued.

"No, you're not. Laura and I are injured, Evy. We aren't at one hundred percent, and we can't keep you safe in our condition. Arthur knows what he's doing. Now say goodbye to Laura and get moving."

Evy held his hand for a few more seconds as she struggled to get her emotions under control. She took a deep breath to steady herself before she let go of Christian's hand. Then she reached up, wrapped her arms around his neck, and pulled him tight. "I'll never forget you. Any of you." She pushed herself away but kept her hands on Christian's shoulders. "I am so sorry about Dexter. I'll never forgive myself."

She turned away from Christian and moved to Laura's bedside. The flight medic was checking Laura's vitals when Evy stepped up and asked him to give her a minute.

Evy leaned down and wrapped her arms around her friend, tears flowing down her cheeks. They whispered quietly to each other until Abby gently touched Evy's shoulder and said, "We have to get moving, Evy. The longer we're on the ground, the more likely someone will take notice."

Evy kissed Laura's cheek and then followed the security team off the aircraft without another word.

Christian watched out the window as Valentine met Evy and the security team at the base of the stairs. They escorted her to a small jet partially hidden inside the hanger connected to the charter flight operations building. Standing guard at the base of the boarding stairs were Liam Harris and Sean O'Brien. When Evy reached the top of the steps, she looked back and waved before disappearing inside.

Once Christian was sure Evy was safely aboard the plane, he moved over and sat next to Laura. He took her hand and said, "Roddy's boys, Liam and Sean, are here. Evy will be fine."

"Where are they taking her?"

"Arthur didn't say, and I didn't ask. Someplace safe."

"We had her 'someplace safe.'" The bitterness of her last two words mirrored Christian's thoughts.

Christian and Laura sat in silence, each lost in their own thoughts. When Abby came out of the cockpit to check on Laura, Christian moved to the front of the cabin to give them some privacy. He took advantage of the break to call Summer. The call was brief and tense. All he could tell her was that things had gone wrong, and he'd be out of touch for a while. He assured her he was fine, but he could tell she didn't believe him when he said he wasn't sure where he'd be. Her confusion and frustration at his refusal to answer her questions were easy to hear in her voice. She hung up without saying goodbye, leaving Christian to wonder if she'd still be there when this was all over. He was sitting quietly, running their conversation through his head and trying to find where he could've done better, when the cabin door opened and Arthur Valentine stepped aboard the plane.

"Stay seated," he said when Christian started to rise to greet him. He shook Christian's hand, then bent down and kissed Laura gently on the cheek before sitting down. He looked at his two operators.

"You may not want to hear this right now, but you two did an outstanding job getting Evy to safety."

Christian snorted. "An outstanding job? The entire team was killed. We barely got her out of there."

"But you did get her out. Her safety was the mission, and now she's on her way to a safe location while the authorities track Fabrizio down."

"Arthur. . ." Laura started to speak.

Valentine held up his hand to stop her. "Let me finish. Yes, we lost people. But you have to remember that each of them was highly trained and knew exactly what he was getting into. It's never easy, but it's part of the life we've chosen."

Christian knew Valentine was right, but he also knew that he was to blame. He had been in charge of the mission. It had been his plan. Worst of all, he'd dragged Dexter along, and it ended up costing his best friend his life. There was no way to avoid those painful truths. He pushed them down deep and locked them away until he could deal with them by himself. For now, they still had things to do.

"So what now?" he asked.

"Now we refuel and head for Iceland."

"Iceland?" Laura's confusion mirrored Christian's. Valentine had never once mentioned Iceland during their planning.

"Why Iceland, Valentine?"

"Roddy's suggestion. He worked closely with the police in Iceland on a terrorist-related weapons trafficking case while he was with MI5. Roddy made some good friends over there. They have no real intelligence service, and they rely mainly on the police for any type of surveillance. Roddy has access to a safe house just south of Reykjavik. He's arranged for us to use the place for as long as we need to get things sorted out."

Before they could ask any questions, Abby poked her head in from the flight deck. "We're all refueled and ready to go. Just say the word."

"Let's get moving then," Arthur replied.

"You're coming with us?" Christian was surprised. He thought Valentine would remain in the States to work on damage control from their running gun battle in Lake Placid. A trail of dead bodies in one of the most famous villages in the Adirondack Mountains was bound to cause a major problem not only for him and his company but for everyone involved in the operation as well.

"I'll fly over with you and make sure you get settled. I was going to put a few of my people there with you for security, but Roddy nixed that idea. He has several former members of the Icelandic Vikingasveitin, or Viking Squad, whom he uses occasionally. The Viking Squad is Iceland's elite counter-terrorism unit," he added when he saw the perplexed look on their faces. "Roddy says the area where the safe house is located has a decent population of expatriates from Europe and the States, so you should blend in okay, but the sudden appearance of a group of Americans might draw unwanted attention. This way, you'll have locals who know their customs and can take care of keeping you supplied and out of sight."

"How long, Arthur?"

"I'm not sure yet, Laura. We're going to have to wait and see how things shake out. I've already spoken to my contacts with the DOJ and Homeland Security. They're working on a national security angle to handle the fallout. All we can do right now is sit tight and keep you two out of reach while we sort things out."

"The United States has an extradition treaty with Iceland, Arthur," Christian pointed out.

"Of course they do. How fortunate that they won't know you're in their beautiful country."

While Valentine was talking, Abby had taxied the plane to the runway and was awaiting clearance to take off. Once the ATC had given them clearance, Abby pushed the throttle lever forward, and the luxury jet began to pick up speed as it rumbled down the runway. The Cessna Longitude needed approximately 4800 feet of runway for takeoff, but Abby had the plane off the runway well before that. The Honeywell HTF700L Turbofan engine produced 7,665 pounds of thrust, and Abby used every bit of it as she guided the sleek aircraft into the sky. The Cessna had a maximum cruising ceiling of 45,000 feet, and Abby leveled the plane out just a thousand feet shy of the top.

"Settle back and relax, folks. ATC reports smooth skies between here and Reykjavik, so feel free to get up and stretch your legs. The flight should take around seven hours."

CHAPTER SEVENTY-FOUR

Gardabaer, Iceland

Christian stood lost in thought. A mug of hot cocoa that had long since gone cold sat forgotten on the table beside him. Outside of the ceiling-to-floor glass wall in front of him, the waters of the North Atlantic roiled violently as wind-driven waves crested at over ten feet, and a wet, heavy rain mixed with snow, driven relentlessly by the winds of yet another winter storm, lashed at the windows.

Mother Nature's fury was a spectacular sight to behold, but it was lost on Christian. Though his eyes stared out at the rain-streaked glass, Christian took no notice. He and Laura had been secluded in the Icelandic safe house that Roddy Fraser had arranged for them for over a month. Christian's wounds were almost completely healed, and although Laura still hobbled a bit when she walked around, her gunshot wound was well on the way to healing as well. They were both in far better shape than when Arthur Valentine had delivered them to their enforced solitude after their battle with Padraig Lowery and his band of mercenaries.

When they first arrived at the beautiful house overlooking the sea, both Laura and Christian had been in bad shape. Now, thanks to a discrete medical team arranged by Roddy Fraser, both he and Laura were well on their way to a full recovery from their numerous injuries.

The safe house they were hiding in was beautiful. It was three stories high, with six bedrooms, eight baths, and a half dozen fireplaces scattered throughout. There was a heated swimming pool as well as a sauna and three hot tubs. The ground floor featured a small but well-equipped gym, which both Christian and Laura were using to speed up their recovery. The entire southern wall of the top floor was designed of glass, offering the breathtaking view Christian now ignored.

Fraser had arranged for a retired couple to take care of the housework and cooking for them. The man and woman kept to themselves, but Christian was able to learn they had both been members of the Reykjavik police force before retiring. For security, Roddy had arranged for former members of Iceland's elite counter-terrorism force, the Viking Squad, to protect the house and its occupants. There were always two members of the team on duty. All in all, it would have been a wonderful place to spend a holiday, but Christian and Laura weren't on a holiday. After a month, it was beginning to feel more like confinement and he and Laura were prisoners.

A great deal had happened back in the States since they had fought off Andino Fabrizio's hired guns and gotten Evora Cota to safety. The legal fallout from the running gun battle that had left dead bodies scattered from Lake Placid to the High Falls Gorge was monumental. Padraig Lowery, the former PIRA commander, and the band of criminals he had hired had left two Lake Placid police officers and three members of the team protecting Evy dead. Also killed were all but two members of Lowery's own people.

The first few days in Iceland brought an emotional mixture of good and bad news. Dexter Choi, Christian's best friend and partner, had been found alive. He'd managed to survive a gunshot wound to his hip as well as a twenty-foot fall into the raging waters of the High Gorge Falls. He was in bad shape, but thanks to Valentine and Christian's mother, Grace Vikstrom, he was getting the best medical care available. Also still alive was Valentine's right-hand man, Steven Paine. Paine had suffered multiple gunshot wounds when Lowery and his people invaded the safe house on Lake Placid, but the former Delta Force member proved himself to be indestructible. Despite suffering six gunshot wounds and losing almost six pints of blood, the man refused to die.

The police had originally taken both Dexter and Paine into

custody and had them under twenty-four-hour police watch at the Albany Medical Center. It had taken Valentine's powerful contacts in D.C. and all of Grace Vikstrom's legal savvy to have both men released from police custody and moved to a different facility better suited to treat their injuries.

Sadly, Valentine confirmed that Jerome Abioye, David Altman, and Pierre Durand had all been killed during the assault on the safe house. Abioye's death hit Christian especially hard. He and the quiet former South African Special Forces soldier had hit it off immediately, becoming friends almost as soon as they'd met.

They also learned that the Lake Placid PD uniforms Lowery's people had used to gain access to the safe house had been taken from the two Lake Placid police officers Chief Nilsen had assigned to watch out for them. The officers' dead bodies had been found stripped of their uniforms and gear and stuffed in the back of their own patrol vehicle.

Two members of Lowery's team had been taken into custody. Both men had suffered life-threatening wounds during the gun battle but were currently recovering in the hospital under a police guard.

The week following the violence was confusing and hectic for law enforcement authorities in New York. Two dead police officers would have been enough to spark a massive investigation, even without all the other violence and deaths connected to their murders. Investigators with the New York State Police and the State Attorney General's office were just beginning to develop a picture of what had transpired when things took an even more complicated turn. Agents with the FBI and Homeland Security arrived in Lake Placid and announced the Department of Justice would be taking over the investigation, citing national security concerns. The ensuing battle between the governor and attorney general of New York and U.S. Attorney General was epic. The governor argued that state sovereignty and state rights should be honored, while the attorney general stuck to his position that the issue was a matter of national security and thus the federal government had jurisdiction.

Christian and Laura had managed to get Evy out of New York without the police even knowing they existed. Nick Atwell had driven back to his home in Blue Mountain Lake after dropping them off at the airport in Plattsburgh without mentioning his part in the day's drama to anyone, and they had all hoped he would be kept out of the investigation.

Unfortunately, when Tyler Matas watched the national news and saw his majestic lakefront home featured prominently in the news stories, he immediately reached out to the Lake Placid Police Department and informed them of who had been renting the home. Thus, by the end of the first week, Christian Vikstrom was named as a person of interest, and a nationwide manhunt ensued.

Christian's thoughts turned to Summer. Roddy Fraser had arranged for an IT specialist to come to the house and set up a system to allow Christian and Laura to communicate with people back home without their communications being monitored or traced. The system had allowed Christian to speak with Summer almost daily since he'd arrived in Iceland. Summer was an intelligent woman, and she'd already figured out Christin was somehow connected to the events in Lake Placid even before rumors of his involvement began to circulate through the Old Forge community.

Summer's original joy at learning Christian was okay and safe slowly turned to frustration and anger as the days and weeks went by, and he refused to tell her where he was or when he'd be home. Christian feared that if he didn't get back home soon, the damage to their relationship would be irrevocable.

A hand touching his shoulder brought Christian back to the present, and he turned to see Laura standing beside him.

"I'm sorry. I didn't mean to startle you."

Even though the doctor was confident Laura would make a full recovery from her wounds, she still looked fragile to Christian. The dark red wool sweater she currently wore only served to highlight how pale she was.

"No worries. I was just standing here daydreaming."

Laura snuggled up next to Christian, and he wrapped an arm around her and drew her close. Her hair smelled of lavender from the shampoo she'd used when she showered. Her normally muscular shoulders were still a little thin, but Christian was certain she'd regain any muscle she'd lost. Prior to her wounds, Laura had been a fitness nut. She'd been in better shape when Christian met her than she was when she was an intelligence officer in the Marine Corps.

"How's Abby doing?"

A smile flashed across Laura's beautiful face, just as it always did when he asked about her wife. "She's fine. I'm hoping I'll see her soon."

"I know the feeling. I'm beginning to think that if I don't get back home soon, Summer may not be waiting anymore."

The comment caught Laura by surprise. She and Christian had become close during the time they'd protected Evy, and they'd grown even closer over the past month, as they had only each other in their seclusion. They spoke often, and she knew how much he cared about Summer.

"What makes you say that?"

"She's getting tired of not knowing what's going on. She knows there are things I can't tell her, and she accepts that on one level. On another level, she feels that if we're going to be intimate and have any chance at a long-term relationship, I should be able to tell her everything. Every time I tell her I can't talk about something, or I don't know when I'll be home, I can feel her pulling a little further away and starting to put up a wall to protect herself."

Laura shifted under Christian's arm, pulling him into a hug. "Stay positive. I think things are about to change." She almost laughed at the confused look that flashed across Christian's face.

"What's that supposed to mean?"

"Arthur called while you were up here brooding." She let the comment hang in the air.

"And?" Christian asked in exasperation when Laura didn't continue.

"He's on his way here. He says he has big news."

"When is it supposed to get here?"

Laura checked her watch, then looked past Christian and said, "Right about now."

Christian turned to see what Laura was looking at, just in time to see a dark gray Land Rover Defender pull through the main gate and stop near the front door. A member of the security detail approached the vehicle to check out the occupants. Christian couldn't hide his surprise when Roddy Fraser and Arthur Valentine climbed out of the big SUV.

Christian gave Laura a hard look, but she held up her hands and said, "Don't look at me. Arthur called and said he and Roddy had just landed at the airport and they'd be here shortly. That was the first time I heard they were coming."

By the time Christian and Laura made it downstairs, Roddy and Arthur were standing in front of the massive fireplace in the living room, warming themselves by the fire. The two men were speaking with one of the security guards currently on duty as they held their hands out toward the crackling fire.

When Roddy saw them enter the room, he walked over to Laura, wrapped her up in a bear hug, and raised her off the floor. "Auck, you're skin and bones, girl!"

"Put me down, you big goof!" Laura laughed despite her protests.

Roddy held the squirming woman a moment longer before setting her down. He put his hands on her shoulders and held her at arm's length as he looked her up and down.

"How are you feeling lass?"

"I'll feel better when we can go home, Roddy."

"Well, then you'll both be happy to hear what I have to tell you," Valentine said as he stepped away from the fireplace. He shook Christian's hand before moving to Laura and giving her a long hug.

"What's going on, Arthur?" Christian asked.

"In the last few days, things have taken a major turn in our favor back home." Arthur moved to one of the overstuffed leather chairs that faced the fireplace. Gesturing to a matching chair and couch, he waved everyone over. "Come on and have a seat. There's a lot to cover."

Christian was growing impatient, but Laura took his arm and guided him over to the couch.

"Okay, Arthur. What's happened?" Laura seemed to sense Christian's impatience and kept a calming hand on his arm.

"Well, to start with, the N.Y. State attorney general has dropped her complaints about the DOJ taking over the investigation."

"That's a surprise," Christian said. "The AG is pure politician. I can't imagine her letting the feds steal her thunder."

"She definitely wasn't happy about it at first, but when we handed her the men who murdered the two Lake Placid police officers on a silver platter, she changed her tune. Now she's spinning it that New York State assisted in the detection and elimination of a major terrorist cell and captured the cop killers."

"How can you be sure who killed the cops? Lowery had a whole team of men. Any one of them could've done it."

"It wasn't easy. In the end, it was the FBI crime lab that broke it open. The troopers found Nate Boyle still alive at the safe house. We think he's the one you struggled with, Christian."

"He was a tough son-of-a-bitch," Christian said.

"Yeah, well, he should be. He and his brother Sammy Boyle were career criminals in Ireland before they moved to Montreal to avoid being arrested back home on murder and weapons charges. Sammy was wearing Officer Teddy Fernsby's uniform when he was killed at the safe house. Anyway, when the troopers found Nate, he still had the knife he used to slit Officer Fernby's throat in his possession. They found Fernsby's DNA on the blade and inside the sheath.

"The guy you shot and left trussed up in the woods by the gorge is Ben Lincoln. He's a Canadian from Montreal. He and the Boyle brothers are known associates of a guy named Brandon Flannery. More about that later. When the trooper searched the vehicle that chased you to the gorge, they found several weapons. One was a 40-caliber handgun. When the weapon was processed, they found Lincoln's fingerprints on it. The lab conducted a ballistics test on it and discovered it was the weapon used to murder Officer Lisa Baker. Nessa Keever was wearing Baker's uniform when Evy killed her in the woods. The assistant U.S. Attorney made the two scumbags an offer they couldn't refuse. Plead guilty to killing the police officers, and the federal government would allow New York State to prosecute them, or deny it and be tried in federal court and face the death penalty."

"What about our guys they killed?" Christian wanted justice for his team.

"The deal is only for the murder of the police officers. Right now, they're both facing murder, weapons, conspiracy, and terrorism-related charges on the federal side. I'm sure the AUSA will offer them life without parole for guilty pleas on all counts."

"How's Evy, Roddy?" Laura asked.

"Much better now that she's back home with her parents in Portugal. She asks about you two constantly, by the way."

"Portugal? Who's protecting her?" Christian asked.

"No one. There's no need," Roddy said.

"So you caught Fabrizio?"

"Sort of, but not really."

"Explain that, please," Laura said.

"Two weeks ago, U.S. Customs and Border Protection received an anonymous tip that there were two bodies floating in the St. Lawrence River between the United States and Cornwall Island. They sent out a boat to investigate. The Border Patrol recovered two bodies from the river. They had chains wrapped around their feet to keep them weighed down, but apparently, whatever the chains were connected to slipped off, and the bodies got hung up on a bunch of driftwood near the shore. According to the CBP report, both bodies were in bad shape. Being submerged in the river for weeks would've been bad enough, but apparently the fish had made a feast of the bodies. The CBP asked the state police for assistance. It took a few days, but they were eventually able to use dental records to identify the remains of one of the guys as James 'Jimmy' King. King is a Native American who lives on the Akwesasne Mohawk Indian Reservation."

"I met him," Laura said quietly.

"Excuse me?" Valentine was clearly surprised.

"He was at the bar in the restaurant at the Whiteface Lodge when we took Evy there. His cousin, Linette King, is the spa manager at the lodge. She introduced me to him at the bar."

"She was working the day Evy slipped away and sent the message to her mother," Christian added.

"Christ!" Arthur cursed. "Any chance she was involved?"

"There's no way to know for sure, but someone should interview her."

"I'll pass that along," Valentine said.

"What about the second body, Arthur?"

"The second body wasn't as easy to identify. There was a French passport on the body identifying him as Claude Du Bois. The passport was an excellent forgery. CBP agents used facial recognition on the passport photo, and that's when they discovered the body was none other than Andino Fabrizio.

"Both men had been shot twice in the back of the head before they were dumped in the river. It appears King worked for a guy named Tyler Jacobs, smuggling things across the border. Jacobs lives on the Canadian side of the Akwesasne Indian Reservation. The tribal police told border patrol agents that there were rumors going around the rez that Jimmy crossed Jacobs, and Jacobs had him killed. It makes sense. If King was tied up with Lowery, Jacobs wouldn't want the kind of heat killing cops would bring being drawn to his activities."

"How'd Fabrizio get tied up with any of these people?"

"I think I have the answer to that," Fraser said. "The best we can piece together by following the money trail Dexter found in Fabrizio's computer system is this: Fabrizio hired a shadowy character in Italy known as L'Avvoltoio, *The Vulture*. *The Vulture* was the head of a small but violent criminal gang known as Le Ombre, or The Shadows, that operates out of Sicily. Either Fabrizio or *The Vulture* hired Padraig Lowery to follow Evy when she came to London for her meeting with Roddy.

"When Evy returned to Rome for the cast party, someone, most likely *The Vulture*, decided that was the time to try to grab her. We have no idea why, but apparently Lowery, Nessa Keever, and Lowery's grandson, Callum Gilboy, traveled to Rome to take part in the kidnapping attempt. You all know how that turned out. Lowery's grandson was killed during that attempt, and according to the two we have in custody, he blamed you,

Christian, for his grandson's death. He wanted you dead bad enough to offer an additional bounty on your head."

"That didn't quite work out for him," Christian said, remembering the feel of the final beats of Lowery's heart through the knife blade he had just impaled the man with.

"Apparently not," Roddy Fraser agreed.

"We believe Lowery used an old PIRA contact in Ireland to arrange for assistance in Canada. Sean Flannery fought alongside Lowery during 'the troubles'. Flannery's grandson, Brandon, emigrated to Canada and ran a small smuggling operation out of Montreal. Flannery's body was found downstream from where Dex was fished from the AuSable River. The knife blade Dex buried in the man's chest was still lodged between his ribs. Other than Nessa Keever, the other men involved in the attack in Lake Placid were all known associates of Brandon."

"Dear God. One man's obsession brought about all of this death." Laura shook her head in disbelief.

"Now what?"

"Now, Christian, we go home."

A Different Life and *Hidden Among the Leaves Part 1*, the first two books in this series, are available online at Amazon and Barnes & Noble. Please leave a positive review on Amazon, Barnes & Noble, and Goodreads.

To the Reader:

First and foremost, thank you for choosing to spend a portion of your precious time with Christian as he and Dexter continue their fight to bring justice to the Adirondacks. Without your support, I wouldn't be able to keep pursuing my dream as an author.

I hope you enjoyed the thrilling conclusion to *Hidden Among the Leaves*. As I explained at the conclusion of Part 1, this book took on a life of its own, and it required two books to tell the entire story properly.

Finally, many of the locations you read about in my books are real. The restaurants, taverns, microbreweries, and tourist/landmark locations do exist. If you recognize some of the locations, you may think to yourself, *That's not right. It's actually like this.* You would be correct. While I use real places, I sometimes change the features to meet the needs of the story.

The people in my stories are a different matter. The people you read about do not exist. Each character in all my books comes directly from my imagination. I may model a character after someone I know or have met. This helps me give the character more depth and relatability. If you think you recognize someone in the book, I'll take that as a compliment, as they are purely a product of my mind.

Again, thank you for choosing to spend some of your precious time exploring the world I've created, and I look forward to bringing you further adventures with Christian Vikstrom and his best friend, Dexter Choi, as they bring justice to the Adirondack Mountains of New York State and beyond.

Jamie Farrington

January 24, 2024

Jamie is a lifelong resident of the beautiful Mohawk Valley. He graduated from Herkimer High School and is an alumnus of The State University of New York at Herkimer where he currently serves on both the Criminal Justice curriculum committee and the Perkins Grant committee. Jamie became a police officer at the age of twenty-three and, after serving ten years as a uniformed patrolman with several agencies, a chance encounter at a local watering hole led to him joining the world-famous United States Marshals Service. For over twenty-four years, Jamie helped track down and arrest the nation's most violent fugitives, with many of his cases taking him all over the world. Jamie began a new chapter in his life when he retired on New Year's Eve 2022. Jamie currently lives in the foothills of the spectacular Adirondack Mountains with his wife, Sherry, and their two rescued fur babies, Brando, the lovable mixed breed dog, and Skid Row, the high-energy Calico kitty, rescued from the abandoned home of an arrested crack dealer.

Made in the USA
Middletown, DE
19 September 2024

60706505R00275